WE CALLED IT MUSIC

A GENERATION OF JAZZ

WE CALLED
IT MUSIC

A GENERATION OF JAZZ

By EDDIE CONDON

Narration by THOMAS SUGRUE

New introduction by GARY GIDDINS

DA CAPO PRESS

Library of Congress Cataloging-in-Publication Data

Condon, Eddie, 1905-1973
  We called it music: a generation of jazz / by Eddie Condon; narration by
Thomas Sugrue; new introduction by Gary Giddins.
    p .   c m .
  Originally published: New York: H. Holt, 1947. With new introd. and an
additional chapter from the British ed. of 1962.
  Includes index.
  ISBN 0-306-80466-2
  1. Condon, Eddie, 1905-1973. 2. Jazz musicians—United
States—Biography. I. Sugrue, Thomas, 1907-   . II. Title.
ML419.C65A3   1992   91-38754
781.65 3 092—dc20   CIP
[B]   MN

First Da Capo Press paperback edition 1992

This Da Capo Press paperback edition of *We Called It Music* is an unabridged
republication of the edition published in New York in 1947, here supplemented
with an additional chapter from the British edition of 1962 and an introduction
by Gary Giddins. It is reprinted by arrangement with Phyllis Condon.

Published by Da Capo Press, Inc.
A member of the Perseus Books Group

INTRODUCTION

E DDIE CONDON was a vigorous jazz activist whose barbed tongue and stubborn beliefs proved to be powerful implements for spreading the jazz gospel as he saw it. More than a decade after his death, the particular kind of music he championed is still widely known as Condon-style. What made his success remarkable was the unorthodox nature of his career. Condon wasn't an important instrumentalist or bandleader, yet he performed on many fine (even important) recordings and fronted countless bands. His accomplishments as a composer were few, yet he helped to codify an enduring school of jazz. He was a radical in his youth and a reactionary ever after, yet he won lasting respect as one of jazz's most effective propagandists, heralding the new music on the bandstand and off, as a musician, organizer, memoirist, radio and TV personality, newspaper columnist, and club-owner.

The Condon-style, also known as Chicago-Dixieland (a phrase he disliked), was born in the late 1920s, reached its apex a decade later, and sustained a popular following throughout the '40s and '50s, even though it had long since jettisoned all signs of progressive development.

Indeed, predictability was part of its allure. What started out as a scrappy, every-man-for-himself music, hellbent on capturing the drive and feeling of pioneer black jazz musicians, became a conservative backwater—a respite from the seeming anarchy of modernism. Played by small ensembles with a driving beat, the Condon-style was a loose-limbed music, inspired by the informality of the jam session and nourished by an intimate ambience that was perhaps too tolerant of journeymen vocalists, roguish bandstand antics, and a petrified repertoire. But it was an honest music, sometimes compellingly so, and it preserved an aura of effortless musical camaraderie that became increasingly rare in modern jazz.

Condon's personality mirrored his music. He worked hard at perfecting a mask of cynicism to hide the sentimentality lurking just below the surface. Had he been the scold he sometimes pretended to be, however, he could hardly have gotten away with as much mischief. A genuinely witty man, he made his impudence palatable even to his victims, who were known to quote Condon's jibes with pleasure. Some of his observations have become part of jazz lore. Consider Condon on French critic Hugues Panassié: "Who does the Frog think he is to tell us how to play? We don't tell him how to jump on a grape." On modern jazz: "The boppers flat their fifths. We consume ours." On Pee Wee Russell: "He's gaining weight—under each eye." On any number of singers: "He once tried to carry a tune across the street and broke both legs." *We Called It Music,* the first and most important of Eddie Condon's three books, includes many lines that have been repeated and rephrased so often many people no longer know where they originated—for example, his elegiac metaphor on first hearing Bix Beiderbecke: "The sound came out like a girl saying yes."

In addition to being a highly entertaining autobiography of a jazz musician, *We Called It Music,* subtitled "A Generation of Jazz" so that everyone would understand what *It* referred to, is a definitive statement on the first generation of white jazzmen and how they saw themselves in relation to the black innovators they emulated. Read today, long after the coming of modern jazz and in light of decades of myth-making revisionism, Condon's memoir brims with more socio-musical ironies than were apparent on first publication, in 1947. Some of that irony is underscored by the strange supplementary chapter written for an English edition in 1962, and reprinted now for the first time in the United States.

The main text makes clear the debt Condon's generation owed Louis Armstrong, King Oliver, Ethel Waters, and Bessie Smith; they were the kings and queens of a new American music. ("When [Jimmy] McPartland mentioned King Oliver," Condon writes, "smoke came out of his eyes.") The contemporary reader expects no less, but it should be noted that in Condon's early years jazz was popularly associated with the likes of Paul Whiteman, Irving Berlin, and George Gershwin. In recognizing the genius of authentic jazz players, Condon and friends were siding with a style of music that was decidedly left of respectable. The pride that animates *We Called It Music* and similar jazz memoirs reflects the satisfaction of men who were considered outlaws in their youth and pioneers as adults. In addition to serving up anecdotal portraits of the titans in action (Oliver at Lincoln Gardens, Jimmie Noone playing for Ravel, Fats Waller preparing a record date), Condon's account captures the excitement of young acolytes learning and, in some cases, mastering a brave new music. He recounts with chauvinistic pleasure the arrival of Beiderbecke and Leon Rappolo, who proved that whites could express themselves through black music, and celebrates the commingling of the Irish, Italians, Jews, and bluebloods who heeded its siren call.

There is a paradox here. If Condon and friends started out as avant-garde renegades ("One of the ladies told me it was just like having the Indians in town again"), intent on playing jazz despite the indifference of "the Republicans" who preferred saccharine fiddle bands, they soon became the most cautious of musical populists. The more respectable and intellectual jazz became, the more they relished their reputations as "natural" musicians — the kind who can readily identify with young Eddie's rather disingenuous question, "What's reading got to do with music?" At times, he seemed to regard jazz as little more than a folk art, a non-stop jam session frequently sustained in an alcoholic mist (the children of the Volstead Act, he explains, inebriated themselves with a vengeance, as if to prove that no government could dictate sobriety). That attitude, bound to appeal to fans suffering from unrequited nostalgia, proved contagious, as witness the gee-whiz prose occasionally served up by commentators in the liner copy of Condon's record albums — e.g., ". . . a dozen good guys having a good time. That is, after all, what it is all about" or "This music *is* roadsters and girls and cutting classes and oranges." It also led to grumbling by ambitious musicians such as Jack Teagarden and Pee Wee Russell, who blamed the Condon-style for stereotyping them and limiting their options. Still, Condon's best work has a spark of its own, and though he sometimes "conducted" more than he played, the bands that bore his name continued to produce memorable work by Russell, Vic Dickenson, Bobby Hackett, Billy Butterfield, Edmund Hall, Bud Freeman, Kenny Davern, and quite a few other Condon regulars.

Back in 1947, when Condon and Thomas Sugrue collaborated on *We Called It Music,* Condon was at the height of his fame as a jazz personality. His nightclub, which opened in 1945, met with great success, as did his Town Hall concerts, radio broadcasts, and records. Sugrue, a newspaper and magazine writer who also wrote fiction, poetry, and a biography of psychic Edgar Cayce, was responsible for the book's strictly historical (italicized) passages; they contain much valuable information, but ought to be read prudently. In excoriating the "theology" of the scholar's approach to jazz, he refuses to distinguish between quaint phrases like "licorice stick" and commonplace musicology on the order of "polyrhythm" and "glissandi." His contention that "the piano began its career in jazz in 1897," the year prostitution was legalized in the French Quarter of New Orleans, is as bizarre as his refusal to admit that racism helped launch the Original Dixieland Jazz Band. Hardly anyone still accepts the idea that "prostitution mothered jazz" or that "the Negro is born with rhythm." There are more mundane errors as well: Paul Whiteman commissioned *Rhapsody in Blue* (hardly "a tune," by the way) for Aeolian Hall not Carnegie; Duke Ellington made his New York debut at Baron Wilkins's Inn not the Kentucky Club; Red Nichols's recordings *are* collectors' items; Condon did not produce the first integrated record date (the New Orleans Rhythm Kings session with Jelly Roll Morton probably has that distinction); "jazz" and "swing" were not mutually exclusive musics. Minor factual errors aside, Sugrue's and Condon's dated ideas have the anthropological value of showing firsthand some common images of jazz in the 1940s.

Perhaps the reader also deserves a warning about the opening section of the book, pertaining to Condon's childhood. Stilted and edgy, it is filled with incidents of sadistic violence that are probably intended to have a Tom Sawyer or Little Rascals flavor. "Halloween was all year around Momence," Condon writes, but the relentless jokeyness wears the reader down, especially when it becomes apparent that he is unwilling to address candidly the subject of his family and upbringing, particularly as concerns Condon's ambivalence about his father and his eagerness to leave home. Interestingly, the same problem obtains in the 1962 addition, "Major and Minor Chords," which was bannered as "a new chapter for the Corgi Edition, answering in no uncertain manner the criticism [Condon] received on his recent tour of Great Britain." Again, the writing is jokey, mannered, sentimental — full of countless references to booze, one-liners that don't come off, and self-serving claims.

Between these opening and closing chapters, the book

comes splendidly alive. From the moment Condon gets his first banjo and leaves home to tour with a band (at 16), the memoir sparkles. When he describes his trip to Cedar Rapids to join Peavey's Jazz Bandits, it is apparent that music will provide Condon with a surrogate family, and an outlet whereby his impish behavior can produce salutary results. He vividly portrays his ascent into the mysterious culture of jazz, finding just the right images to convey the thrill of those "mackinaw days," when everyone seemed to be dancing, spooning, and playing music on countless lake resorts all over the midwest. The peculiar claims that come later, such as his insistence that Benny Goodman didn't play real jazz at Carnegie Hall in 1938, or that by 1947 there were no more than 50 "first class players" (including Ralph Sutton and Johnny Blowers, of course, but not Charlie Parker and Dizzy Gillespie), must be read in the context of Condon's faith in the music that captured his imagination and liberated him from Momence, Indiana, in the early '20s. Credit him with keeping the faith and doing his damnedest to sustain some of the innocence at the heart of jazz as he knew and loved it.

Condon kept active in the years following the appearance of *We Called It Music*. Although his nightclub changed premises in 1958 — relocating from West 3rd Street to East 56th Street — it managed to stay in business until 1967, for an impressive total of 22 years. He collaborated on two more books: *Eddie Condon's Treasury of Jazz* (1956), an ambitious anthology of writings on the subject, edited by Condon and Richard Gehman; and *Eddie Condon's Scrapbook of Jazz* (1973), a hugely entertaining collection of pictures and captions, collated by Condon and Hank O'Neal. From 1964 on, illness prevented him from traveling much, though he embarked on occasional tours and appeared from time to time in clubs and at festivals — his last performance was at a tribute to him at the Newport Jazz Festival-New York in 1972, a year before his death. Less than two years later, bassist Red Balaban opened a new jazz club called Eddie Condon's on 54th Street. The walls were covered with enlarged photographs of Condon and his favorite musicians. The music was Condon-style, plain and simple.

— GARY GIDDINS
New York City
March, 1986

Note: The "Informal Discography" reprinted here from the original edition of *We Called It Music* only goes up to 1946, of course, and doesn't pretend to be complete even for the years it covers. Many of Condon's best recordings have been re-released in recent years, and although some have once again disappeared from the record bins, the interested reader may want to keep an eye out for the following gems (all issued under Condon's name): *Eddie Condon's World of Jazz* (1927-54/Columbia), *Windy City Seven and Jam Sessions* (1938/Commodore), *The Liederkranz Sessions* (1939-40/Commodore), *A Good Band Is Hard to Find* (1938-42/Commodore), *Gershwin Program* (1941-45/MCA), *The Best of Eddie Condon*

(1944-50/MCA), *Jammin' at Condon's* (1954/Columbia), *Ringside at Condon's* (1955/Savoy), *In Japan* (1964/Chiaroscuro).

G.G.
1986

ADDENDUM

Since the introduction to the hardcover edition of this book was written, the LP has been all but supplanted by the CD, alas. Eddie Condon's music was quick to make the technological leap. Many of the finest of his Commodore recordings are collected on *Jammin' at Commodore* (1938-39/Commodore). The ambitious and well-heeled Condon completist can now obtain all of his — and everyone else's — work for that label on *The Complete Commodore Jazz Recordings*, a three-volume (46 LPs) edition available from the mail-order company Mosaic Records in Stamford, CT. His radio transcriptions have thus far been issued on *The Definitive Eddie Condon, Vol. 1* (1944/Stash). *That Toddlin' Town*, subtitled Chicago Jazz Revisited, has been reissued (1959/Atlantic). Expanded editions of his later concerts are found on *Eddie Condon in Japan* (1964/Chiaroscuro) and *Live at the New School* (1972/Chiaroscuro).

G.G
1991

CONTENTS

FOR BIX
I hope he isn't wearing a cap

"Sing unto him a new song; play skilfully with a loud noise."

Psalm 33:3

A PAIR OF
ENGLISH SHOES

IT WAS Sunday, semi-evening. Maggie was back from the park. Liza was in her play pen, muttering at a doll. Phyllis was in the kitchen dyeing a couple of rugs. I had just decided not to light a cigarette; I was too lazy to inhale the smoke. The telephone rang. It was John McNulty calling from somewhere north of Forty-second Street.

"I have just fallen off the wagon after eight years and you are the first person I called up," he said. "I want to show you my English shoes. I'll be right down."

I hung up and said to Maggie, "John McNulty is coming to see us."

She was dubious. "Is he a man?" she asked.

"He is a writer," I said.

She accepted the qualification. "May I hit him with my hammer?" she asked.

McNulty had changed; his face was sunburned and he was enthusiastic about daylight. "You just lie down in it and it fills you with energy," he explained. "I didn't think it would work but it does."

We examined the English shoes. They were standard, conservative, and apparently a good fit. We had a drink. McNulty looked at Maggie and edged his chair a little toward me.

1

"I never quite figured you as a family man," he said in an undertone.

"My father-in-law is a lawyer and one of the best rifle shots in the country," I said. "He once held the national title for marksmanship."

McNulty nodded. "A man should settle down," he said.

We drank quietly. "So you have your own saloon now," he said, "and your own band, and a wife and two daughters. Your mother would be proud of you."

We had another drink. "I heard your program, 'Eddie Condon's Jazz Concert' while I was in California," John said. "Why was it taken off the air? I knew men who stayed home from poker games on Saturday afternoon to listen to it."

I told him the story. Johnny O'Connor, Fred Waring's manager, rammed us down the Blue Network's throat. We used the network's electricity and studios, nothing else. We filed program notes with the script department each week, then tore them up. We brought in our own announcer, Fred Robbins, a man who understands jazz. We ad libbed the program verbally and musically. We got our own guest speakers—John O'Hara, the author; Joe McCarthy, of Yank magazine; George Frazier, of Life magazine. The show was transcribed each week and sent abroad to be played for the armed forces; it won first place in both the European and Pacific GI popularity polls. It ran for forty-eight weeks; then some new executive blood was poured into the Blue Network and it was decided that something had to be done about the program. Its rating had picked up; soldiers everywhere preferred it to the "Hit Parade," which they voted second, and "Command Performance," which was their third choice; its mail was sensational. The soldier letters all said the same thing, "Your music is the next best thing to a

2

trip home." Ernie Anderson and I met with representatives of the sales and script departments, and with the new executives.

There was a lot of talk. Finally one of the executives said he thought the name of the program ought to be changed.

"What do you suggest calling it?" Ernie asked.

" 'Saturday Afternoon Senior Swing,' " the executive said.

"Why?" Ernie asked.

"The present title is too long," the executive said.

Ernie looked at me. I was counting on my fingers. "Eddie Condon's Jazz Concert" contained twenty-three letters; "Saturday Afternoon Senior Swing" had twenty-eight.

"These guys are real executives," I whispered to Ernie. "Watch out."

After a while one of the other executives said, "I think we ought to bring in a comedian. I suggest Jackie Kelk."

"Who is Jackie Kelk?" I asked.

The executive stared at me. "Jackie Kelk is Homer on the 'Aldrich Family'," he said.

"What is that?" I said.

The executive's lips tightened. "You don't know of the 'Aldrich Family'?" he asked, leaning toward me a little.

Ernie kicked me under the table.

"I only know two things about radio," I said, "how to use it to set my watch and how to turn it off."

There was more talk and then the ultimatum was delivered —we could accept a new format for the show, including a comedian, or we could quit. One of the older executives tried to be helpful.

"There is no need to decide immediately," he said. "Take a few days to think it over, then let us know."

3

"We don't need a few days," Ernie said. "We can give you our answer now. It's no, in italics."

McNulty nodded when I finished. "I was afraid I was going to have to change my opinion of radio when they let you play jazz without doing anything to louse it up," he said. "I'm glad radio hasn't changed. It gives me a feeling of security."

Maggie came over and leaned against John's knee. We had another drink. John had something on his mind. "There is going to be a book," he said. "They are going to collect those pieces I wrote for *The New Yorker* about Tim's place and put them in a volume. I think they are going to call it *Third Avenue, New York*." He turned the glass in his hand and looked at his English shoes. Then it came. "You've got to write a book too," he said.

We had another drink. Maggie got bored with us and went to help Liza take the play pen apart. "How am I going to do it and what am I going to write about?" I said. John stood up. "Is there a typewriter in the house?" he asked. "In the kitchen," I said. "In the bread box."

We went into the kitchen, opened the bread box, and lifted the typewriter out of it. John put a sheet of paper in the machine.

"Where and when were you born?" he said to me.

I told him. On the sheet he typed: Goodland, Indiana, November 16, 1905.

He spaced and wrote another line: Present address, Washington Square North, New York City.

"Now all you've got to do," he said, "is put down on paper what happened between those two lines. Try it. What do you remember?"

4

I pulled up the kitchen stool and John sat on it. Together we stared at the sheet of paper.

"Put down cat," I said.

John typed the word.

When we lived in Momence, Illinois, we had a cat named Geronimo. One day my sister, Martina, went to the shed in the backyard where we kept the corncobs and sat down in a chair. She fell over backward and struck Geronimo and broke his back. He wasn't dead so my brother John hit him with a baseball bat. Then we dug a grave and buried him and put a cross over him. We got some kernels of corn and wrote his name in the soft dirt. When we came back after eating dinner, the neighbor's chickens had come over and eaten all the corn. They had almost eaten Geronimo, too.

"Remember the time we took the cottage at Normandy Beach near Barnegat Bay and the hurricane came and blew four doors off the garage and the lights went out and the water came up the street?" Phyllis said. She was still dyeing rugs.

"Put down shoes," I said.

John typed the word.

One night John Steinbeck came into the saloon and said to me, "Eddie, why don't you go back to playing the banjo? It's the only American instrument and it ought to be used to play the only American music. Why do you play a lover's instrument, a guitar?" I said, "John, the banjo went out with button shoes." John bent over and whispered in my good ear, "Eddie, button shoes are coming back."

"Remember the time Mezzrow was rooming with you and it was the Fourth of July and you had a date with me and we had nothing to do all day and Mezzrow said, 'Don't worry,

5

I know a delicatessen that will be open at five o'clock and we can get some turkey necks'?" Phyllis said.

"Put down Lord," I said.

John typed the word.

Jimmy Lord was a young Chicago boy who played clarinet and saxophone and arranged music. He used to sit in with us at the Palace Gardens in Chicago; he had a yellow Marmon car and once I tried to drive it and stripped the gears. One summer his mother, Ann Lord, rented an apartment in New York, on the east side next to River House. I was broke and she let me stay there. I hadn't carfare to get across town but when I arrived there was a Japanese butler to look after me. There was a large library in the apartment; it included a stack of social registers eight feet high. I did almost my whole life's reading that summer.

The last time I saw Jimmy was at Princeton, where I played at a house party with Red McKenzie's Mound City Blue Blowers. Jimmy had walked out of a tuberculosis sanitarium determined to cure himself by will power. He wanted to play the Princeton date with us and insisted he was well enough. After the party we found him sitting halfway up the stairs, resting before attempting the next step.

"Let us help you, Jimmy," McKenzie said. "We'll carry you up."

Jimmy refused. "I've got to do this by myself," he said. "There is no other way."

The next week he died.

"Do you remember the time we drove to Minneapolis and my brother Sam couldn't stay awake at the wheel and you went through all the luggage to get a benzedrine tablet that was at the bottom of the last bag and Sam took it and went

6

right to sleep and didn't wake up for ten hours?" Phyllis said.

I took McNulty back into the living room.

"Why do you want me to write a book?" I asked.

"I'm lonesome," he said.

After he left Maggie climbed up on my lap. "He was a nice man," she said. "I didn't hit him." She put my arm where she wanted it and fell asleep. I dozed with her.

What do you remember? I thought. When Joe McCarthy appeared on the radio show we had to clear his script with the State Department, and for once we had to read what was prepared for us. There was a joke. I said, "Joe, I understand you're from Boston." Joe said, "Yes, Eddie, I'm one of the lace curtain Irish from Massachusetts." I said, "Lace curtain? What kind of Irish are they?" Joe said, "Lace curtain Irish are the kind who have fresh fruit in the house when nobody is even sick." The State Department refused to pass it. Ireland, a neutral country, might be offended.

Vinton Freedley refused to pass the script for a stage version of Dorothy Baker's *Young Man With A Horn*, a novel inspired by the career of Bix Beiderbecke. It was a wise decision. Burgess Meredith was to play the part of Bix, whose name in the book was Rick. Margaret Sullavan was Rick's girl friend, Amy North. I was offered the role of a banjo player called Bobby LaPorte; my mission in the plot was to keep Rick from drinking too much. At one point I was to walk into a studio wearing a wrap-around topcoat, look up at the skylight, and say, "Man, what a trick joint this is! I wonder how they ever get those curtains down." Charles MacArthur was called in to doctor the script; he began writing Paris scenes. Dorothy Baker went off to have a baby and Freedley came to his senses. The show was abandoned and Bix was saved.

Meredith had an alternate idea. He called me from New York on the telephone while I was playing at the Brass Rail in Chicago. "You're going to open a club of your own," he said. "You can be your own boss and hire your own band and play jazz the way you want to play it. Tyrone Power and I are going to be your backers."

"How much do you and Ty know about running a restaurant or a saloon?" I asked. "Could either of you buy a shell of beef intelligently?"

"No," he said.

"Neither could I," I said. "I think you and Ty are nice guys and I believe you have some money. When I get back to New York let's take it into a crap game. We can lose it faster that way and we'll have more fun."

"We'll open a club," Meredith said. He is short and determined.

But we didn't; the night-club business isn't for amateurs; it's as tricky as trading stocks on margin. Several years later Pete Pesci, half-owner of Julius', said to me one night during a period of excommunication from Nick's, "Why don't you open your own place?" It was the offer I had been waiting for. "Will you be my manager?" I asked. He smiled. "Why not?" he said. "I like your music. I might as well have it where I can hear it and do my work at the same time." Pete knew how to buy a shell of beef, and he knew how to run a saloon.

We rented the old Howdy Club at 47 West Third Street. I signed the lease on Friday, July 13, 1945. "This will be lucky for us," Pete said. "We will have a lot of customers." We opened on December 20th. "What will you wear on the stand?" Bud Freeman asked. "Shoes," I said. The band had Wild Bill Davison, Joe Marsala, Dave Tough, Gene Schroeder

8

on piano, Brad Gowans on trombone, and Bob Casey on bass. Joe Sullivan alternated with the band, playing piano solos. Jack Bland, Max Kaminsky, Tommy Dorsey, and George Wettling dropped in. There were seven Smiths from Minneapolis scattered through the crowd. People stood in the hallway waiting to get in. We had the biggest vestibule business in town.

A special trio of Julius' patrons came—Chelsea Queely, Dan Qualey (with a long a), and Jake Qualey (with a short a). Having them with me in a bar always gave me a sense of security; when I couldn't introduce them to somebody without getting the names mixed up I knew it was time to change to beer.

"This is it," Phyllis said as she looked at the crowd. "Your life is beginning at forty."

"It's a compromise," I said, "Town Hall with booze."

Pa would have liked it; he had to come home from his saloon to hear music, and to play it. After dinner he would get out his fiddle; one of the girls would accompany him on the piano. Sometimes my brother Cliff played the alto horn. There was always music in the house. I hummed Turkey In The Straw before I said mama; Pa rode me on his foot while he sang it.

Friends and relatives from Indiana were always visiting us. They apparently had a lot of business to attend to in Illinois. Indiana was a dry state. Sometimes my uncles came. They stayed with us and I heard them talking about the old farm in Indiana, and about Grandfather David Condon, who came from Ireland and who died before I was born. He must have been a great man, I thought; his sons were big and strong but they talked about their father as if he were bigger and stronger than all of them put together. They talked also about the saloon Pa had in Goodland, Indiana, before the state went dry, and after a while they got up and went to visit the saloon Pa had in Momence, Illinois.

The saloon was on one side or the other depending on how the people voted. Range Street ran through the middle of Momence, and down the middle of Range Street went . . .

THE FAMILY BIBLE

DAVID CONDON, born Jan. 1, 1827, County Limerick, Ireland

MARGARET HAYES CONDON, born Dec. 15, 1834, County Limerick, Ireland

Married Aug. 19, 1855, Springfield, Mass.

JOHN CONDON, born Jan. 1, 1861, Ottawa, Illinois

MARGARET McGRATH CONDON, born Feb. 11, 1865, Ottawa, Illinois

Married Feb. 11, 1885, Benton County, Indiana

CLIFFORD CONDON, born Nov. 27, 1885, Benton County, Indiana

LUCILLE CONDON, born March 17, 1887, Benton County, Indiana

FLORENCE (DOT) CONDON, born Oct. 2, 1889, Benton County, Indiana

GRACE CONDON, born Dec. 24, 1891, Benton County, Indiana

HELENA CONDON, born May 2, 1895, Benton County, Indiana

MARTINA CONDON, born May 10, 1899, Benton County, Indiana

JOHN CONDON, born June 28, 1901, Benton County, Indiana

JAMES (PAT) CONDON, born July 29, 1903, Benton County, Indiana

ALBERT EDWIN (EDDIE) CONDON, born Nov. 16, 1905, Benton County, Indiana

DAVID CONDON was born a twin on the first day of January, 1827, in County Limerick, Ireland. He had an early wisdom and left for America when he was twenty-one, in the year of the famine, crossing to New York in six weeks on a sailing vessel. Margaret Hayes was born on the fifteenth of December, 1834, also in County Limerick. She was waked for America at eighteen and set out with an older brother on a ship which drifted from its course and spent fourteen weeks on the Atlantic, during all of which Margaret was seasick. In Springfield, Massachusetts, she met David Condon, who had come there from New York to work in a factory. They were married on the nineteenth of August, 1855. Eleven children were born to them: one in Massachusetts, one in New York State, four in Illinois, and five in Indiana. Their names were Thomas, Dennis, John, James, Catherine, Johannah, Mary, Michael, Margaret, Elizabeth, and David. The six sons were all over six feet tall; the five daughters just missed this mark.

In 1859 David and Margaret and their two Eastern-born sons, Thomas and Dennis, arrived in the town of Ottawa, Illinois. The next year David went down the Mississippi and worked on the levees at New Orleans. He wrote to Margaret that the city was the most pleasant he had encountered, and that particularly it had a great deal of music, which would please her. The Negroes, he said, sang especially well, and had many songs and dances of their own. The climate was not healthful but the weather was soft; he hoped to remain there and send for her and the children. The next spring there was trouble between the states. David had no desire to fight for slavery against a government which guaranteed his freedom. To avoid the Confederate draft he walked home. He traveled by night, hiding in cornfields and canebrakes during the day. He was fed by slaves who smuggled food to him "hidden in their bosoms." He arrived home barefoot.

For seven years he labored in the coal mines of Illinois, with neither Rachel nor a raise for recompense. In 1868 he loaded his belongings and a plow into a covered wagon, and with Margaret and their six children set out for the prairies of Indiana, there to break the land at three dollars an acre for Abner Strawn of Ottawa. He plowed prairie for two years, dug and walled wells for twenty-five dollars each, and in 1871 was able to buy for himself three horses and eighty acres of slough land in Union Township, Benton County. To build his home he felled timber and hauled it sixteen miles. The house was a single room, sixteen by sixteen, with a floored attic; it was located on the only dry land on the farm. The stables were thatched with slough grass; there were two cows, a few hogs, and some poultry. The farming implements were a sod plow and an old linchpin wagon. The land was covered with pussy willows, and there were boulders everywhere, some of them tons in weight. The next year David bought forty more acres, also swamp. He cleared the pussy willows, removed or buried the boulders, dug ditches to drain the water, planted corn, and by the third year had a yield of from seventy-five to one hundred bushels per acre. He bought forty additional acres and planted them in flax and buckwheat. He grew tobacco and built a cane mill, a corn sheller, and a hay press. He raised his own sugar cane, made his own molasses and buckwheat flour, shipped baled hay, and rented his cornstalks

14

to herders at a dollar an acre. As his sons grew they worked with him.

The winters were cold and filled with snow. Blizzards swept across the prairie and piled drifts so high that fences were covered and roads were impassable for weeks. The farmers scooped out openings with four-horse teams and drove back and forth over the trails with empty wagons until the snow was beaten solid. One drift on the Condon farm, ten feet deep and on the east side of a high hedge fence, was not completely melted by the Fourth of July. In the spring and fall there were dense fogs. David and his sons were lost in mist on three occasions, once all day, once all night, and once for eighteen hours while driving cattle to Delphi. Many of the cattle were never found.

For twenty-seven years Margaret was never without a baby in her arms; when her youngest child was three years old she took her eight-day-old granddaughter to raise. That was her only bottle baby. She also took care of the poultry and the young animals on the farm. Once she reached into a hen's nest for eggs and found a rattlesnake. Once a mule became entangled in a barbed wire fence; it took six men to extricate her; she stood then with her flank horribly lacerated. The men felled her but none could bear to sew the wound. Margaret did it with a darning needle and some wrapping twine.

She washed with well water which she pumped and carried 125 feet, and which she softened with ashes from the corncobs which burned in her kitchen stove. She pounded the clothes with an eight-inch square of wood attached to a broom handle. She made her own soap and used flour for starch. She white-washed the walls and ceilings of her house, to which rooms were added as the years passed. She scrubbed the soft pine floors with

15

a brush made of twisted slough grass. She did all the family sewing by hand, making work clothes for the boys of heavy jean and hickory cloth, fashioning dresses for the girls with numberless tucks and ruffles which she hemmed with a whip stitch. She made all the bedding, including ticks, quilts, and comforts. She plucked feathers from the geese and ducks for pillows and ticks. She sewed rag carpets and washed them by hand once a year. She knitted socks, stockings, and mittens. In the early years she sewed mostly at night by the light of a piece of cloth laid in a saucer of grease. After the tenth child she bought a Howe sewing machine; by then she also had kerosene lamps.

She cooked on an old-fashioned stove with cobs and wood for fuel. She baked bread for her family and for a neighboring widower and his two children. She boarded the schoolteacher in the winter and took in her brother's motherless children from Chicago in the summer. Through all this she sang. Music was her complete joy. Her voice was clear and sweet; thousands of frogs in the slough gave it background. She encouraged her children to play instruments—combs, jew's-harps, accordions, violins, harmonicas, banjos. David bought her an organ at an auction; it became the altar where she offered up her contentment. In summer she made a chime of horseshoes in the grape arbor, graduating the shoes to form a scale. Safe in the shade the children beat out tunes with a wagon-wheel spoke.

David died on March 22, 1898. He caught a cold while delivering corn for a neighbor during severe weather in February; it went into pleurisy. His final request was that his oldest horse, Dave, be looked after well. Dave was the last colt of the farm's first team. His dam and sire saved their master and mistress once while crossing a frozen creek. The ice broke and the team and wagon went through; with only their nostrils above water the horses kept going. Dave lived to be twenty-eight and his hide was made into a robe which is still in the family. Margaret outlived her husband by twelve years.

The Condon children were the first Catholics to attend school in Union Township; they all went through the grades and Mayme Condon, the granddaughter raised from infancy, was graduated from high school the afternoon David died. All of the family attended the local Catholic church until one Sunday when Thomas, disagreeing with the argument of a sermon, walked out. His sister Mary followed him as a sympathizer. Neither ever returned. Mary left her money to the Moody Bible Institute. Three of the sons were set up in farming by their father; three of the daughters taught in county schools. The family was highly self-educated; David, anxious to raise them properly, once drove home with a circulating library he had purchased.

The sons were noted for their strength. When carnivals came through the county towns in summer the Condon boys followed them and tormented the proprietors of the muscle-testing machines. Dave, the youngest—he was the same age as Dave the horse—was finally barred from the shows. He not only won all the prizes, he broke the equipment. Once at home while talking on the party line he was annoyed by a neighbor who, listening in, disagreed with him. Dave tore the telephone off the wall and tossed it through a window. Once in a saloon in Kentland, Indiana, he picked up a base-burner—it had a fire in it—and dumped it over a man's head. John was gentler; he threw a beer stein at the town marshal, but missed. He was the best fiddler in Benton County; he organized the orchestra for Saturday night dances and acted as its leader. It was customary for a farmer, when requesting a favorite number, to bribe the leader

17

with a bite of chewing tobacco. John did not chew himself, but he accepted each proffered plug, cut off a reasonable section, and put it in his side pocket. The night's take went to Dave, who chewed any brand with vigor.

Among the Saturday night dancers were the sons and daughters of Patrick McGrath, who was born in County Tipperary, Ireland, in 1832, and who married Anna Grady, also of Tipperary, in 1860. The McGraths arrived in Ottawa, Illinois, a month before David Condon left for New Orleans. Patrick worked in the coal mines for sixteen years, then took his family to Indiana, where eventually he settled in Union Township on a farm of 240 acres. There were seven children: William, John, Margaret, Anna, Mary, Jerry, and Dennis. John Condon, over the bridge of his fiddle, watched Margaret McGrath dancing and began to court her. He carried her in his horse and buggy to the dances and drove her home afterward. Once, getting into the carriage on a winter evening, she sat on the bow of his fiddle and broke it. John cut a willow and, so the legend goes, had a makeshift bow ready by the time the dance began, having cut the hairs for it from his horse's tail. He married Margaret McGrath on February 11, 1885, the bride's twentieth birthday. The groom was twenty-four, having been born on his father's thirty-fourth birthday. The next November a son, Clifford, was born to them. There followed, at intervals, five daughters: Lucille, Florence, Grace, Helena, and Martina. In 1901 and in 1903 sons arrived, John and James. In the fall of 1905 preparations were made for the birth of a ninth child.

Clifford, who was approaching his twentieth birthday, showed an almost paternal interest in the event. When on November 16th it turned out to be a boy he wanted him named for Edmund Hayes, a cousin then starring in vaudeville as "The

18

Piano Mover." After a good deal of discussion this suggestion was partially accepted; the baby was named Albert Edwin. He was the last child and he was born in Goodland, where his father had gone to conduct a saloon. His right ear never grew nor had a drum.

The music which David Condon admired in New Orleans went through a metamorphosis following the war in which he refused to take part. Many of the emancipated Negroes, leaving the plantations, took to the roads and gathered in the cities. They carried their music with them—work songs, spirituals, ballads, and blues which had developed through generations of slavery from native African forms. In New Orleans, always a tolerant town, some of the former slaves found jobs. In pawn-shops and secondhand stores they bought musical instruments; for the first time they tried their talents on the cornet and the trombone. No one taught them; they could not read music. They played as they felt and they made the instruments do what they believed all music should do—talk. They organized bands and dressed themselves in uniforms. They played at funerals and other social gatherings; they took whatever tunes they heard and played them in their own way. For them it was a natural way; for music it was something new. It was jazz.

Modern interest in jazz as an art form—which indeed it is—has burdened this early period of birth and development with the awe accorded sacred history. Scholars and apostles have devised a theology so complicated and a ritual so incense-laden that the most pompous of pedants is forced to his knees in vene-ration of a mystery he cannot understand. Religious mania, inarticulation, confusion of tongues, schisms, witch hunts, damnation of heretics—all these are part of the jazz cult. There is fratricidal warfare between the Fundamentalists and the Modernists; there are those who swear on the hallowed memory of Buddy Bolden that only Negroes can play authentic jazz; there are those who assert that real jazz began in Chicago and was first played by white men. There are the discographers, who search for classic jazz records as if they were fragments of the true cross. There are the jazz players themselves, frightened into incoherence by glib students of their art who refer to a clarinet as a "licorice stiçk" and who stud their conversations with such terms as polyrhythm, glissandi, antiphony, and microtonality. One immortal and mentally normal jazz player, after listening for seventy minutes to a jazz-maniac discourse on the subtleties of the art, said moodily to his employer, "He makes it sound like I'm committing a sin. Maybe I ought to quit."

In a partial, unsatisfactory way, the complex terms of European music do describe jazz. There is polyrhythm; there is microtonality; there are slurrings which can be described as glissandi. But since the prophets of jazz loudly declare the new art's divorcement from European tradition, the description of it critically in terms of that tradition is paradoxical. The average American knows what jazz is because he has been listening to it for a generation. The definitions of it he now reads, devised from the language used to laud the performances of the Boston Symphony Orchestra and the Toscanini broadcasts, confound and confuse him. He knows what he hears until he reads a description of it; then he realizes he did not hear it at all. What he heard was something else: microtonality, polyrhythm, antiphony. Yet what jazz is—good jazz, bad jazz, imitation jazz—can be put into understandable terms.

The West African Negroes who came to the United States as slaves brought with them a music fully developed and sharply opposed to the European art of song. The disparity represented a difference not of color or culture, but of consciousness. From the general stream of mind which forms all men the European had labored to isolate himself as an individual, organizing the world around him according to standards and values proceeding from his personal understanding and reason. The Negro, long ago pushed gently to the bank of the mental stream, still rested there with his feet in the water. He showed no desire to go away from what the European called the unconscious or subconscious mind. It was full of fascinating things—fairies, goblins, devils, elementals, and as it flowed it made music.

The European, far away from the stream, heard only the strong sounds and set them down according to his understanding and his reason, organizing them by theory and what remembrance he still possessed. Those who could not hear at all any more were able by studying and practice to reproduce artificially what the more keen-eared had discerned. The Negro, on the bank of the stream, had little need for remembrance or theory. He heard all the sounds, weak and strong; humming and singing, he reproduced them. Tapping on drums, he kept time with the rhythm of the river's flow. He imitated what he heard, and what he heard contained polyrhythms, inner-rhythms, over-rhythms, microtonality, and glissandi. What the European heard contained melody and harmony; he built his system on these, with instruments for reproduction of the carefully written sounds or notes. His music became a highly self-conscious art, demanding experts for its composition and its execution. Negro music continued to be an expression of the unconscious, employing the fluid, malleable self-consciousness of the performers as a medium. The drummers and singers and dancers contrived forms which were self-conscious, but which were activated and directed by the unconscious. In the twentieth century the European, revaluing the unconscious under the inspiration of Sigmund Freud, adapted this technique to all of his arts—painting, writing, sculpture, music, etc. The revolution, led by such men as Picasso, Joyce, Epstein, and Stravinsky, is still in progress. The Negro, by way of Appomattox, New Orleans, and Chicago, contributed to the rebellion by giving it his traditional, unspoiled, highly artistic music—free, uninhibited, continuously creative, spontaneously improvised, polyrhythmic, microtonal, and straight from the unconscious.

Creative thought proceeds from the unconscious to the conscious; whether it is the making of a symphony, a sonnet, or a song, the process is the same. The writer or composer sets up on the point of his concentration an idea, a mood, or a theme. By various techniques of stimulation and meditation he evokes, from his unconscious, patterns for the development, embellishment, elaboration, strengthening, and completion of the idea or mood or theme. The selection and arrangement are problems for the self-consciousness, and represent the skill and style of the writer or composer; the thoughts themselves, their richness, depth, aptness, beauty, luminosity, represent the talent or genius of the man. The European concentrated on skill and style; he built a highly self-conscious art. The Negro let the unconscious have its way with him; form remained a skeleton covered with a new body each time he sang or danced or beat his ceremonial drums. In West Africa every singer, every dancer, every drummer, was a composer in his own right, weaving a fresh creation each time he performed. When a group of these personal artists played together each man improvised his contribution. The result was a mixture of sounds in various states of relationship—complementary, supplementary, oppositional. There were subtle shadings of tone and pitch to avoid duplication of sound. There were rhythmic beats purposely held in order to vary and modify and complicate the pattern. With a dozen or more composers audibly and in gathered company creating independently on an agreed general theme, an art of co-operative avoidance grew up. Stimulated mutually, clinging to a single idea, they composed individually while politely avoiding collision with each other's pattern.

In Africa all this was done with voices, drums, and dancing. The voices called questions and shouted answers. This was antiphony. As the calls and responses gradually overlapped and intermingled polyphony developed, the melodies of the calls and responses operating at the same time. With the rhythm flowing and mixing between these interweaving lines of melody, with the notes changing and the pitch fluctuating, the music changed and moved like the color of summer clouds reflecting a sunset, brilliant and beautiful and brief, never again repeated in quite the same way. European music was like a moment of such a sunset, painted by Turner and reproduced to hang in numberless homes, a never-changing view seen always through the eyes of a single artist.

In America the music of the Negro naturally endured change. Ceremonial dancing and drumming had to be abandoned; the Negro was a slave, his culture was savagery. In the fields, laboring through long summer days, he developed the work song; in his whitewashed Christian church he transformed Scottish and English hymns into spirituals; in his cabin he sang the blues. The few, simple notes of the European melodies were broken up by him into a variety of subtle, quivering, sliding tones. Between E and F and between B and C on the scale he injected quarter tones, which he slurred at times so that they swung like a cry in the night—blue notes. Around these, and through the full, rich field of tone built into his voice, he improvised the story of his exile, his loneliness, his sorrow, and his despair. Nobody knew the trouble he'd seen, nobody knew but Jesus. He woke up in the morning and his woman was gone away. He worked all day and the sun never cooled a bit. But something within whispered glory to come, something within banished sorrow and pain. He would go to the river someday and cross, he would enter Beulah Land. He would walk all over God's heaven, and his shoes would be shiny bright. It had to be that way; there must be a God somewhere.

No one cared about his music; it was primitive, unorganized, without melody or harmony. So, being worthless, it was not taken from him. Besides, it solaced him, and sometimes, employed to interpret an old hymn, it had a not unpleasant sound. Obviously it could do no harm.

Freedom and city life and instruments gave surge and change and development to the music, but its manner and its expression remained the same. The performer was a medium through which the sounds exorcised from his unconscious were articulated; the instrument he played became an extension of himself; he talked or sang through it. He imparted to it the variety of tone and pitch native to his voice. He placed the theme or mood or rhythmic pattern or melody lightly on the point of his concentration and let his unconscious improvise around it. He did not need notes written on a page; he had a million of them in his head.

So jazz began, somewhere in the vicinity of 1870 in the city of New Orleans. The instruments of its expression were the cornet, the clarinet, the trombone, and the drums. The street bands, the earliest development, had alto and baritone horns. The dance bands, beginning in the 1890's, added piano, banjo, and tuba. All kinds of music went into the mold—work songs, hymns, blues, marches, ballads, minstrel tunes, and folk songs brought to America by Italian, Irish, Spanish, and French immigrants. It all came out jazz. The players also originated basic melodies and performed them for their fellow musicians, who contributed their improvisations, different each time the tune was played. Later this technique was adapted to any popular song. The melody was just an idea, a base on which to build variations.

The bands played for parades, for picnics, for funerals, in honky-tonks, at carnivals, and on the river boats. Often they climbed into wagons and drove through the streets to advertise the dances at which they were to play at night. The tailboard of the wagon was dropped and there, his feet hanging over, the trombone player sat. A trombone in a jazz band is still referred to as "tailgate." When two rival bands met at a street corner they locked wagon wheels and "cut" each other, blasting away with their instruments until one or the other group, winded and temporarily deaf, gave up and pulled away. The remaining band was declared victorious by the gathered crowd and its dance that night was the better attended. The best of the bands was Buddy Bolden's. Bolden was a barber by profession; he also published a scandal sheet and was a heller with women. When his band marched down the street he had a woman to carry his coat, a woman to carry his cap, and a woman to carry his horn when he wasn't playing. He easily won both of the popular titles, Kid and King. He enjoyed his fame, worked hard to enhance it, and went mad during a parade in 1907.

There was a funeral almost every day. In New Orleans where people must be buried above ground because of the marshy soil, interment is dramatic. Burial societies abounded among the

25

Negroes, and a man had to be a pauper not to go to his mausoleum with music. On the way to the cemetery the band played appropriately; one of the stock pieces was When The Saints Go Marching In. When the ceremony was finished and the march back home began, tempo quickened. The cornets sounded an introduction to Didn't He Ramble, He Rambled Round The Town Till The Butcher Cut Him Down. After that anything went, while the "second line" of admiring urchins danced and accompanied the musicians with their own improvisations on homemade instruments. On Sundays there were baseball games in Washington Park and picnics at Milneberg on. Lake Pontchartrain. In the repertory of every band was Milneberg Joys. Among the famous bands were the Excelsior, the Eagle, the Diamond, and the Reliance. After King Bolden the best cornet players were Freddie Keppard, Joe Oliver, and Louis Armstrong.

The cornet player was the boss man because he played the lead. He blew it loud and be blew it strong. When Keppard played vaudeville with the Creole Band no one could sit in the front rows of the orchestra. He blew them back to the middle of the house. The clarinet raced around the melody like a highstrung child, dashing in and out, climbing and falling on its face. The trombone, slurring, insinuating, and marking the time, was sometimes a part of the rhythm section, sometimes a contestant in the melodic commentary. The drums and bass and banjo and, later, the piano, marked the beat. The method of slapping the bass fiddle had an obvious origin. A player broke his bow during a performance and had to resort to plucking the strings; the result was so efficacious, rhythmically, that it became standard practice for jazz band players. The snare and bass drums of the marching band acquired appurtenances when they

26

no longer had to be played and carried at the same time; tom-toms, wood blocks, and triangles grew on them like Spanish moss. The piano, naturally a solo instrument, began edging its way into solo parts as soon as it was adopted by the dance bands.

The piano began its career in jazz in 1897. That year New Orleans decided to confine prostitution within a certain area. Twelve blocks were marked out in the French Quarter, one of them Basin Street. The ordinance creating the section was introduced by an alderman named Sidney Story; the most famous red-light district in the world was therefore called Story-ville. It was fabulous from the beginning. It had its own "blue book"; it had quadroons and octoroons, some of them beautiful beyond belief; it had rows of fifty-cent cribs and five-dollar houses with interiors resembling Hapsburg palaces; it had barrel houses where for a nickel customers filled their glasses from a cask and the spigot dripped whiskey into a gut bucket on the floor. There were gambling joints, cabarets, honky-tonks, and approximately two hundred places where, on a basic theme and with a sliding price scale, love was improvised. It was just the right place for a vital, uninhibited, noisy, growing art.

The bands played in the cabarets; they were too loud and dis-tracting for the bordellos; the madams preferred string ensem-bles and piano players. One of these pianists was Jelly Roll Mor-ton, composer of Milneberg Joys; another was Clarence Williams, who wrote I Ain't Gonna Give Nobody None Of My Jelly Roll. Another was Tony Jackson, who had a song called I've Got Elgin Movements In My Hips With Twenty Years' Guarantee. Morton wrote many tunes, as did Williams; it was Morton who adapted Tiger Rag from a French quadrille. At the cabarets pianos were included in the bands; among these cabarets were Peter Lalla's 25 Club, The 101 Ranch, The 28 Club, Rice's,

27

and The Tuxedo Dance Hall. In them during the early years of the century could be heard such men as Joe Oliver, Kid Ory, Jimmy Noone, Johnny and Baby Dodds, Freddie Keppard, Sidney Bechet, and Louis Armstrong. The oldest profession sponsored the newest of the arts; jazz grew and flowered in Storyville; its finest virtuosi were nourished there. In 1917 a Navy order to suppress all open prostitution brought its brief, brazen history to an end.

The high-priced girls rode off in style; the residents of the cribs marched away with their mattresses on their backs. The musicians scattered, looking for jobs. The remaining river boats, converted into excursion steamers, took some of the bands and carried them up the Mississippi and along its tributaries. They played their music at all the river towns; in the afternoon there was an excursion with dancing and picnic lunches, with mothers and nurses and children; in the evening young couples went on a moonlight cruise. Far up in Iowa, at Davenport, a boy in short pants named Beiderbecke sneaked back to listen to the band at night. At Cape Girardeau a youngster named Jess Stacy met each boat; later he played piano on one of them. Joe Oliver went to Chicago; Ma Rainey and Bessie Smith were on the road, singing the blues. Nobody knew what the music was, or what it meant, but it was getting around; it was being heard; it was even on records.

The first jazz on phonographs was played by white men, but this was not because of discrimination. In 1911 Freddie Keppard took some men from the Olympia band, formed the Creole Band, and went on a vaudeville tour over the entire country. It was the bass player in this band, Bill Johnson, who broke his bow and began the slap technique; the place, for history's information, was Shreveport. In New York in 1916 the Victor

28

Company asked Keppard to make some records. Keppard's reply is justly famous. "Nothing doing," he said. "We won't put our stuff on records for everybody to steal." So Victor passed the offer on to a group of white players then performing at Reisenweber's. The offer was accepted, the records were made, and the Original Dixieland Jazz Band introduced the music of New Orleans to the world. The band skyrocketed to fame, went to London, and returned in triumph. The Jazz Age was begun.

The members of the Original Dixieland Jazz Band were from New Orleans, where they had played in various groups under the direction of Jack Laine, the father of white jazz. Laine grew up under the influence of ragtime and such brass bands as King Bolden's. Improvisation attracted him as it did other white musicians, and although he and his men had to operate backwards, fighting through the habits and prejudices of musical training and education, they arrived at something which closely paralleled the Negro music they admired. Later young white players came along who did not bother to take lessons on their instruments; they went to the cabarets, listened to the Negroes, and practiced or "woodshedded," trying to reproduce the effects they heard. Under the leadership of Tom Brown a group of them went to Chicago in 1915 to play at the Lamb's Café. There was some union trouble, and the band found itself the victim of a campaign of slander. People were told that what they played was "jass" music. The word "jass" was known in Chicago, particularly in the red-light district, where only in a remote and very poetic way was it attached to music. The idea of "jass" music suddenly became fascinating; the slander backfired; the Lamb's Café was crowded every night. In its advertisements the café proudly spoke of its "Jass Band." The next year, when another band came to Chicago from New Orleans, it was known

29

as the "Dixie Land Jass Band." This was the organization which went on to New York and Reisenweber's.

When Storyville was shuttered Joe Oliver went to Chicago and began playing in the "black and tan" cafés of the south side. White jazz players from New Orleans also went to Chicago; they worked at the Friars' Inn under the name of the New Orleans Rhythm Kings. The war ended and prohibition began; suddenly the new music had another home, the speakeasy. In the damp, smoky atmosphere of a determined, common, and shared illegality the second great era of jazz began. While the Capone mob was forming itself to take control of the alcohol traffic, youngsters from Chicago high schools were listening in awe to King Oliver's trumpet and Leon Rappolo's clarinet, the drumming of Baby Dodds, the singing of Bessie Smith. Jazz was up the river; it had a beachhead on Lake Michigan.

National prohibition was the third strike for John Condon. He had moved from Goodland in 1907, when Indiana went dry, settling in Momence, Illinois, on the Kankakee River. Momence had also, after a while, gone dry; he had emigrated to Chicago Heights, a settlement twenty-five miles north of Momence and twenty-five miles south of Chicago. There he bowed to Andrew Volstead and accepted the inevitable; he became a policeman. The work was tedious but otherwise enjoyable. Sitting at home in the parlor after a day on the beat he sometimes said to his youngest son, "Albert, why don't you take that banjo and go down to the cellar and let me hear myself think while I'm reading the paper?" Albert went, and Mr. Condon pursued the reports of President Wilson's efforts to form a League of Nations and write a peace treaty while in Paris, the chords of Ida drifting up faintly as an obbligato to his thoughts. The despatches from Paris were pessimistic, but Mr. Condon was not a man easily discouraged. He had survived the failure, successively, of three banks, each containing all of his funds. When news of the last crash came he was taking a nap. Lucille, his eldest daughter, woke him up. "The bank's failed," she said. Her father yawned. "Some more good news," he said, and went back to sleep. He considered President Wilson a great leader, with a good chance of success. That was in 1919.

MOMENCE

THE SALOON was on one side of the street or the other, depending on how the people voted. Range Street ran through the middle of Momence, and down the middle of Range Street went the line dividing Momence Township from Ganeer Township. Local option was a popular political diversion and one or the other of the townships was always voting the drys in and the wets out, or the wets in and the drys out. A girl named Laura Brady had a hat shop across the street from the saloon, and that's the way it stayed. If Laura's side was wet and Pa's side was dry, she changed shops with him. If Pa's side then went dry and Laura's went wet, they switched again. Either way Laura's shop was opposite the saloon, and Pa's customers only had to remember to turn left or right when they came up the street in order to get a beer instead of a hat. Finally both sides went dry and Pa had to give up. But that was later.

Pennies were never put in the cash register; Pa had a superstition about spending them for anything except charity. He put them in a mixing bowl at the far end of the bar, and instructed his bartenders to do likewise. I sent the kids around back to wait for me. Then I went in from the street, walked through the cool beer smell to the end of the bar, watched my chance, stuck my hand in the mixing bowl, grabbed a fistful of pennies, and ran for the rear entrance. Then we hit every gum-ball machine in town.

Sometimes we bumped into Cliff, my oldest brother. He worked for the power company and was apt to be anywhere, climbing a pole or fixing a short. We listened to him sing; Allan von der Schmidt would come along and play the cornet. Cliff operated the moving picture machines at the Bijou at night. During the first and second shows, while his assistant was rewinding the film, he went down front and sang the song of the day, with illustrated slides, in color. On his way to work in the morning he stopped at the drugstore where the film was delivered. He unpacked the slides containing the song of the day and studied them; somewhere along the line he would run into Allan and get him to pick out the melody on his cornet. If we found Cliff when he had the song learned he was good for a nickel or a dime. Cliff could sing all the way from tenor to bass; he was front man in the choir at St. Patrick's Church, with the rest of the Condon mob behind him.

In a high wind Momence had three thousand people and some floating chickens. There were a lot of French, Polish, and Condons. Our family operated on a democratic principle; outside we were united against the world, inside we fought each other for exercise. When one of us got a chore from Ma he could either do it or try to get one of the others to do it. Ma would say to Dot (she was christened Florence but refused to answer to it), "Go down and look at the furnace." Just then I would come through the front door on my way to the back door—it was shorter than going around the house and there was always a chance of nudging Ma for a cookie or a slab of cake. "Go down and look at the furnace," Dot would say to me. I would detour to the cellar door, go halfway down the steps, come back up, say, "It's still there," and duck out. According to our rules that was fair.

33

I had protective coloration in a way; I was all khaki—pants, shirt, shoes, skin, and hair. Sometimes Ma couldn't see me when I was almost in front of her and would grab Jim, the next oldest, for a job. We had to bring in the corncobs Ma used for starting the fire in the kitchen range. When we argued about which was going to lug the basket Ma would say, "Carry it together or I'll cut your hair." Once she did cut our hair, and we were ashamed for weeks whenever we went out. When we were old enough Jim and I had to dry the dishes; we dropped a lot of them, but it was an old gag by that time and nobody took the towels away from us. "Just don't drop the Pluggy Mitchell bowl," Ma would say. I didn't know why it was called the Pluggy Mitchell bowl but I figured Pluggy must be quite a guy so I didn't drop it.

There was a lot of internal language in the family. A drink of liquor was referred to as "Mr. Smith's other." Somewhere in Indiana there was a Mrs. Smith who each day took a noon lunch to Mr. Smith. The lunchbox contained meat, potatoes, bread, pie, coffee, and "Mr. Smith's other," a half pint of whiskey. Criticism of anything or anybody was opposed by saying, "What's the matter with Hank?" I had a pal named Hank; his father was much older than his mother. Once I overheard one of my sisters saying it was "funny" about Hank's father being so old and having a strapping boy like Hank. I went charging into the kitchen with my fists up. "What's the matter with Hank?" I said. We also had a double talk called Hudge Gudge. We learned it from George Bourjois, a Frenchman who jabbered English so fast and with such an accent that you had to study what he said as if it were a foreign language. We also spoke English, particularly among our friends—Boonya Bydalek, Nine-toes Demack, Pig Jarvis, Nighthawk and "88" Mitchell,

34

Goat Bukoski, Bulldog Reynolds, Snake Kirby, Posy Gibeault, Rats Bukoski, and Kittyboo Chipman.

We all sat down at table together and if anyone got up to fetch something he had forgotten he was licked for the meal. Everyone else had something for him to get; if he got back into his chair before dessert he was a gazelle. Ma did all the baking, with the girls to help her—bread, pies, cakes, tarts, muffins. Pa usually brought a guest for dinner; somebody from dry Indiana was always passing through. He would have a touch of "Mr. Smith's other" and sit down to eat with us. One old family friend from Goodland got sentimental as he was leaving; he shook Pa's hand and said, "Come out to visit me and bring—" then he looked around and saw all of us staring at him—"and bring some of the children," he finished.

Occasionally we saw Uncle Jerr, one of Ma's brothers. Jerr figured there were two ways to live; a man could enjoy himself, or he could work. Jerr preferred to enjoy himself, so the family tied up his inheritance and rationed it to him little by little. It amused Jerr, particularly when some of the men involved in the rationing master-minded a bank into failure. "The only difference between me and Dennis," Jerr used to say in reference to one of his working and economically cautious brothers, "is that Dennis has a crease in his pants." Once Jerr actually went to work for some people back in the woods. He returned quickly. "Never saw anything like it," he said. "No reading matter except what's printed on sugar sacks and wrapping paper. Rottenest cook I ever ate after—fried the bacon so hard if you stuck it with a fork it would fly up and knock your eye out. And for that they expected me to work all day."

Jerr wore a crew-neck jersey, a derby, tennis shoes, and a gentleman's mustache. As soon as he received a ration from his inheritance he went from dry Indiana to wet Illinois. Once he was missing for some time. Then a body was found floating face down in a stone quarry near Kankakee. The size, the garb, the mustache, and a lip scar, all fitted Jerr. He was identified and carried back to Indiana. The family put a fancy suit of clothes on him and started a high-class wake; the best cooks in Benton County sent specimens of their work; people came from three states—friends, relatives, and gourmets. Everything was fine until Jerr walked in; nobody heard him because of his sneakers. He went right up to his sister Mary and said, "What the hell do you mean by not inviting me to my own wake? Am I that bad?" Women hit the floor like raindrops. When those who hadn't fainted saw that Jerr wasn't followed by a string of rats and wasn't dripping water from his clothes they realized he was alive. It was quite a party after that.

Jerr finally died in a hospital, winning a bet with the man in the next bed; Jerr bet he would go first, and he did. He entered the horizontal house wearing a red vest; he had a low opinion of death. Once when a farm hand in Indiana went berserk and killed his employer, Jerr was informed that the man had been sentenced to be hanged. "Hell," Jerr said, "they ought to do worse to him than that. They ought to take his chewing tobacco away."

We swam in a quarry near Momence. The first ledge was ten feet under water so you couldn't ease in. You learned to swim in the river; the quarry was not for beginners. There was a narrow gauge track running down into it and this was used for initiation into the gang. If you could dive down, get your hands on the track, pull yourself hand over hand to the bottom and throw a switch, you were in. The kids on top could hear the click as the switch closed down below.

36

In the river we fished, boated, swam, and ran trot lines. A trot line ran almost from bank to bank and was held under water by weights. It had hooks running all along its length. You just baited the hooks and came back twice a day to collect the fish. If there wasn't a good catch on our line we visited others, particularly those belonging to the Prairies. The Prairies were a large family living on the river; Pa said they had their names stamped on every fish in the Kankakee. We couldn't find the mark, though at one time or another we examined the fish on every Prairie trot line. Finally the Prairies came with shotguns and sat on the riverbank, and we gave up our scientific investigation.

There were shallow places in the river and one of them, about three miles south of town, had a sandy bottom; we swam there during the summer. John had to wear a brace to correct an injured kneecap and a tricky hip socket. Martina did his fighting for him and we all helped him get the brace off so he could swim. Ma wondered why he was so tired at night, but swimming did the trick. He finally threw away the brace and began to walk without help. There was a bridge over the river at the center of town. One day Jim and I hung Lloyd Black from it. He wouldn't give us his new pocketknife. We put a rope through his belt, lowered him, and left him there. Somebody saw us and told Pa. He went to the bridge and pulled Lloyd up; then he came and found us. We were trying out the knife, carving our initials on the window sills of a new house the town banker was building.

They had finally made me go to school. All the Catholic kids in town went to St. Patrick's Academy. There were mostly boarding students in the classes and they were jealous of us. We came to school eating apples and went home to our parents

37

every day. Their parents were separated, or were traveling people. When we started home one of them would chuck something at us. In winter we fought with snowballs; every snowball had a stone in it. In spring we played hooky on Friday and got whacked with a ruler on Monday by Father LaBrie. It was worth it to go walking in the woods and prowling on the river. In the woods we picked violets.

The Catholics in town were mostly French-Canadian. Father LaBrie. It was worth it to go walking in the woods and prowl-Sunday. We had religious instruction at home. There was an old family crucifix heavy as a lead pipe, with a small skull and bones at its base. One day Ma took me in her lap, put the crucifix on the table, and told me about Jesus. When she was finished she said, "Is there anything you would like to ask me?" I pointed at the skull and crossbones. "Who's that little fool down there?" I said.

Eventually I had to make my first communion. The day before the event I went to church and told my sins to Father LaBrie. When I got back I went into the kitchen. Ma was working around the stove. "Did you make a good confession?" she asked.

"Oh sure," I said, "it was swell."

"What did you tell Father LaBrie?"

"Oh, all that stuff about what I'm not supposed to do."

"About not doing what I tell you and being late for dinner and telling tales and fighting with Jim?"

"Sure, all that stuff."

"Did you tell him about the time you were pitching horse-shoes with Jim and you argued about a leaner, and you threw the horseshoe at him?"

38

"Jim doesn't care. I missed him and he hit me and broke my tooth."

"Well, what else did you tell Father LaBrie?"

"Oh, the usual stuff, like adultery."

"Adultery?" She opened the oven and stuck her head inside to look at some corn bread.

"Sure, fourteen times."

"That's quite a lot. What did Father LaBrie say?"

"He told me I ought not to do it so much. He said I ought to try to control myself."

"Well, I hope you will. Just how do you happen to commit adultery so often?" She couldn't seem to figure out whether the bread was doing all right; she kept sticking her head in the oven.

"Well, it's when I'm by myself."

"By yourself? Oh yes, of course. I forgot for a moment that's how you commit adultery."

"Sure, I get off by myself in a corner and cuss like the dickens. It's pretty bad."

"Yes, I guess it is. I'm afraid you will have to control yourself."

Martina got a bum steer on prayers. Grace taught her; Martina repeated the words after her each night. One night Grace was rolling along with "Hail Mary, full of grace—" when Martina interrupted her. "I can say my prayers by myself now," she said. "You go away." Grace was willing; she figured the job was done; the nuns at St. Patrick's would add the trimmings. It wasn't until years later that Ma overheard Martina saying, "Hail Mary, full of Martina. . . ."

Martina was the youngest sister; she did John's fighting for him, but only with nonrelatives. At home Jim would punch me, I would tell John, John would punch Jim, then Jim would tell Martina and Martina would punch John. Since I was the youngest and smallest there was nobody I could hang it on except Byron Tenant. Byron was a little odd, but he was good company. When we picked grapes he ate the skins and threw away the rest. He stuffed his nostrils with pebbles and went around that way all day. Once Byron and I got a contract from Ma to clean the cellar. We found a lot of pretty bottles on a shelf. The stuff in them was beautifully colored; some of it was green, some of it was yellow, some of it was white. We drank a little from each bottle. Ma found us sleeping under a cherry tree in the backyard, full of absinthe, crème de menthe, fernet branca, strega, benedictine, and chartreuse.

Before I went to church for the first time I had a vague idea that Mass was a songfest. Every Sunday morning the program of the choir was rehearsed from all parts of our house; chunks of it came from the kitchen, the dining room, and the various bedrooms. Anyone passing through the parlor hit a chord on the piano to set the pitch. On my first visit to St. Patrick's I sat in the family pew with Ma. It was quite a while before I discovered, behind and above me, the choir. Then I hollered, "Hi, Lucille!" Ma told me to turn around and keep quiet. "Why do we have to look the other way?" I wanted to know. I couldn't figure out why the people stared at the altar when the music was coming from the opposite direction. As soon as I got things straightened out I wanted to be an altar boy. I was too young but I persuaded the acolytes to break me in on Benediction, as a candle boy. They rehearsed me secretly and ran me on one Sunday afternoon. Everything was fine until it was time for Father LaBrie to sit down at the side of the altar. By then I was ready to sit down myself, so I looked around, picked a chair, and climbed into it. Father LaBrie sat on top of me. It was his chair.

"Don't be so ambitious," he whispered when we got ourselves untangled. "You are too young to be a bishop."

Father LaBrie looked like a good-natured bulldog. Pa said he was the only civilized man in Momence. He had a soft, wet handshake and a nephew named Gabriel who was thinking of studying for the priesthood. Once Gabriel took us down cellar and we tried the sacramental wine. Some of it was dry, some of it was sweet. We drank both kinds. Nothing happened. We were not changed. Gabriel decided not to become a priest.

Jim and I had a pal named Andy Peterson, who was indestructible. We had a feud with Andy once; Jim and I hid behind some hedges and when Andy went by on his scooter we dropped rocks on his head. He got off the scooter and looked at us with a very sad expression. "That's a hell of a thing to do," he said. "I thought you guys were my friends."

We all went together when the first frost came and gathered black walnuts. One fall day we were up a tree when Andy got an idea. "If I had an umbrella I could use it for a parachute and jump from here," he said. "Go home and get me one, Albert." Our house was only a block away so I ran back and hooked an umbrella from the hall. We all got down on the ground to watch Andy. He opened the umbrella, wriggled to the end of the highest branch, and jumped. As far as I can remember he came straight down. When we picked him up he said to me, "That wasn't the right kind of umbrella. Go home and get me a bigger one and I'll try it again."

Andy was with us the day Jim and I got our first second-hand bicycle. The handlebars were loose and we had trouble

41

tightening the nut sufficiently so they would stay in place. We put a wrench on the nut and when we couldn't move it any more Jim got a baseball bat. "Hold the bike steady and I'll hit the wrench," he said. Then he put both hands on the bat and swung backward with all his strength. He hit Andy, who was standing behind him, squarely on the head. "Excuse me," Andy said, "I didn't know I was in the way."

We took the bicycle down by the river to try it out and all the Prairie kids came after us. There were fifteen of them and they all wanted to ride. We gave in to the biggest one because we figured we couldn't lick him. He was wearing a cap; he fixed it at a jaunty angle and got on the bike. Just as he started the handlebars slipped again and he pitched forward. His cap fell over his eyes and he rode straight into the river. "The fish will know who he is," Jim said. "They're all related to him."

We objected to the Prairies because they used homemade bombs to stun the fish. They filled jugs with lime, put in water, jammed the corks, and dropped the jugs into the river. Trot lines were bad enough; we made them out of telephone wire and each one had about fifty hooks. We started from one bank in a rowboat and worked slowly to the other bank, pulling the line into the boat, taking the fish off the hooks and rebaiting them. There were catfish, redhorse, bass, bullheads, pickerel, and carp. We used a lot of bird meat for bait. Telephone lines from the town ran across the river and there were always a lot of swallows sitting on them. We knocked them off with slingshots, picked them out of the water, and cut them up. Andy Peterson showed us where to get the best shot for our slings. There was a factory in town which made ladders. One of the finishing processes consisted of saw-

42

ing small metal slugs off the ends of the rungs. A slug fitted perfectly into a sling; if you had a strong arm it was almost as good as a rifle bullet.

There was a man named Holycross who had a camp on an island down the river. Once during a summer he had to go away with his family to attend a funeral; it was a week's trip and he asked us to take care of the camp during his absence. We did—John, Jim, Martina, and I. On one side of the island the channel was shallow; cattle waded over from the mainland to graze during the day. We milked all the cows dry and wrestled the young bulls until they were exhausted. Near by on the other bank was a farm with a large chicken yard. We crossed in a boat, crawled through the underbrush, and with a .22 rifle shot three fryers a day for our dinner. When Mr. Holycross returned the farmers from both banks converged on him, and he went to Pa.

Pa had a lot of patience and a lot of humor. One day he received a letter from a state official, bringing to his attention the staggering number of unexplained absences from school compiled by his sons. The letterhead was embellished with a fancy seal, something to do with the department of education. Pa sat down and wrote a reply. What he said none of us ever knew, but when he finished it he took a silver dollar from his pocket, placed it at the top of the sheet of stationery, and hit it as hard as he could with a hammer. Then under his signature he scribbled, "P.S. Please take note of my seal." The hammer he used to hit the dollar was the same one Lucille used on him. When she was a baby she found it on the parlor floor and dragged it out to the porch, where Pa was sleeping in the hammock. By using both hands she managed to lift it and hit Pa right between the eyes. Ma always referred to it as the

43

time Pa exhibited his great command of the English language. The only time I heard him show off his vocabulary was the night someone forgot to put the marbles away. We had a large collection of aggies, migs, and snotties. They were supposed to be kept in a lard can, but one night they were strewn along the top of the stairs. Pa had long, narrow feet, but they weren't narrow enough to miss the migs. I heard him as he ricocheted off the banister; I was enchanted by the words.

We always wondered how he knew where we were and what we were doing, but running a saloon all day it was a fairly simple matter; someone would drop in for a beer and casually mention that Jim and I were fishing in the river or that Martina was practicing on the sparrows with Pa's new shotgun. Pa was an expert hunter; he kept the nuns at school supplied with ducks and game during the various seasons. He had a large collection of firearms, some of them antiques. When my brother John and Jack Clegg went on a canoe trip to New Orleans—down the Kankakee, the Illinois, and the Mississippi—John was careful not to take any of the antiques. He took the new guns, the finest Pa had ever owned. Their eighteen-foot Old Town canoe turned over during the trip. John and Jack came up all right; the shotguns stayed down.

Pa had a real worry one day. The Kankakee was at spring high; my sisters Grace and Dot went down it in a flat-bottom boat with only a push paddle, which they lost. They waved frantically to farmers on shore but the farmers thought they were just being friendly and waved back. Betty, our brown and white Irish setter, ran along the bank, then jumped into the water and swam behind the boat until she was exhausted. Grace and Dot dragged her aboard. Pa heard the girls were on the river and got some buggies to ride along both sides until

44

the drivers spotted the boat. It was in the current and going at a good clip. When the farmers found out from the drivers of the buggies what was wrong one of them phoned ahead to a man named Hoag, who dragged a boat from his haymow and went to the rescue. By the time he managed to get the girls ashore we were on the spot, having ridden down in a carriage. Grace and Dot were badly scared but Martina thought it was all great fun. "Hey, Mr. Hoag," she said, "how about taking me for a ride now?"

The time came when Betty got so old she had to be shot. We talked about it for weeks, trying to figure some way of avoiding the execution. For twelve years Betty had been a member of the family. Once on a rainy night when I was small Ma put a raincoat over her head and went into the backyard for something. I heard Betty bark at her. I ran to the door and said, "Why, Betty Condon, don't you know your own mother?" When I wandered from the house Betty went to look for me; if I got in the road she nudged me back to the sidewalk; she pushed me home when she thought I ought to go there. When I got lost one day during a political rally it was Betty who found me up on the speakers' platform, sitting in Governor Dunn's lap. The boys got mad and the girls went around sniffling all the time we were talking about the execution. Finally Martina said, "I'll do it!" She put one of Pa's .38 revolvers in her blouse, called to Betty, and went off with her down the river. When she returned one bullet had been fired from the pistol and Betty was dead.

But Martina didn't shoot Betty. We found that out long afterward. She got to a lonely place on the river and pulled out the gun and pointed it at Betty. Betty crawled to her, looked up, and whimpered. Martina couldn't pull the trigger.

45

She sat on a rock and cried until George Terrell, a boy she knew, came along carrying a .32 rifle. He shot Betty and threw her body into the river while Martina blubbered. After it was over Martina dried her eyes and fired a shot into the air and went home.

I believed Martina shot Betty and I thought it was very brave of her. I remembered the time Martina had to choose between saving me or Betty from drowning; she made up her mind to rescue both of us and she did. It was winter and Martina, Betty, and I went to the river to look for shinny sticks, which we made by bending willows, charring them at the turn, then cutting them off at the base.

The ice was treacherous; there had been a freeze, a thaw, and then another freeze. There was a thin layer of ice, a lot of water, and then solid ice. Martina and I started to cross to the opposite bank. The ice was cracking but we thought we could make it; then Betty came after us and her weight was too much; the three of us went into the water. Martina was tall enough to stand on the solid ice beneath the water but she had to hold me up so I could breathe and break a path through the thin ice to shore. She was doing all right until she noticed that Betty, who was heavy and old, was having trouble staying up. Automatically she loosened her grip on me and reached for Betty; then she remembered and grabbed me again. Later she admitted wondering which of us it was more worth while to save. While making up her mind she kept pushing me ahead, breaking the ice, and turning to give Betty a pull. Somehow all three of us got to shore; Martina was exhausted for days and Betty and I had colds. After Betty's assassination Martina and I caught a mongrel and turned him into a fox terrier. I held him and Martina chopped off his tail.

46

Winter came early to Momence; we had snow by Thanksgiving and it settled down for the season like an old woman at a wake. We played shinny and skated on the river and went sledding wherever we found a slight incline. In the mornings we hopped out of bed and raced for the base-burner downstairs. It was the only place where we could get dressed without breaking in two from the cold. The girls pressed their hair ribbons on the hot stovepipe. Everyone who came to the house, whether for business or pleasure, stepped in for a session at the base-burner and a nip from one of the fancy bottles on the sideboard. One day Pete Nichols came to deliver eggs. He was dressed to the eyes in a bearskin coat. Pa asked him to step to the base-burner and have a touch of "Mr. Smith's other." Pete was slightly taciturn; he had mastered a single sentence and that was all he ever spoke: "Well, that's all right, far's that's concerned." After the first drink Pa asked him to have another. "Well," Pete said, "that's all right, far's that's concerned." Meanwhile he didn't take off his coat or even unbutton it and he stayed smack up against the base-burner, which was in high gear. Pa offered a third drink and Pete said, "Well, that's all right, far's that's concerned." I noticed that he was disappearing into his bearskin coat. After the fifth drink I could see nothing of his head at all (I was close to the floor, looking up at a sharp angle) but I could hear a voice coming up through the coat, saying, "Well-l-l-l, thass l'right, farzzatz concerrn."

Saloonkeepers in those days received fancy liqueurs and cordials as gifts from the brewery and distillery salesmen. Pa brought them home and Ma put them on the sideboard. One Christmas Lucille fell in love with a very elaborate bottle and asked Ma if she could have it when it was empty. Ma said she

47

could but the stuff disappeared slowly; the boys at the base-burner preferred straight whiskey. One day while Ma was away Lucille decided to take things in her own hands; she emptied the bottle. When Ma got home her oldest daughter was hanging over the picket fence, passed out cold. After that Lucille never drank anything stronger than lukewarm water.

There were always fellows coming to see the girls. One night Dot was entertaining a particularly bashful young man in the parlor. Martina, always helpful, leaned over the banister and called down to her: "Dot, if you'll put the pot on the stairs I'll come down and get it." Grace had a friend from Chicago who was a real city boy. When he saw the basket of cobs in the kitchen near the stove he asked Ma what it was. "It's a kind of cereal we use here in the country," Ma said. "Unless you eat it you can't survive a winter in this climate." The boy was worried. "I'm only going to be here over the week end," he said. "Do you think I ought to eat some?" Ma thought it over. "No," she said finally, "I don't think it will be necessary. But when you go outside don't breathe deeply." "I won't," the boy promised.

Helena was tall and slender; one spring day she took me to a carnival. There was a dwarf playing a calliope. He was worried because he had lost the sheet music to a song he had to learn—*Down Among The Sheltering Palms*. Helena knew the lyrics so she offered to teach him. I stuck around, chewing an apple and squirting juice over the keyboard. The dwarf finally got so mad at me he tossed me out of the park. I went straight home and told Ma: "There's a little poop at the tent show trying to shine up to Helena." Helena was not flattered. "Albert just doesn't appreciate music," she said.

They all called me Albert then. I thought it was a fine name; I like elegance. There was a rim of stained glass around our

48

parlor windows; that was for me. One day I came home from school at noon and asked Ma for a quarter; there were a lot of things needed in the church and in the school and the nuns put the bite on us pretty often. "Sister Mary Carmel says for us to bring a quarter and the poor kids can bring a dime," I said. It was the usual deal; Ma had been shelling out quarters for years. She must have been a little fed up because that day when I got ready to go back for the afternoon session she handed me a dime. She didn't say anything, just gave it to me. I went out on the front porch and sat down. I couldn't go to school; it was too awful. How could we be poor with that stained glass? Didn't Pa buy all the tickets to the church bazaars and weren't we always sending things to the nuns? I couldn't figure it out.

Suddenly the door opened and Ma came out. "What are you doing here, Albert?" she said. I went up and grabbed her hand—she was a soft touch usually. "I can't go to school with only a dime," I said. "Sister Mary Carmel will think we are poor." Ma shook me off. "You get off this porch right this minute and go to school. Give Sister Mary Carmel the dime and tell her your mother said the more often she asks the less it will be. Now get!"

The first job I had was working for Father LaBrie. A new church was being built, with a slate roof. The slate was very handy; we broke it up and made arrowheads and shot the neighbors' chickens. I was picking up some slate one summer day when Father LaBrie asked me if I would like a job carrying water for the workmen. I reported next morning and lugged pails up ladders all day; at five o'clock I was told that the job was too dangerous for me. Father LaBrie paid me off; he wrote out a check for one dollar. The next day I went to the bank to cash it. The teller took it and disappeared from

49

his cage. Then Mr. Parish, the president of the bank, came out and asked me into his office. I sat down in a big leather chair.

"I am glad you have come to us with this transaction, Albert," he said. "However, we do not normally handle deals of such magnitude."

I thought he meant it was too small, so I said, "Haven't you got a little guy who can do it?"

He shook his head. "I think our biggest man should expedite this," he said. Then he went out and brought back the tallest man in the place. The man shook hands with me and we all had a nice talk. Finally I got my dollar, a brand new one, and Mr. Parish saw me to the door.

"If you have any business in the future, I hope you will remember us," he said.

My first real job was at Melby's combination furniture store and undertaking parlor. I had a shoeshine stand outside and I watched the stiffs for Mr. Melby while he was away. We had a lot of interesting bodies; they floated down the Kankakee, especially in good weather. Once we got several from an automobile wreck, which in those days was an uncommon event. "They must have been swell people," I reported to Ma. "There's silk underwear all over the place." With my first earnings I went to Clegg's and ordered a pair of English shoes. Nothing else would satisfy me. Pa took one look at the pointed toes and said, "I know what those shoes are for—kicking a snake in the behind."

During the summers we visited our aunts and uncles on their Indiana farms. We liked Mary Condon Garvin, who was a Holy Roller when we were young. Another of Pa's sisters was Lizzie Garrity. Aunt Lizzie sent her washing to a colored woman who sent her two small boys with a wagon to pick up the clothes. They told Aunt Lizzie their name was Casey. Aunt Lizzie said, "My, my, there must be a little Irish in you." The next week the boys came back and said, "Our mother said to tell you that our grandfather was Irish and that we ain't one bit ashamed of it."

Our neighbors in Momence were, in the order of their appearance, Swedish, French, and Jewish. The Swedish lady kept chickens and an old horse and was always losing her false teeth. One day she found an old upper plate in the chicken yard. She put it right in her mouth in place of the new one, which didn't fit. When her horse died she cried for three days. The French lady had a vicious pet bulldog whose greatest ambition was to eat the Condon kids. Every afternoon his mistress served him tea and toast on the porch.

Beyond our street the farms began. The first of them was L-shaped, with a cornfield and an orchard near the street. We robbed the orchard and cut down, just before husking time, thirty square yards in the middle of the cornfield for a camp. We couldn't be seen from the street; we lived a fine life in our tepees.

Halloween was all year around in Momence. One of the happy moments I remember was the evening we stuck a fishing pole through Mr. Clark's wire fence and set the other end in the fork of a young tree, bridging the sidewalk. It was just getting dark and the biggest Prairie boy was coming home from work, carrying his lunchbox and whistling *There'll Be A Hot Time In The Old Town Tonight*. He hit the pole and a high note at the same time. I can still hear the lunchbox hitting the sidewalk. It made a wonderful sound.

The drys were trying to get both sides of Range Street. One of them ran a dry goods store. He worked very hard one spring.

51

Still the wets won. On election night Cliff took his quartet to the dry goods store and serenaded it with, *Don't worry, keep on smiling and the world will smile with you.* The last line was, *The sun will shine tomorrow and we'll all drink beer.* The quartet consisted, in addition to Cliff, of Henry Contois, a Frenchman; Dutch Gelino, a German; and Johnny Morgan, a Negro.

In 1914 the drys finally won in both townships and Pa had to close up. He decided to move to Chicago Heights. By that time the kids were calling me Eddie and I was playing piano by ear, in the key of F.

CHICAGO HEIGHTS

THE LAW kept Pa on the move. He went to Chicago Heights ahead of the family and opened a place. One night a young dude from Momence dropped in with his girl. "What will you have?" Pa said to the girl. "I believe I shall drink some whiskey," said the girl. "Like hell you will," Pa said. "You'll drink beer while you're in here." Saloonkeepers like that were a menace to progress; they were reactionary. In a few years they were outlawed. After that anybody could drink anything.

Back in Momence Jim and I helped to lose a race at the Kankakee County Fair. We had a friend named Daisy Baby. Daisy Baby's father had a barn, and one of his father's friends kept a horse in the barn. The horse was being trained to run in the big race at the fair. We looked him over one day and decided to give him a workout. We hitched him to a buggy and drove him down the road, fording the river at a shallow place and trotting along the road on the opposite bank. Suddenly another horse and buggy loomed up; Baby's father was driving it. He spotted us and let out a howl of rage. We turned around and started for home, breaking the horse into a gallop. We went through the ford without slackening pace and beat Baby's father to the barn. The horse seemed winded; maybe we pushed him too hard. He entered the race but his rival won the event going away. Later some man who lost a lot of money on our horse played a dirty trick on Baby. He tied him to a tree and held snuff under his nose; every time Baby sneezed he hit his head against the trunk.

How to make money was a continuous problem. A man we called "Rags" had a junk yard down by the river; there was so much stuff scattered around that he never knew how much or what he had. One day on the river Jim and I pushed a few solid pieces off the bank into our boat. Then we rode to the bridge, carried the junk around the corner, and presented it to Rags. He bought it, carried it out back, and set it down again. Whenever our backs were strong enough we picked it up and sold it to him again.

Pa finally found a house in Chicago Heights that was big enough and solid enough to hold his family, and sufficiently isolated to protect his neighbors. It was on top of a hill; after a rain there were wonderful puddles down below. I wanted to impress the neighborhood kids so one day after a thunderstorm I put on Pa's new hunting boots and went down to show off. I was lost in them; I tied the straps over my shoulders. I was doing fine though, getting a lot of attention, when I heard a voice from the top of the hill—my father's. He called just once: "Albert!" Never before had he referred to me as anything but "The Indian." I pulled out of the puddle and walked up the hill. It seemed a long way; all the kids knew I was going to catch hell; so did I. Pa pulled me out of the boots and for the first and only time gave me a lacing. Knowing what he had to endure I consider this a remarkable record.

Chicago Heights was a big city to me—25,000 people. We made the rounds of the factories, checked the candy stores, and fought with local kids. One of them sunk his teeth in John's eyebrow but didn't bite it off; it happened to be Good Friday, a strict fast. We attended St. Agnes' church and went to public school. I found a way to make money—caddying at Olympia Fields, a golf club three miles from town. There were four courses, all served by a creek which acted as a natural water hazard. On week days I caddied; on week ends I worked at the water holes. Early in the morning I went to the most dangerous spot on the creek, put on my bathing suit, and waited. Every time a ball landed in the water I jumped in and retrieved it; the tip was usually a quarter. A lot of the players were duffers, but they were too proud to use a ball that floated—that was for beginners. They wanted something that would carry far and sink deep; so did I.

In the evenings I played twilight golf with Hughie Siren, the caddy master; I also made friends with Bill Lowry, the club steward. One day Bill offered me a job taking care of the service bar in the dining room. One of my chores was to come in early in the morning and mop up. The second day I got interested in the fancy liqueur bottles on the shelf. I took a sip from each by way of education. When Bill came in he couldn't tell me from the mop. He offered me my resignation; I accepted it and went to sleep.

Shortly after we moved to Chicago Heights Ma had a stroke. She was in bed for a few months; then she began to get around in a wheel chair. Every afternoon I pushed her to church and waited while she said the stations of the cross and lighted a votive candle. I could usually get enough out of her to support me at a candy store while I waited; I put the bite on while I was lacing her shoes or pulling her corset tight—the corset was a good touch for movie money, too. One day we got all the way to church and I was still broke. "I suppose you haven't got a dime?" I said. "No," she said, "I haven't." "How about the candles you light?" I said. "They cost a dime." "I have a charge account," Ma said.

We got along very well together. She had lost her sense of smell, so she couldn't check on my breath for evidence of cigarette smoking; and I was deaf in my right ear, so I couldn't hear certain things she told me not to do. The girls had to take over the housework for her and theoretically they had charge of me, but there were so many of them that I always had a defender as well as an accuser. I began cribbing puffs from John's cigarettes; Jim and I hung around whenever he lighted one. "Be polite about it," Jim said. "Wait until the match goes out before you ask him." We had to look after the furnace; every night Cliff complained that we used too much coal, and we kept on using too much, but it was like dropping dishes; it didn't get us fired. One night when it was my turn to go down into the cellar Jim said, "Don't forget to count the lumps." He kept the cellar door open and I hollered up to him, "One, two, three, four, five . . ." but Cliff sat and paid no attention; he was too smart for us.

Jim went into the seventh grade and I went into the sixth. The next year I went into the seventh grade and Jim stayed in it. The next year when school opened and we said good-by to Ma on the first day she said, "Well, Jim, are you going to be in the seventh grade again?" "Yes," Jim said. "How nice," Ma said. "Why don't you teach it this year?"

One day recess for the seventh grade coincided with a passing freight train and Jim decided to take a course in bumology. Among the things he left behind was a ukulele, a present from Mary Burgel, one of the various friends of my various sisters. There were girls all over our house all of the time—washing hair, making fudge, beating on the piano, sewing, talking a lot

56

of stuff which made no sense to me. All of my sisters played the piano except Martina. Lucille played by ear. Dot, Grace, and Helena took lessons; so did John. Helena and Grace didn't get along with their teachers; they ragged the scales they were supposed to learn and played notes that weren't in the score. I kept after them to speed it up, to play something "fast." Then I'd get *Oceana Roll* or *If He Can Fight Like He Can Love— What A Soldier Boy He'll Be.* The girls learned to accompany Pa while he played his fiddle. He had a repertoire that included *Fisher's Hornpipe, Rye Waltz, Irish Washerwoman, Pop Goes The Weasel,* and *Casey Jones.* He played them over and over, beating time with his number twelve feet. Ma's favorite tune was *Nobody Knows And Nobody Seems To Care.* It was a perfect commentary on her mob.

I began to play Jim's ukulele; it was a good instrument, a Lyon and Healy, costing about fifty dollars. It wasn't hard to learn; all my life I had heard chords and I could play them on the piano. With Pa on the fiddle, Cliff on the alto horn, and one of the girls at the piano it was easy for me to sneak in and play the rhythm; with all that noise nobody knew I was there.

Cliff and the girls sang in the church choir and helped out when the parish put on a home talent show to pay the coal bill. I went to see them perform one night and sat next to a sad-faced man who didn't applaud or laugh or even smile. Since I was giving everybody a big hand, even those who were not related to me by blood, I got a little annoyed, particularly since the man was giving me a cold eye every time I laughed or clapped. After one of Cliff's solos I caught the guy looking at me and gave him the eye right back. "Say," I said, "what's the matter with you? I came here to have some fun and I'm going to have it, whether you like it or not." He hissed right back at me, "Hams! You're all hams!" I didn't know what to say because I couldn't figure out what he meant; I was afraid it was a new kind of word for a Catholic, or a saloonkeeper's kid. Later I told Ma and she explained. "It just means you're a Condon," she said.

In the eighth grade my scholastic integrity was tempted and it fell. The class was taught by the principal of the school, a good-looking man who lectured on the evils of smoking and who was an aspirin fiend. One day I and my pal, Joe Klingaman, finished an umbrella stand in manual training and decided to give it to the principal for a present. We took it to his private house, knocked at the door, and were let in. We walked into the living room and found him smoking a cigarette. We didn't say anything, just gave him the umbrella stand, but after that I was always called from class and sent out to get him some aspirin. Both of us understood that I was to take my bicycle and ride around town for as long as I liked before coming back. No matter what I did I got high marks, so I didn't bother to learn algebra or much of anything else. I was graduated with honors at the age of twelve.

The next fall I entered high school. I didn't know anything about algebra; I smoked cigarettes; I was nuts about music; I hung around with older boys; and I could shoot pool, play golf, fight, and give the worst Swedish massage west of Pough-keepsie—I did it for Ma. Jim came home after his year of bumology and brought some phonograph records. I had never heard anything like the music that was on them—*Muscle Shoals Blues* and *Aunt Hagar's Children's Blues* by Mamie Smith and Her Jass Hounds. "What's that?" I asked Jim. "It's a new kind of music," Jim said. "How do you like it?" I listened for a while. "It doesn't bother me," I said. Jim got some more records and we played them over and over, blues and popular tunes by the

Paul Biese Trio, Wilbur Sweatman's band, Ted Lewis, Art Hickman and the Edison Trio. The new kind of music had all of us listening. Lucille had signed up for a course in ragtime in Chicago; after the second lesson her teacher asked her not to come back; he told her she was far ahead of him. She had been playing at home, under her own inspiration, for so long and for such a hard mob of critics that she was better than any of us thought. Now she began picking tricks off the new records, adding them to the technique she had developed playing *That International Rag* and *Maple Leaf Rag*.

There was a lot of battle stuff to play around that time— *Tipperary, Keep The Home Fires Burning, Pack Up Your Troubles, Rose Of No Man's Land, Liberty Bell It's Time To Ring Again, Oh How I Hate To Get Up In The Morning, K-K-K-Katy, Over There, Till We Meet Again.* The brush fire in Europe was stamped out temporarily on November 11, 1918. I was a cheerleader at high school by then, practically in charge of the entire armistice celebration, so I thought. After the war there was a reconversion of aluminum pots to kitchen use—the kids who had been using them for trench helmets gave them back to their mothers. The girls stopped knitting sweaters and went back to talking about Mary Pickford, Pearl White, Theda Bara, and Norma Talmadge. I ran into a kid named Jimmy Ainscough, who played the piano and wanted to start a band. Jack Dunn gave Jim a short-necked tenor banjo and I kept the ukulele. With Jimmy on the piano we beat out *Pretty Baby, For Me And My Gal, The Darktown Strutters' Ball,* and a couple of new tunes called *Hindustan* and *Ja-Da*. I realized that Ma had the right idea; according to her anything we played could be called by her favorite title, *Nobody Knows And Nobody Seems To Care.*

59

While the boys were away at war some of the ladies and gentlemen at home succeeded in putting over the Eighteenth Amendment; the law finally had Pa tied to the tracks. He closed up; trucks came and took the stock away. It had always been a successful and popular saloon although the books never showed it. Pa was a soft touch; he kept a portion of what he made only because nobody asked him for it. Now he made a logical move; he joined the police. They asked him to take a marksmanship test. He stepped up with an old .45 six-shooter and made six bulls'-eyes. He got the job but almost immediately was in trouble. Two men he arrested, one white and one colored, were brought before a local judge. The judge turned the white man loose and sent the Negro to jail. Pa told the judge what he thought of him in language which the court clerk refused to take down; he said there were no shorthand symbols for it. A couple of years later the diatribe paid off. Three white thugs jumped Pa one night and had him in a bad way. Two Negroes came along and saved him.

Another freight train came along and Jim grabbed it. I got the tenor banjo. I practiced in the living room until Pa came home; then I went down into the cellar so he could read the newspaper in peace. "It's not what I hear that bothers me, it's how much of it," he explained. "How are you doing?" "Fine," I said. "How is that guy Wilson doing over in Paris?" "Fine," Pa said. "You can't beat the Democrats, even if they are Presbyterians."

In the cellar I opened the furnace door to give myself some light. Then I pulled up a wheelbarrow and sat in it. It was like being in front of a fireplace; I practiced chords until my fingers got tired, then I watched the flames. Usually I ended by falling asleep. Ma would miss me and send one of the girls down to wake me and drag me upstairs to bed.

Jimmy Ainscough found a saxophone player and a kid who owned a set of drums. We organized a band and began practicing, usually at our house. One day Jimmy grabbed me in school. His eyes were halfway out of his face. "We've got a job!" he whispered. It was like being tipped off that we were being scouted by the White Sox. I swallowed whatever was in my mouth and said, "Where?" "The Odd Fellows," Jimmy said. I leaned against the wall. "What'll we play?" I asked. Jimmy bent down so no one could overhear his plan. "We'll start out each time on a different tune," he said. "If we get lost everybody go into *Ida* in the key of C."

We played the date and *Ida* sounded wonderful, at least to us. We got other dates, and I began to save my money to buy a pair of long pants. Jimmy and I were the only permanent members of the band; the others changed from date to date and the outfit never had a name. It just showed up at the appointed time and played *Dardanella, I'm Forever Blowing Bubbles, Swanee, Avalon, Japanese Sandman, Whispering, I'm Sorry I Made You Cry, Alice Blue Gown, How Ya Gonna Keep 'Em Down On The Farm?* I sat out in front where I could see the dancers and watch the boys tossing their lines at the girls. It was wonderful. There were two things in the world which obviously were fun: music and girls. I would get to the girls as soon as I got the long pants.

The one-armed cornet player Wingy Mannone once said, "You can't work all night and fight all day." I realized this in 1919; I began losing sleep then and I have never been able since to pay myself any more than the interest on the debt. I began falling asleep in school. I fell asleep under the dining-room table after breakfast, before I even got to school. At the end of the first term I was given a quarter credit in gymnasium;

61

everything else was a blank. At the end of the second term I got another quarter credit for gymnasium—I was always present and my blood was circulating. The only other credits I got were negative; the principal, whom we called The Duke, considered me the source of all the evil in the school. No matter what happened he would say, "Albert cooked that one up," and grab me. If I met him in the hall he would say, "Well, Albert, are you still smoking?" Then he would stick his hand in my pocket and take my cigarettes. My pals were juniors and seniors in the school; The Duke believed that I taught them to smoke and to chew tobacco. He also believed that I was their source of cigarettes. "Albert," he would say to me, "I believe you have a father and a mother?" "Yes, sir, one of each," I would say. "I suppose they have plans for your future, and hopes?" he would ask. "They hope I will come home from school today," I would answer.

Finally Pa said to me, "Don't you think you ought to do better in your studies?" I told him the truth. "I want to be a musician," I said. "Well," he said, "there is nothing wrong with that, except that if you are a bad musician you may not be able to make a living and probably you will be hanged. You had better go down cellar and practice some more. Right now you are terrible and you can't read music." I looked at him in astonishment. "What's that got to do with being a musician?" I asked.

Just over the Indiana line there was a summer resort called Cedar Lake, with a pavilion for dancing and an orchestra seven nights a week. Some of the good bands came there and I went every night to listen and to dance (I had long pants now). This took a lot of time and I spent most of the day sleeping. As soon as I got up I practiced. Jimmy was the only member of the band who could read music. He played over the melodies and helped me on chordal structure. The reed and horn players, if we had any, picked up the melody, and the drummer slugged it out for himself. Jimmy got the job and we were paid seven or eight dollars each. Chicago Heights was split in two by the main line of the Chicago and Eastern Illinois Railroad; on the east side of the tracks were factories, a colored section, and an Italian settlement. The factories were mostly subsidiary steel plants and the workers were only gentlemen up to a point. It was fun to play for them but it was wise to set up the instruments near a door or an open window. We were still playing *Ida* in the key of C.

The country dances outside of town were also apt to be athletic. One Sunday morning after church Jim and I met a group of friends who had been to a barn dance the night before. "You sure missed it," one of them said to us. "We had a wonderful time! One of the guys got hit over the head with a wagon tongue."

The girls finally began to put pressure on me. Dot refused to launder my white shirts. She figured I was a dude and that as soon as I ran out of clean shirts I would come to terms. The terms were that I stay home on certain nights, get in early on other nights, get up at a reasonable hour, and contribute to the communal labor. I rejected the offer. I had a lot of shirts and I began to take good care of the collars and cuffs. I worked out the spots on them and ironed them on the breadboard I had made for Ma in manual training. "I'll get you yet," Dot said. "You can't keep that up forever."

Sisters are harder to manipulate than mothers; I could always get around Ma, or at least I thought I could. She tricked me once in Momence and I didn't realize it for a year. I went to her one day and said, "I never get to do anything. Yesterday Leo

Barsaleau almost got to go to Kankakee on the wagon." Ma said, "Well, maybe I have been a little hard on you. I don't think Leo Barsaleau should have something that you haven't got. Tomorrow you can almost get to go on the wagon to Kankakee." I was completely satisfied.

I was still ironing collars and cuffs on the breadboard when Cliff came home for a visit. He had been away most of the time since the beginning of the war, when he went to work for the government as an electrician. Now he was in Cedar Rapids, Iowa, working for Uncle Dave. Uncle Dave had been put in a pesthouse during an epidemic of smallpox and while incarcerated had amused himself by inventing a vault lock for banks. It was so efficient it changed the working hours of bandits in three states; they had to pull their stickups during the day, while the vaults were open for business; at night they couldn't crack Uncle Dave's lock. He found he could manufacture them for fifteen dollars; with Cliff to do the installing, the price to a bank was three hundred dollars. Uncle Dave got well* and set up a shop in Cedar Rapids.

Pa was proud of Uncle Dave. "He's done a wonderful thing for those bandits," he told Cliff. "Now they'll be able to spend the evenings with their families and live a normal life. Maybe after a while the police will be able to do the same thing." Then I told Cliff about Jim. Jim had bummed his way to California and enlisted in the cavalry. He had sent us a group picture of his company; the picture was three feet long and it took us seventeen days to find Jim. "Jim is no fool," Pa said. "In the next war the only safe place in the world will be on a horse."

"What's Albert doing?" Cliff asked.

"You can call me Eddie," I said.

* became prosperous

"He isn't doing a thing," Pa said. "He won't go to school and he can't play the banjo."

"I can play *Ida* good now," I said.

"He can iron shirts, too," Dot said. "Get him a job in a laundry, Cliff."

"I worked two weeks in the mill," I said.

"You were fired for falling asleep," Pa pointed out.

"Well, maybe we ought to have one professional musician in the family," Cliff said. "The rest of us do it for nothing."

"How can he be a professional musician when he can't read music?" This was a pitch from somebody in the next room.

"He doesn't have to read music; he can play it." This came from somebody in the hall.

"Has anybody looked at the fire? It seems to be going out." This came from the kitchen.

"I worked two weeks in the mill," I insisted.

"How many tons of coal have you ordered for the winter?" Cliff said to Pa.

"I haven't made up my mind," Pa said. "It depends on how many Albert needs to keep him warm while he practices."

"You can call me Eddie," I said.

"Why don't you get him a job in a bank, Cliff? He can keep the robbers away by playing his banjo." This was from somebody on his way upstairs, leaning over the banister.

"I can play *Ida* good," I said.

"Has anybody seen the music for *Kitten On The Keys?*" one of the girls asked.

"Who can play it?" Cliff asked.

"I can play *I'm Just Wild About Harry*," I said, "in the key of F."

"What do you think of Harding?" Pa said.

65

"I think he is President," I said.

"That is a personal opinion," Pa answered.

"Maybe I can get you a job in Cedar Rapids," Cliff said.

"Would you like to hear me sing *My Man?*" Dot asked.

Cliff went back to Cedar Rapids and a few weeks later Pa said, "I have a letter from Cliff. He has a job for Albert in Cedar Rapids." I said, "I don't want a job. I want to be a musician. I worked two weeks in the mill." Pa handed me the letter. "That's what the job is. You're going to play in an orchestra." I sat down fast. After a while I said, a little quietly, "I can't read music." Pa said, "You don't have to read music; they just want you to play the banjo."

Suddenly I jumped up and grabbed Dot. "If you wash and iron all my white shirts for me I'll give you five dollars from my first week's pay," I said. "I'll do it," she said, "but only because you are my brother. I'll never see the five dollars." For two days we had white Christmas in the backyard. Then I packed up my banjo and shirts and took the train to Cedar Rapids. It was September, 1921.

PEAVEY'S
JAZZ BANDITS

IT WAS the longest trip I had ever taken and I was all by myself. I smoked cigarettes and didn't care who saw me. This is the nuts, I thought, regular transcontinental stuff. Cedar Rapids was the big time for me—60,000 people all day, standing or sitting. Cliff met me at the station. "Did you meet any beautiful women on the train?" he asked. "I had my dough in my shoe," I said.

Uncle Dave had a family and lived with it; Cliff had a furnished room and shared it with me. Every morning we walked together to the business section; Cliff went to a bank and I went to a poolroom. I always figured it was a good idea to have a secondary skill, something to fall back on for room rent. I learned to shoot pool stealing shots in Momence, during a brief matriculation as pin boy in the local bowling alley. Now I could hold my own with any stranger unless he had three arms. There were only a few of these around.

The day after I arrived Cliff introduced me to Bill Engleman, a local businessman who liked music and had a dance band. "This is the brother I was telling you about who isn't doing anything and plays the banjo," Cliff said. Engleman indicated that he would be interested in how I was feeling and I told him I was fine. "We're playing a dance at the Odd Fellows tomorrow night," he said. "Would you care to start that soon?" "No Odd Fellows dance is complete without me," I said. I was back where I started. Where was the glamour of the big city?

Engleman had an orthodox band. It played popular music the way it was written; its basic number was *Missouri Waltz*. Engleman played trumpet and saxophone; there was a drummer, a fiddler, and a piano player named Lena whose husband made Bohemian home brew. Lena was young and good looking and I loved to hear her play *I'm Always Chasing Rainbows*. We worked three or four times a week at club dances, socials, lodge parties, and gatherings at Coe College. We gave them fox trots and waltzes—*A Kiss In The Dark, Whispering, Avalon, Say It With Music, Mr. Gallagher And Mr. Shean, Japanese Sandman, A Pretty Girl Is Like A Melody*. They jiggled for the fox trots and swished for the waltzes. The girls were hoisting their skirts inch by inch; they were bobbing their hair, and some of them used lipstick. Some of them wore silk stockings. Legs dressed in this fashion were exciting.

A few weeks after I started with Engleman a large package arrived for Cliff. When I got home he unwrapped it. I was sitting on a chair practicing some chords, watching my fingers and trying to make them obey my mind. Suddenly I realized Cliff was standing in front of me.

"Why don't you try this?" he said. "Maybe it will sound better."

In his hands he held a shiny new long-necked plectrum Vega banjo. The tenor banjo skidded off my knee and hit the floor.

"Where shall I put it," Cliff asked, "in your mouth or in your lap?"

I hugged it for ten minutes before I stopped shaking sufficiently to try a C-Major chord. A small choir of angels
68

threw it right back at me from the plectrum. To hell with the poolroom, I thought; this is heaven. "It cost $180," Cliff said. "You can pay me when you play the Palace in New York."

I loved that Vega like a Stutz Bearcat. Every day in Uncle Dave's office I practiced in the middle of nuts and bolts and locks. I had to learn all the chords I knew over again; the tenor banjo was strung like a ukulele, the Vega was tuned BDGC. In a few weeks I completed the switch and took the White Lady—that was the name stamped on the Vega—into the band for the holiday season. I was sixteen and definitely a whiz bang; those were the mackinaw days. I sent Dot five dollars for washing my shirts.

On New Year's Eve we went into the heart of the Babbitt section to play at Charles City, Iowa. This was one of the three times each year the inhabitants got drunk and had a good time; they came up to the bandstand and asked for their favorite songs —war tunes for the veterans, waltzes for the ladies, ragtime for the kids, and ballads for the crying drunks. They gathered in front of Engleman and hollered for *Sweet Adeline, Smiles, Let The Rest Of The World Go By, Moonlight Bay, Sweetheart Of Sigma Chi.* The White Lady was wonderful; she didn't miss a beat. We got 1922 under way with nothing worse than a slight hangover.

All that winter I practiced by day and played with Engleman at night; when there was no job we gathered at Lena's to drink home brew and play cribbage. One spring day I ran into Fat Rank, a local dance promoter. He told me about a man from Waterloo who was in town looking for a banjo player. "Fellow named Peavey," Fat explained. "He had a band in Waterloo before the war. He wants to play jazz music. I told him you might be a man for him." Play jazz? I and the White Lady dreamed about it. We had nightmares. I went to see Peavey.

He turned out to be a good-looking, amiable young man; some time previously he had been born in Riceville, Iowa, and christened Hollis. My handicaps were just what he wanted. "There is no use trying to convert the older musicians to jazz," he said. "Since you can't read music you have nothing to unlearn. The question is, can we get you in the union?" We went to the local headquarters and found out. The answer was simple. I couldn't read music; I couldn't join the union.

"Can Gabriel read music?" Peavey said to the man in charge.

"Is he playing in your band?" the man asked.

"Never mind," Peavey said. "We'll fix it up in Waterloo."

I packed the White Lady and my white shirts and went to Waterloo with him. On the way he told me his idea for the band. Jazz had been something far away and foreign to him in 1918, when he had an orchestra playing at the Electric Park Pavilion in Waterloo. The army kept drafting his violinists and finally he joined up himself. He was put in the band at Camp Dodge, Des Moines, under the leadership of John Valentine Eppel, the man who got together the *Missouri Waltz*. After the armistice he went back to Waterloo, organized a new dance band, and fell in love with its pianist, Doris Enney. They were married in the fall of 1920 and during the winter went to Houston, Texas, on their honeymoon. There Peavey went to work with his saxophone and clarinet in a band at the Main Street auditorium.

"First thing I knew," Peavey said, "some one said 'Blues in F' and everyone began to play—no music, just a basic twelve bar theme. The whole thing was improvised as we went along, and every chorus was better than the one before. Each instrument took a chorus, with the others playing around it. We got some

70

wonderful hot breaks. After a blues number we would take an intermission and go out and talk it over.

"When Doris and I came back to Waterloo we just couldn't leave that music behind. We had to organize a band that could play it, and that's what we're doing. We'll play the other stuff, too, of course, but we'll go out this summer without a fiddler."

"No fiddler? Will the Republicans like that?" I asked.

"They'll never know," Peavey said. "We'll just play for the common people."

Doris was beautiful and a fine musician. She spent a lot of time teaching me chords and modulations; Peavey instructed me in the afterbeat and the structure of the blues. Together we listened to records by the Original Dixieland Jazz Band; day after day we practiced jazz tunes—Panama, Clarinet Marmalade, Jazz Me Blues, Tiger Rag, Livery Stable Blues, Sensation Rag, Skeleton Jangle, Royal Garden Blues, Eccentric Rag, Muskrat Ramble, Satanic Blues. A trombone player named Louie Arndt joined us; a drummer named Harold Cranford, of Minneapolis, advertised in a musical journal that he played drums, wanted a job, and could, "read, fake, improvise, and play jazz." "That's our boy," Peavey said, and wrote to him. Cranford turned up a week later, fat, good-natured, hard-working, conscientious, and as good a drummer as he claimed to be. He sang a little, and Peavey decided to make him a vocalist. I sang a little too; I didn't know any better. Peavey told me to split the job of killing the lyrics with Cranford. Then we all piled into a seven-passenger Cadillac sedan and set out to fight the roads and entertain the people of Iowa, Wisconsin, and Minnesota. We called ourselves Peavey's Jazz Bandits. With no paved roads, no violin, and a determination to inflict jazz on the biggest and strongest people in the United States, it was a brave expedi-

71

tion. In my pocket was a card signifying that I was a member of Local No. 334, American Federation of Musicians. Peavey had worked it somehow; the price was twenty dollars.

Peavey, I discovered, was an ideal commander in chief. First of all he packed us into the car—instruments, luggage, musicians. Each person, each instrument, each piece of luggage, had to be in a certain spot or the whole plan would fall apart. It was a perfect puzzle; only Peavey could solve it. He did the driving; we covered twelve thousand miles that first summer and didn't scratch a fender. We never got caught with a blowout and no spare tire; we never had to sleep in the car. Peavey studied maps as if they were chessboards; no matter where we played he drove us, before or afterward, to a good hotel. His pockets were filled with old letters, telegrams, programs, and other documents, all covered with notes and figures in pencil. Wherever we were he spent a lot of time on the telephone; wherever we went the arrangements were perfect. "Join Peavey's Jazz Bandits and see the world through the side curtains," we wrote on our post cards. It was a libel. With Peavey we saw everything through rose-colored glasses.

The people liked the jazz we played; they didn't even ask for the fiddle. Usually we set up at an open-air pavilion situated between towns. It might be five miles from one place, eight miles from another, and two or three miles from a third. Usually it was in the middle of a field and was constructed of rough lumber. On dance nights the cows and the dead men stayed home; everyone else got to the pavilion by foot, horse, or wheel. A Model T Ford normally carried twelve; a hay wagon took longer but brought more. Some of the farmers came in overalls, but most of them knew about white shirts and blue serge suits. They were all big (there must be something in that corn besides

72

what goes into whiskey) and they always enjoyed themselves, even when I was singing. They all loved *Roses Of Picardy*, and so did I, but the police should have stopped it.

During intermissions we met the local girls at the refreshment stand. Harold Cranford showed me a simple technique: look along the hot dog stand until you spot a group of single girls, then go there to buy your refreshments. Inquire solicitously whether the music is too fast or too slow. The rest is elementary. Back on the stand courtship was simple; we played *All By Myself, Ain't We Got Fun, Make Believe,* and then got up and sang *Ma, He's Makin' Eyes At Me.* . . .

Intermission lasted thirty minutes. Any musician who was not back on the stand at the end of that time was fined five dollars. The first time it happened to me I was disgusted with myself; swapping bad gags with a girl in a middie blouse isn't worth five bucks. But when payday came Peavey said to me, "I'm giving you a five dollar raise this week." He was so soft-hearted he couldn't keep the fine. After that I preyed on his good nature; I was late after intermission, was fined, and got the money back as a bonus at the end of the week. Back in Chicago Heights Jim came home and heard I was getting forty-five dollars a week for playing a long-necked banjo. He bought one the next day and sent me a wire: "How do you tune it?"

Our route finally brought us to Rochester, Minnesota, and we were asked to play for the staff of the Mayo Brothers Clinic. There were a lot of boys from out-of-town* interning at the clinic and they wanted to know whether we would appear in appropriate formal dress for our concert. "I do not allow my musicians to dress in the same manner as waiters," Peavey told them. He had a couple of dressmakers run up some clown suits

* foreigners

for us and we showed up looking like a bad hand of bridge. After we broke into *Tiger Rag* the out-of-town boys began to edge toward the door; they knew a deck of cards from the strait-jacket ward when they saw it. But they asked us to come back again, and we did, every time we hit Rochester. It was the best town on our route; the streets were paved.

On the third of July we played an open air pavilion at Fort Dodge, Iowa. We had a long jump from there to Riceville, Peavey's home town, where we were to play the next afternoon and night. When the car was loaded I was missing. Peavey went looking for me and finally trailed me to a local restaurant. I was in a booth with two girls, each one considerably bigger than I. Peavey shamed me.

"Why don't you pick on someone your size?" he said to the girls. "You ought to have more pride than to force a defenseless boy to go with you! Everywhere I take my band it's the same story. Just because he's cute you think you can run off with him and do what you like. If this nonsense doesn't stop I'm going to send for his mother and have her chaperone him."

The girls lowered their heads and I sneaked out. Peavey laughed all the way to Riceville, but the next day he was penitent. "I'll give you a five-dollar raise," he said. I got back my honor that afternoon. The Ladies Aid Society of the Methodist Church served dinner to us in the basement of the edifice. Just as we sat down there was a crash. A pint bottle of white mule had fallen from my pocket and broken on the floor. Peavey looked at me and I looked at him. "Now who's cute?" I said.

That was the best meal I ever had, though I ate many to almost equal it afterward, prepared by the same cook. She was Mrs. Carrie Wilkes, a friend of Peavey's and the best woman over a stove I ever knew. What she served was simple—chicken, dumplings, biscuit, shortcake—but what she put into preparing these dishes was straight voodoo.

We ate well wherever we were; a good meal cost fifty cents, the best steak was no more than a dollar. A pint of fresh strawberries with cream could be had for fifteen cents. One thing disappointed me. I expected to find corn liquor in the corn country, but there was none; the crop apparently was used for secondary purposes. There was a little phony rye around but a musician can't take a chance on having his fingernails melt. We made our own lubricant, drugstore alcohol and distilled water in equal proportions. When distilled water was unavailable we boiled plain water and let it go at that. The alcohol cost two dollars a pint at a drugstore or poolroom. Peavey didn't object to the use of it so long as we paced ourselves and didn't perch on the rafters.

Harold Cranford started after the girls as we drove into the main street. I considered it polite to wait until I was in town half an hour. Then I threw out the net: "I don't suppose you picked that dress yourself because a girl as young as you wouldn't know how pretty it makes her look." "I suppose you're going to let me go and eat a banana split all by myself and get indigestion." "Do you think if I cross the street I might be able to keep from falling in love with you?" If there was a lake and a canoe it was simple: "Don't you know it's dangerous for a person to go out in a canoe alone?" "But I'm not going out in a canoe alone," she would answer. "But I am," was the clincher. She went along to save me.

The best line I had was something I didn't realize at the time. I was from over the hill and wasn't staying long in town; that made me attractive and it made me safe. I had a girl in Eau Claire with red hair and beautiful eyes. Every time we were resident I took her canoeing on Half Moon Lake—corduroy cushions and *When My Baby Smiles At Me.* When I found out she was the daughter of the local chief of police I realized why I had so little competition; I was barging in where the yokels feared to tread. One day in Menomonie, Wisconsin, I walked out of a Greek restaurant which specialized in banana cream pie and saw three girls coming down the street. They were students from Stout Institute. One of them looked like Pola Negri's kid sister. I forgot the banana cream pie, though it was hardly past my shoulders. "Who is that?" I said to one of the home guards. He waved me away. "Don't waste your time," he said. "She won't give anybody a tumble. She's waiting for the Prince of Wales." I watched her go by and went back to get some more pie. Two Greeks ran the restaurant; when we were in town one of them spent his mornings at the Y.M.C.A. boxing with our trombone player, Don Burnett. That afternoon I went to a local tent bazaar pitched by a lake. The local band was playing for dancing; we were to take over at night. Suddenly I spotted Pola standing at the edge of the crowd. I walked right up to her and said, "If you have no objection to dancing with me I have no objection to dancing with you." She dropped her lashes a few feet and said, "Students aren't allowed to dance at public gatherings." "Too bad we both can swim," I said. "Otherwise we could go out in a canoe and drown." That was it. She was waiting for an importation; she didn't want to expose her style to the local boys. She even tried to impress me by saying she was from St. Louis, but later she admitted she came from Beaver Dam, Wisconsin. Then I told her about paved streets.

We covered the circuit three times during the summer; by August the crops were so rich you could live by inhaling them. The people were so healthy dissipation was almost a medicine, something to keep them from jumping out of their skin. We gave them jazz, which they loved, and the popular tunes which were singeing the corn silk that summer: *China Boy, Hot Lips, On The Gin-Gin-Ginny Shore, Stumbling, Carolina In The Morning,* and *Way Down Yonder In New Orleans.* Songs lasted more than a season then; we were still playing *Ain't We Got Fun, Second-Hand Rose, Yoo-Hoo,* and, several times a night, *The Sheik.* Without being asked we went into *Wabash Blues, Wang Wang Blues, Avalon, Margie, Whispering, Hindustan,* and one that began to look like a perennial, *Somebody Stole My Gal.* Early in the evening the old folks danced and we gave them *That Naughty Waltz, I'm Forever Blowing Bubbles, Alice Blue Gown, The World Is Waiting For The Sunrise,* and *A Kiss In The Dark.* If they stayed later they had requests: *When I Sailed Away To Norway, Gypsy Love Song, Kiss Me Again, At Dawning, Meet Me Tonight In Dreamland, By The Light Of The Silvery Moon, Down By The Old Mill Stream, Melancholy Baby.*

We had to do the war songs: *Keep The Home Fires Burning, Pack Up Your Troubles In Your Old Kit Bag, There's A Long, Long Trail, Roses Of Picardy, Joan Of Arc They Are Calling You, Where Do We Go From Here?, Just A Baby's Prayer At Twilight, Madelon, K-K-K-Katy, Hello, Central, Give Me No Man's Land, Oh How I Hate To Get Up In The Morning, Rose Of No Man's Land, Oh How I Wish I Could Sleep Until My Daddy Comes Home.* By half past eleven there was more corn in the pavilion than in the fields. Harold Cranford and I sang the lyrics in simple, unadorned, phony style: *Dear Old Pal Of Mine, I'm Always Chasing Rainbows, Old Pal Why Don't You Answer Me?, My Buddy.*

Harold liked women, food, and drink—in that order. One

77

evening at dusk he rolled into our hotel with half a dozen choice watermelons. "We'll put these on ice and eat them after the dance," he said. His eyes were shining and his lips were a little damp with anticipation. As soon as we hit the last note of *Good Night Ladies* I put my banjo away and looked for Harold. He was tying up two girls with his best line, long-tested and never known to break at a crucial moment. "Hi, Harold," I called, "let's get back to the hotel. We've got those watermelons waiting." Harold raised his head and pointed his nose at the rafters. "Really, Eddie," he said, "I seldom take nourishment at this hour. I find that it isn't conducive to good health. I don't believe I shall join you." He was dying for the watermelons, I knew, but he wanted the girls more.

"Harold never thinks of anything but women," I said to Peavey as we sat eating the watermelons.

"I'm glad you have such a good sense of values," Peavey said, spitting out a seed.

A few minutes later I lurched to my feet; I was loaded to the Adam's apple with melon.

"Where are you going?" Peavey said.

"I have a date," I said.

Peavey spat out another seed. "Four hundred million bushels of corn and eleven thousand lakes," he said, "and you spend your time looking for girls."

"They're hard to find," I said.

But they weren't; there was always at least one around with a soft eye and an easy laugh. Usually she lived in a large house with a wide front porch and a hammock. The later the season and the bigger the moon the more romantic she became. One night in early September I sat on a porch and saw, in the moonlight, apples shining on a tree in the front yard. I forgot romance

78

and picked a few. As I sat in the hammock munching noisily the girl said, a little coldly I thought, "If you find a worm don't eat it. Today is Friday."

The second time we hit Rochester we ran into opposition. Another band was playing a dance the same night; it was headed by Al Gable, a pianist. Peavey hired a truck and we piled into it with our instruments and drove around town giving out samples of our music. Gable did the same thing; we passed him several times. We also passed several of the out-of-town boys from Mayo's; I knew them by their beards. Now they are sure we are nuts, I thought to myself. "This is the way they do it in New Orleans," Peavey said. He was having a good time, and he was sure we would win. We did; our dance outdrew the one at which Gable played. We ran into his band several more times that summer; in each case Peavey hired a truck and we peddled our wares. Once Gable beat us; he got the crowd, we got the night off.

One day we pulled into Winona and found a river boat tied up at the wharf. She was the *Capitol*, of the J. S. Strekfus Lines, and her band was Tony's Iowans, headed by Tony Cattalina, a cornet player. We piled aboard for the afternoon excursion up the river; there were children and mothers and nurses and old folks and youngsters who stood by the band with their ears and mouths open. This is it, I thought—you know what the melody is but you don't hear it. The cornet and the clarinet, and sometimes the trombone, treat it like a girl. They hang around it, doing handsprings and all sorts of other tricks, always keeping an eye on it and trying to make an impression. The rhythm section provides transportation, everything floats on its beat. This was what we've been trying to play all summer. This is jazz. "Now I know why we are bandits," I said to Peavey. He didn't answer; his eyes were glazed. He was loaded* with the music.

The boat went up the river a way, turned around, and was nudging into the wharf again by suppertime. At night there was a moonlight excursion. This was the dinger; the young folks went aboard arm in arm. The boys wore knickers, white shirts, and bow ties. Most of the golfers gave up knickers that year after the ribbon counters took them over. Harding stuck to them, but he was a ragtime President.

We made another river boat at LaCrosse; this one was the *J.S.*, named for Strekfus himself. The boats moved north with the summer. Most of the musicians were from New Orleans, but gradually youngsters in the river towns learned the music and got jobs on the excursion steamers. Peavey kept talking about the trombone player in Tony's Iowans, a young fellow named Tal Sexton. "I wish we had him with us," he said.

The weather held through most of September and we finished our run up and down the Mississippi, from Northeastern Iowa to Rice Lake, Wisconsin, hitting Chippewa Falls, Eau Claire, Menomonie, and LaCrosse, Wisconsin; Rochester, Owatonna, and Winona, Minnesota; Waterloo, Oelwein, Independence, Elkader, Volga City, McGregor, and Cresco, Iowa. One day we drove into Cy Thompson's Chicken Ranch at LeRoy, Minnesota, where we were to play a dance that night. Peavey was wanted on the long distance telephone; it was Johnny Lane, manager of the Arcadia Ballroom in St. Paul. He wanted to try us out for a winter job at the Arcadia. We drove to St. Paul and at nine o'clock on a Sunday morning stopped the Cadillac in front of Lane's house. Peavey rapped on the door and was

* drunk

admitted. We piled in after him. Lane looked as if the last thing he wanted to hear was a jazz band.

We set our instruments in the living room; the drum spurs fitted nicely into the oriental rug. The whole street was quiet as a tomb. Then Peavey nodded and we broke into a jazz version of *Meet Me Tonight In Dreamland*. Nobody played the melody, of course, and the time was four-four. Right in the middle of Sunday morning it sounded as if thirty people were getting their throats cut in Lane's front room. He sat in a chair and hung on, rocking softly with the pain. When it was over he whispered to Peavey, "Could you try something soft and slow, something like *Meet Me Tonight In Dreamland?*" "Certainly," Peavey said. "We play that number often." He gave us the wink and we turned on the maple sugar; even the drums played the melody. We left with a seven months' contract and an opening date two weeks away.

Suddenly I was homesick. "I think I'll go down to Chicago Heights for a while," I said to Peavey. "An excellent idea," he said. "Don't forget to tell your mother everything you did during the summer. She'll be proud of you."

"I will," I promised, "and I'll tell her that I always got permission from you."

YOUNG MAN
WITH A CAP

THINGS hadn't changed in Chicago Heights; most of the people still stood up to walk. One day Pee Wee Rank, a drummer, called me from Chicago. "How would you like to play in Syracuse?" he said. It sounded as far away as Moscow. "At the Alhambra Ballroom," Pee Wee went on. "The piano player is a holdover. I'm making up the rest of the band." He was on his way to the Tri-Cities—Rock Island, Moline, and Davenport—to round up talent. "Call me when you get there," I said. I was eating three times a day. Why go to Moscow?

Pee Wee called from Davenport. "I've got the greatest band you ever heard," he said. "You can't miss playing with this outfit. Meet me at the LaSalle Street station in Chicago tomorrow night at eight o'clock. We'll be a sensation in Syracuse."

He sold me. At eight o'clock the next night I stood in the station and watched Pee Wee come at me with three other guys. One was a dude, one was an ordinary human being. The third was a kid in a cap with the peak broken. He had on a green overcoat from the walk-up-one-and-save-ten district; the collar was off his neck. He had a round face and eyes that had no desire to focus on what was in front of him. Pee Wee introduced us. The guy in the cap was first.

82

"This is Bix Beiderbecke."

I've made a mistake, I thought. I'm stuck with this clam digger for two months.

"Hello," Beiderbecke said. Great talker, I thought.

The dude was next; his name was Wayne Hostetter. The ordinary human being was Johnny Eberhardt. Eberhardt was the saxophone player; Hostetter played clarinet and violin. Nobody said anything about Beiderbecke's instrument.

"We have a couple of hours before the train leaves for Syracuse," Pee Wee said. "Bix wants to go to the College Inn and see Louis Panico. Let's walk over."

The College Inn was in the Sherman House, a loop hotel. Louis Panico was playing trumpet in Isham Jones' band. He was only eighteen, and had written Wabash Blues, and was getting $350 a week. They'll never let us in, I thought. This corncobber probably has heard Louis on a record and hasn't any better sense than to think he can march in wearing that cap and hear him play. I fell back and walked with Hostetter, the dude.

"Is Beiderbecke our cornet player?" I asked.

"By way of understatement, yes," Hostetter said. "Wait until you hear him play. You'll go nuts."

I can believe it, I thought. What kind of music have these guys heard? What is their standard? How can a guy in a cap and a green overcoat play anything civilized?

We walked right into the College Inn without being stopped. Pee Wee and Beiderbecke pushed their way up to the band stand. I spotted Panico about the time he saw Beiderbecke. His face lighted up like a drunk on Christmas Eve.

"Bix!" he yelled. He leaned over to shake hands and the boys in the band looked around as if free drinks had been announced. Beiderbecke must be something, I thought, but what?

83

Louis played his *Wabash Blues* and *Hot Lips*. There was more brass and class in the joint than I had ever seen. My eyes were just getting used to the glare when Pee Wee said, "Bix wants to go to the Friars' Inn."

Well, I thought, they let us in here, why not the Friars' Inn? The Friars' Inn was a flashy cabaret for big spenders. For music it had the New Orleans Rhythm Kings, the famous white jazz band. I had heard their records on Gennett. If any of the Rhythm Kings spoke to Beiderbecke he was somebody, cap and all. On the way over Hostetter and I talked about the Rhythm Kings. They had Leon Rappolo on the clarinet; he was already a legend. Jack Pettis played the C-melody saxophone, Elmer Schoebel the piano, Frank Snyder the drums. The trombonist was George Brunies, the banjo player Lewie Black. On the string bass was Arnold Loyocano; Don Murray played tenor saxophone. Hostetter repeated the names as if he were nominating an all-American football team. "This is really a band," he said. "Definitely the nuts. There's nothing better." Then he added, as if it was something I ought to know and keep quiet about, "Schoebel reads music."

We walked in and kept on going again, right up to the band stand. The players fell over themselves greeting Beiderbecke. Have I got to buy a cap to make good, I thought?

"How about sitting in, Bix?" one of the players said.

Beiderbecke smiled like an embarrassed kid and muttered something. Then he got up on the stand and walked over and sat down—at the piano. "*Clarinet Marmalade*," somebody said. Bix nodded and hit the keys.

Then it happened. All my life I had been listening to music, particularly on the piano. But I had never heard anything remotely resembling what Beiderbecke played. For the first time

I realized that music isn't all the same, that some people play so differently from others that it becomes an entirely new set of sounds. That was the first time I heard the New Orleans Rhythm Kings, except on records, but I actually didn't hear them at all; I listened to Beiderbecke. When we rushed out to grab our train I was completely confused. Trying to get to sleep in an upper berth I kept thinking—what about the cornet, can he play that too?

The next day we got up as the train came into Cleveland. With nothing to do but sit and stare at the scenery from there to Buffalo I began to wonder again about the cornet. I got out my banjo. Eberhardt dug up his saxophone and doodled along with me. Finally Beiderbecke took out a silver cornet. He put it to his lips and blew a phrase. The sound came out like a girl saying yes. Eberhardt smiled at me. "How about *Panama?*" he said. I was still shivering and licking my insides, tasting the last of the phrase. "All right," Beiderbecke said, "*Panama.*" By itself, so it seemed, my banjo took up the rhythm. At last I was playing music; so far as I was concerned it could go on forever.

We disrupted the train. People crowded in from the other coaches; they stood in the aisles and on the seats. We played all the way to Buffalo—*Tiger Rag, Jelly Roll Blues, Hot Lips, China Boy, Wabash Blues, Royal Garden Blues, Wang Wang Blues, Jazz Me Blues,* I couldn't wait to get to Syracuse; I hoped I would be stuck forever with Beiderbecke.

We checked into the St. James Apartments, a new and fashionable building. Hostetter sent Beiderbecke down to get the key to the incinerator. Bix went. Hostetter, we discovered, was a chiropractor. He had a portable treatment table with him and he used us to practice on. "I'll keep you all in good shape," he said. There was no use protesting; if you didn't want the

85

treatment you got it anyhow, on the floor or wherever you happened to be when you gave up the struggle. It was wiser to lie down on the table and get it over with. We lasted in the St. James a week; the noise we made, the music we played, and the hours we kept drove the other tenants to an ultimatum: we could get out or we could have our throats cut. We moved.

I was the happiest kid in the world. Every night I played with Bix at the Alhambra; when I heard his horn nothing could possibly bother me. Often at six o'clock in the morning I tried to get him out of bed to play the piano for me. "Please, Bix," I would say, "just for a little while. Then you can take a nap." He was as amiable as a pup. He would sit at the big grand piano and play by the hour—Eastwood Lane's *Adirondack Sketches* and MacDowell's things. He played his own way, with his own phrasing. The way he voiced an ordinary 7th chord was the joy and wonder of my life. The way he dressed was my despair. His wardrobe consisted of two suits, a tuxedo for the job and a baggy outfit to wear in between. He had one pair of shoes, a few shirts, and a couple of four-in-hand ties. The green overcoat and the cap with the broken peak completed his ensemble. Nothing new was ever added. Bix couldn't be bothered. He had other things to do and to think about. At the back of the Alhambra Ballroom there was a ski ball concession. Bix decided that it was his destiny, during intermissions, to beat the game. He put a large part of his salary each week into trying; he ended with two teddy bears and a box of chocolates.

We were paid forty-five dollars a week; we found a speakeasy where we could get beer for ten cents. This was the most economical deal we could find in Syracuse, ten beers for a dollar. Hostetter figured it out by calculus. "We can get loaded every night," he said, "but Bix will have to cut down his contribution

THE CONDON FAMILY
Left to right—back row: Clifford, Florence, Lucille, Grace; front
row: Helena, James, Pa, John, Ma, Eddie, Martina

PEAVEY'S JAZZ BANDITS

Eddie is seated next to Doris Peavey, holding accordian. The drummer is Harold Cranford, the trombonist Tal Sexton. Standing, holding saxophone, is Hollis M. Peavey, now Mayor of Huntington Park, Cal.

JAM SESSION AT JIMMY RYAN'S

Left to right—Marty Marsala (off stand, under "Ladies"), Eddie Condon, guitar; George Wettling, drums; Sandy Williams, trombone; Max Kaminsky, trumpet; Bobby Hackett (behind Kaminsky), trumpet; Pee Wee Russell, clarinet; Joe Sullivan, piano; Al Morgan, bass; Al Hall, bass. *(Photo: Charles Peterson)*

OPENING NIGHT
AT EDDIE CONDON'S
Eddie, Joe Marsala,
Bud Freeman

(Harper's Bazaar)

Town Hall audience
—bobby soxers?   (Charles Peterson)

TOWN HALL CONCERT
—EDDIE CONDON LEADS
Left to right—Dave Tough, drums; Billy
Butterfield, Bobby Hackett, Max Kamin-
sky, Hot Lips Page, trumpets (George
Wettling in background); John Sim-
mons, bass; Pee Wee Russell, Ed Hall,
clarinets; J. C. Higginbotham, Miff Mole,
trombones; Cliff Jackson, piano; Bob
Casey, bass; Kansas Fields, drums
(Photo: Charles Peterson)

Louis Armstrong in dressing gown. Left to right—Tommy Dorsey, trombone; Bud Freeman, saxophone; Pops Foster, bass; Eddie Condon, guitar; Henry Allen, trumpet; George Wettling, drums. *(Photo: Charles Peterson)*

SIDNEY BECHET ·
(Skippy Adelman)

JAMES P. JOHNSON
Piano decorations by
Ludwig Bemelmans
(John Francis O'Reilly)

ZUTTY SINGLETON
*(Charles Peterson — Reprinted from Spot Magazine. Copyright 1942 by
Fawcett Publications, Inc.*

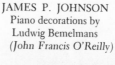

CARNEGIE HALL
Left to right—Hot Lips Page, Billy Butterfield,
Muggsy Spanier, Yank Lausen
(Photo: Skippy Adelman)

THE FAMOUS DOOR
Red McKenzie sings in the key
of F, due to the limitation of
his accompanist, Eddie Condon (pre-Polyclinic). (Photo:
Charles Peterson)

Eddie and his brother Pat on the Empress of
Britain. (Photo: Paul Smith)

Eddie and Pee Wee exchange
felicitations while Ernie
Anderson looks on and Ernie
Caceres plays a baritone saxo-
phone accompaniment
(Photo: Skippy Adelman)

Students of the Walt
Whitman School listen to
a lecture on American Cul-
ture. Joe Sullivan, piano;
Pee Wee Russell, clarinet;
Louis Armstrong, trumpet;
Zutty Singleton, drums;
Bobby Hackett, trumpet;
Brad Gowans, trombone;
Eddie Condon, guitar; Max
Kaminsky, trumpet
(Photo: Charles Peterson)

JACK TEAGARDEN

TOWN HALL
Ed Hall listens to leader Condon while Jess Stacy tries the piano. *(Photo: Skippy Adelman)*

FATS WALLER
(Photo: Otto Hess)

RUNNING THROUGH A NUMBER AT TOWN HALL
Left to right—Ernie Caceres, clarinet; Gene Schroeder, piano; Eddie Condon, Gene Krupa, Pee Wee Russell, Muggsy Spanier. *(Photo: Skippy Adelman)*

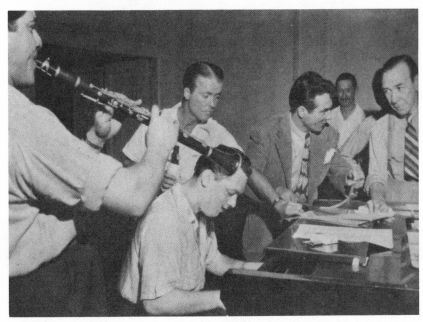

EDDIE AND MAGGIE   (Photo: *Lisette Model*)

to the ski ball." "Oh, I can lick it," Bix said. "I've almost got the system figured out now."

On payday we visited some of the other bars. Hostetter had charts of all the parts of the body, including a blow-up of the eye. This he folded and took with him when we visited strange speakeasies. After the first drink he put it on the bar and studied it. Invariably the bartender became interested. Hostetter explained that it was a system for telling fortunes by examining the eye. Pretty soon the bartender asked Hostetter to have a look at his eye. Hostetter leaned over the bar and stared for a long time. Finally he said, "Hmmm, I see that you have had a social disease." That was the end of the examination; we got drinks on the house for the rest of the night.

For days after my arrival something about Syracuse puzzled me. Every other car in the streets was a Franklin, air-cooled, with a sloping hood in front. Finally Hostetter enlightened me. "They make them here," he said. There were a lot of canals in Syracuse too; one night Hostetter and Bix stopped as we were crossing one of them on a bridge. "Let's throw Eddie in," Bix said. "Sure," Hostetter said. "We can always get another banjo player. Besides, his spine has too few vertebrae in the cervical area and too many in the lumbar. He'll never grow and will live to be past ninety and become a burden to his family." They grabbed me—I was five feet six and weighed a hundred and ten—and held me over the bridge.

"Will there be any punishment for this?" Bix said.

"Not unless it can be proved that he is a human being," Hostetter said.

"He sings," Bix suggested.

"Irrelevant, inconsequential, and incompetent as evidence," Hostetter said.

"He still has two dollars in his pocket," Bix said.

"A point for the defense," Hostetter said.

"He makes forty-five dollars a week and we can borrow all but his room rent," Bix said.

"Reprieve granted," Hostetter said.

They lifted me back on the bridge and set me on my feet. "Give us the two dollars," Hostetter said. I handed it over and we went back to the ten-for-a-dollar place and split twenty beers between us.

We ate in a self-service restaurant where the customer paid a fee, took a napkin, and was free to eat anything that didn't eat him. The napkins were of good quality and rather dainty in size; we didn't buy any handkerchiefs while we were in Syracuse. Except for the beer, drinking material was a problem. The best we could manage was a half pint of alcohol mixed with a half pint of cherry pop; this cost two dollars. Alcohol and distilled water with a little anisette passed for gin. As Christmas came on the liquor, the self-service food, and the melancholy Bix put into his piano playing began to work on me. Just before the holidays the band broke up; Johnny Eberhardt and I went back to Chicago; Bix headed for New York to hear the Original Dixieland Jazz Band, particularly Nick La Rocca, its cornet player.

Back home I told everyone about Bix. "He must be a great guy," Jim said. "What does he do with his old clothes?" Peavey and the boys were doing well in the Arcadia Ballroom in St. Paul. It was the first time a jazz band had worked steadily in either of the Twin Cities; the crowds were making Johnny Lane happy. I decided to get in on the fun; after a quiet New Year's Eve with several thousand people Jim escorted me to the station. We leaned against each other until the train came in. Then I got into a day coach and Jim walked off into 1923. Several ways of relieving the monotony of my hangover occurred to me as the day wore on, but all of them required money. Again and again I went through my pockets; I even looked in my shoes. I had no money at all, not even a nickel to call Peavey from the station in St. Paul. "I'll ask a cop for a nickel," I said to myself. "He'll either give it to me or arrest me; either way I'll get out of the station."

Peavey, the perfect man, was there to meet me. With him was Johnny Lane; they had a hired limousine; I got between them in the back seat and tried to shake quietly. Lane looked at me closely, then reached into an inside pocket and pulled out a pint of whiskey. "Better have a drink on the new year," he said. "That is, if you drink." Peavey didn't smile. "Well," I said, "I don't mind breaking a rule for a special occasion." Sixty seconds later I was alive. I began telling Peavey about Bix.

The Arcadia Ballroom was a tea party, Boston style. We had signals with the lights. If we were off the stand when a fight started the lights flickered twice and we rushed to our instruments and played loud and fast to distract the crowd's attention. The crowds were large and on Saturday night when everyone joined in the chorus of Yes, We Have No Bananas, things were a little left of center mentally. There was another tune they sang, Barney Google. Billy Rose is still doing penance for writing that one. The floor boss of the joint stood at the edge of the band stand and jiggled with the music. The bouncers rocked and swayed. In between sets everybody stood around and talked about how Tommy Gibbons was going to lick Jack Dempsey and bring the world's heavyweight championship to St. Paul. After two

89

drinks even the girls would demonstrate how Tommy was going to do it. It was safer in Minneapolis, where we went to broadcast over station WLAG (now WCCO) at the Oak Grove Hotel. This was our first experience with radio; nobody knew much about it, not even the people who were running it. We told Harold Cranford that all broadcasts were formal affairs; he showed up in his tuxedo. What disappointed him was the absence of girls in the studio; radio as a means of entertainment never regained stature with him.

Peavey finally surrendered in the matter of Bix. "I'll write and offer him a job if you'll promise to stop talking about him," he said. "I don't want to be a bore," I said, "but what is the point in playing instruments four or five hours every night unless we have a musician in the band?" Bix finally answered Peavey's letter. He wrote in pencil on the back of a penny post card, "I will come to work for you for $75 a week." Originally he had put down sixty-five; there was a smudge where he had erased the six, but it was still plainly visible under the seven. Peavey handed me the card and watched me fidget. "I don't think I want him in my band," he said.

But he did hire Tal Sexton, whom we had heard on the river boat Capitol. Sexton was to join us during the summer tour, for which Peavey bought a new Packard. The car had more nickel and paint than an Indian plumber; we were the cynosure of local eyes wherever we went. Garages in the small towns were still converted livery stables; mechanics and horse experts were interchangeable parts; the Packard attracted them both—it was as good looking as a horse and it was more automobile than they had previously seen. That summer Peavey made another perfect record as a driver—fifteen thousand miles without bruising the nickel. We covered the same circuit, stayed in the same hotels, dated the same girls, and played the same tunes, with a few additions—*Bambalina, I Love You, Just A Girl That Men Forget, Linger Awhile, Swingin' Down The Lane, You Gotta See Mama Every Night.* At the Barron County Fair at Rice Lake, Wisconsin, Peavey billed me as "The world's youngest banjo player."

The boys in the band all carried fishing tackle; they argued constantly about artificial bait; they tried their theories while we rode ferries across rivers. Peavey, who was in the middle of every discussion, decided to give all of us a week's vacation at Miller's Lodge in northern Wisconsin, so we could settle our disputes. We fished all day and played poker all night, and finally Peavey had to take us back on the job so we could get some rest. We made a tour of northern Minnesota and southern Ontario, playing Hibbing, Eveleth, and Chisholm. Then we went north to International Falls on the Canadian border. Just south of it we ran into a herd of deer on the road; forest fires were burning along both sides of the highway. We drove through to Emo, Ontario, where we played a concert.

At dinner the old fellow who was our host poured cream into his coffee. He put his finger across the spout of the pitcher to hold back the flies which had fallen into the cream. Doris pushed back her chair and got up; she wasn't hungry. "You never feel that way when you give us castor oil," I said. She was health officer for the band; at the slightest indication of trouble we were lined up and fed castor oil. We were a jazz band, which meant that none of us could be replaced. There were musicians in the country through which we were traveling, but they were not jazz players; they read music. We operated as a group mind, improvising together on a selected theme or melody.

Doris figured that a group mind meant a group body. If one of us sneezed we were all sick.

From Ontario we went to Appleton, Wisconsin, to play at the Terrace Gardens, a roadhouse. Tal Sexton joined us there; we played seven nights a week and on Sunday afternoons. Business was bad. On Sundays the place was deserted; if a car was seen coming down the road we ran to the stand and broke into *Tiger Rag*. If the car stopped we continued to play; if it went by we stopped. Finally we got a three days' notice that the job was closing on Friday. The final pay check bounced at the bank; the manager of the place had gone to Chicago to get a new band and a floor show. We met him at the station when he returned and escorted him to the hotel. We sat around quietly, with him in the middle, until another check was written, taken to the bank, cashed, and the money brought back. Then just as we were about to leave on Saturday the manager came and asked us to stay for the week end; the new band hadn't arrived. Peavey agreed but demanded that we be paid each night. We were paid on Saturday, but that night someone threw the furniture out of the dormitory in which the band was housed, and the Jazz Bandits were blamed.

We settled by playing free the next night and then started for St. Paul in the Packard. Harold Cranford went ahead by train to see about getting us a job. When we arrived he had a tryout lined up at the State Theater, in Minneapolis. Stage presentations were in vogue; could we improvise a revue? "We can do anything," Peavey said, "but only in Latin." The management liked our music; we settled down to rehearse a show.

The setting was a tearoom. As the curtain rose the musicians were draped over the piano. I was singing *That Old Gang Of Mine*. Then we did individual bits: Doris was a Salvation

92

Army lass; Tal Sexton went through a policeman routine; Peavey, Harold, and I were a drunk trio, clinging to a prop lamppost, singing *Sweet Adeline*. We did a split week at the Strand Theater in Sioux Falls, South Dakota. While we were there we received a telegram from Jack McGee, manager of the Roseland Dance Gardens in Winnipeg, offering us a job for the winter. Peavey wired that we would arrive as soon as our theater engagement ended.

We returned to Minneapolis and opened at the State. William Warvell Nelson was in the pit conducting the orchestra; a violinist named Rubinoff was his concertmaster. Our act was a hit, though Peavey, Harold, and I were accused of overacting. We played our second week in the Capitol Theater, St. Paul; I was lucky all week. On the street near our hotel ladders were propped against a building for several days. Tal Sexton regarded them with fear; he kept to the edge of the sidewalk and made me go ahead of him, keeping a hand on my shoulder. One day I wriggled away from him and ran under the ladders. Tal caught up with me as I walked into the hotel lobby; he was moaning and prophesying horrible things. We walked up to the cigar counter and I picked up a punchboard we had both been trying to hit all week. While Tal watched me I won twenty-two dollars and the prize box of candy. "You'll never live to eat it," Tal said. I also won a red silk dressing gown, only slightly too big for me. A lush in the hotel had fallen in love with *Carolina In The Morning*; he called me at all hours of the night to come to his room and play it for him. Finally one morning about dawn, when I had played it over and over again and was exhausted, he said, "Just once more—and I'll give you this." He took off the dressing gown he always wore for the serenade. I took it and

93

played for another hour. Finally Peavey woke up and came and found me. He escorted me down the hall, holding my train. I had the robe for years, but I never grew into it.

At breakfast Sunday morning on the train to Winnipeg I met a salesman from Cedar Rapids, a former pug named Jack. "Winnipeg has Blue Sunday," he told me. "There's nothing to do but go to the band concert at the Alhambra. Meet me there and I'll show you around." We checked into the Vendome Hotel on Fort Street; it wasn't cold yet, only about ten degrees below. I went to the Alhambra and met Jack. He introduced me to a gorgeous girl in a mink coat; she was older than I and didn't look as if she was living at home. Her name was Charmaine. We listened to the band concert and Charmaine asked me how I liked Canada. Come up and see me and bring your own towels, her voice seemed to say. I said Canada could stand a little coal on the fire. She smiled.

We opened the next night at Roseland. McGee had been in the habit of hiring musicians individually and putting his own band together. When he heard us play *That's A'Plenty, San, Farewell Blues, Panama, Eccentric Rag, Dippermouth Blues*, he was confused. "I've never heard anything like it," he told Peavey. "One minute it is beautiful and the next it is terrible. You don't seem to have any musicians. I can't pick out one who seems to know what he's doing." Meanwhile the crowd was applauding and gathering around the bandstand. McGee shook his head. "As long as they keep coming it's all right with me," he said, "but I don't know what you're doing." We eased him for a while with popular tunes—*Last Night On The Back Porch, It Ain't Gonna Rain No More, Just A Girl That Men Forget, Wonderful One,* and *Charleston.* But just

94

as he thought things were back to normal we broke out with our version of *Runnin' Wild* and he shook his head again.

Just before we played the last set there was a telephone call for the banjo player. It was Charmaine. "Are you going to be busy after closing?" she asked. "Would you like to go out for a ride?" I was strictly in the dark about her so I stalled. "I've been in a bad card game," I said. "The panic is on." She laughed, and it didn't chill my blood. "You won't need any money," she said. "I'll pick you up in half an hour." In thirty-one minutes she was in front of the Roseland with a car and chauffeur. We went to a small, intimate roadhouse. Charmaine confided in me, deep thoughts and high dreams. "What about Jack?" I asked, remembering his eight years in the ring, practically all of them vertical. Charmaine sighed. "Jack is a businessman," she said. I knew where I was then; on third base.

One night I dropped into a café after work. I had my coat half off when I saw Jack walking toward me. "What the hell do you mean by stealing my girl?" he said. About the same time he hit me on the mouth and knocked me under the table. The table fell over and I grabbed a large salt shaker. Why soil my bare hands, I figured. Before much more happened we were separated and Jack began to apologize and say how sorry he was and no girl was worth a friendship and couldn't we forget it and have a drink. Then he left and Harold Cranford came in. "My pal!" Harold moaned. "They can't do this to my pal!" I couldn't say anything because my mouth was rising like a hot muffin. "Let's find him," Harold said. He charged into the street and I went after him. We were on Portage Avenue, the main drag of Winnipeg. Suddenly we saw Jack coming, wrapped in his camel's hair coat. Harold stepped up to him and said, "You can't hit my pal." Jack tried to explain.

He didn't want any more trouble. "Put 'em up!" Harold demanded. Jack sighed. "I hate to do this," he said. Then he hit Harold on the mouth. The next night neither of us sang; the other boys had to take over *That Old Gang Of Mine* and *Old Pal Why Don't You Answer Me?* "Couple of tough boys from the States," Peavey said. "Take it easy on these poor foreigners."

We all went in for winter sports—skating, tobogganing, and bobsledding at forty degrees below zero on River Park. Starting from ice chutes the sleds went for a mile up and down the river. Somewhere along the course I met Yvonne, a young French-Canadian girl who was more to my style than Charmaine, though after I left Winnipeg she married a saxophone player.

McGee finally decided that Doris was a good musician; later he spotted Sexton, and gradually he got around to the other members of the band. We broadcast over station CKY and also, by telephone, over CJGX at Saskatchewan, five hundred miles away. Listeners sent telegrams and letters requesting numbers; one of the favorites was a waltz written by the Peaveys, called *Summertime*. One of our occasional customers was a tycoon from Calgary; he came to town about twice a month; his hobby was the banjo and he was a nut on tortoise shell. Every time he came he brought me tortoise shell picks; his pockets were full of them. At the time I was using a two-pick system, with no tortoise involved. On my thumb I wore a pick made of composition material; on my forefinger I wore a metal pick. Kid Tortoise never seemed to notice that I never used the picks he brought me; he just kept giving them to me and I kept putting them in my pocket.

Our music wasn't bad but I couldn't forget Bix. I kept

thinking of the New Orleans Rhythm Kings, too. Chicago was full of hot music; King Oliver's Creole Jazz Band was playing at the Lincoln Gardens; every cabaret on the south side kept an outfit worth hearing. "I think I'll go south for the rest of the winter," I said to Peavey. "To Florida?" he asked. "No," I said, "to Chicago." "Remember me when you go to confession," he said. That was the last I saw of the Jazz Bandits. "So long, pal," Harold Cranford said. "If you ever need anyone to get in and punch for you just let me know."

CHICAGO'S SOUTH SIDE gave jazz a sincere welcome. When King Joe Oliver arrived in 1918 representatives of two bands met him at the station. Eddie Venson wanted him to play at the Royal Gardens Café with Jimmy Noone; Bill Johnson and Sidney Bechet were on hand to persuade him to join them at the Dreamland. The discussion shifted from the station to a bar and reached an amiable decision. Oliver joined both bands, playing early with one, late with the other. There was no one to challenge his title of King except Freddie Keppard. Keppard dropped in at the Royal Gardens one night and Oliver took him on in a "cutting" contest. The consensus was that, "Joe Oliver beat the socks off Keppard."

Back in New Orleans, where he was born in 1885, Oliver learned music slowly. He began in formal fashion, reading notes and playing with a children's band. Once the children's band went on tour and Joe returned with a scar over one eye; someone had struck him with a broomstick. For a while he was called "Bad Eye" Joe. When he first played with the Eagle Band he was sent home because he played "so loud and so bad." He was confused because the players improvised instead of following the score. Gradually he learned the technique of improvisation and eventually produced a stomp of his own, called Dippermouth.

He went to work in Storyville, and there he heard nothing but praise for Freddie Keppard and Manuel Perez. It irritated him; in his own opinion he was better than both men. He played in a cabaret at the corner of Bienville and Marais Streets, with Big Eye Louis on clarinet, Deedee Chandler on drums, and Richard Jones at the piano. One night between numbers the musicians began talking about Keppard and Perez. Oliver stood up and walked to the piano. "Jones," he said, "beat it out in B flat."

Jones began and Joe put his cornet to his lips and blew. He walked out into the street and pointed his horn first at the cabaret where Keppard worked, then at the café where Perez was playing. He blew with such power that every bed and bar in the neighborhood emptied. People poured into the street and crowded around Joe, while he blew and blew, swinging his cornet from one target to the other. When everyone knew what he was doing and was satisfied with the way he was doing it, he turned and led the people inside. After that he was King Joe.

In Chicago in 1920 he organized his own Creole Jazz Band and took it to California. Returning to the south side he went again to the Royal Gardens, now re-christened the Lincoln Gardens. In 1922 he decided to send for his boy Louis Armstrong to play second cornet. Louis arrived and stood outside the café listening to the music, afraid to go in. He couldn't believe he was in Chicago, hired to play in a band with Papa Joe Oliver.

Louis Armstrong learned to play a cornet in the Waif's Home in New Orleans, to which he was sent for firing a pistol within the city limits on New Year's Day, 1913. Before that he haunted Storyville at night, singing in an urchins' quartet, playing on a guitar made from a cigar box. As he grew he played in cabarets, gin mills, and barrel houses. He spent two seasons with Fate Marable's band on the Strekfus river boats.

99

He composed a tune which later became very popular and sold it for fifty dollars. He was twenty-two when he arrived in Chicago on the night of July 8th. Listening to Papa Joe he thought, "I wonder if I'm good enough to play in that band." He was. People used to say to Oliver, "That boy will blow you out of business." Joe would smile and say, "He won't hurt me while he's in my band."

Before prohibition poured white patrons into the south side cafés there were white boys gathered around the bandstands at the Dreamland and Lincoln Gardens, some of them startlingly young. Musicians were discovering the new music and listening to its masters. Members of the New Orleans Rhythm Kings, the white jazz orchestra at Friars' Inn, came to listen to their old Storyville colleagues. They listened so well that one of their recordings, Tin Roof Blues, contained more than a surface resemblance to King Oliver's Jazzin' Babies' Blues.

The younger white boys were high-school students—Dave Tough, George Wettling, Francis Muggsy Spanier, Benny Goodman, and a group from Austin High on the west side: Jimmy MacPartland, Lawrence Bud Freeman, Frank Teschmaker, and Jim Lannigan. At home these boys practiced and listened to records by the Rhythm Kings and the Oliver band; they were determined to play jazz. They formed small orchestras, played at school dances, and went to the south side or to Friars' Inn to take lessons from the masters of their respective instruments—Baby Dodds on drums, Jimmy Noone and Johnny Dodds and Leon Rappolo on clarinet, Joe and Louis on cornet, George Brunies on trombone.

The star of the New Orleans Rhythm Kings was Leon Rappolo, who played clarinet; the driving force of the band was George Brunies, the trombone player. Both were from

New Orleans; both were from musical families; both were veterans of Storyville. Rappolo ran away from home when he was fourteen and played in a band with Bee Palmer's act on the Orpheum circuit; the police found him and sent him home. He worked then at the Halfway House in Storyville with Abbie Brunies, George's brother. In Chicago in 1920 he and George and Paul Mares played at the Cascades Ballroom, where the piano was half a tone off. They organized the New Orleans Rhythm Kings and got a job at Friars' Inn on the strength of their version of Wabash Blues. So enchanted were the Rhythm Kings with Chicago life that after work in the early dawn they rode around for hours on the elevated. Rappolo slowly went mad; he liked to lean against a telephone pole with his clarinet and improvise on the rhythm he heard humming in the wires. He stood on the stand at the Friars' Inn and played chorus after chorus while the customers stopped dancing to listen. The manager begged him to stop so the people could sit down and spend some money. When he was harmlessly insane he went back to New Orleans and Abbie Brunies took him again into the band at the Halfway House and looked after him.

They all knew Bix Beiderbecke, the round-eyed, eager-faced youngster from Davenport with the mousy hair and the marvelous ear. They knew the Condon kid from Chicago Heights, too; he was small, quick-moving, clothes-conscious, sharp-tongued, seldom still, and forever organizing parties, dates, and excursions to the south side. They called him "Slick." He was innocently frank with phonies; otherwise he talked in a mixture of understatement and hyperbole. About Louis Armstrong's cornet playing he would say, "It doesn't bother me." In describing Gene Krupa to George Wettling he said, "He's got a seventy-two-inch heart." He was passionately, deeply devoted to jazz, proselyted constantly in its behalf, refused to solo on his own instrument, and pioneered in the appreciation of Beiderbecke. Bix's playing never bothered him; Bix's indifference to clothes and fresh linen and romance did.

Bix was never actually a person; he was a living legend. Nothing which has been invented about him is as accurately symbolical as the everyday things he did. Without effort he personified jazz; by natural selection he devoted himself to the outstanding characteristics of the music he loved. He was obsessed with it; with the aid of prohibition and its artifacts he drove away all other things—food, sleep, women, ambition, vanity, desire. He played the piano and the cornet, that was all; when he was sick the Whiteman band kept an empty chair for him; when he died no one was glad and many wept.

He was born Leon Bismarck Beiderbecke on March 10, 1903, in Davenport, Iowa. As a child he reached to the keyboard and picked out tunes; he knew the air of The Second Hungarian Rhapsody when he was three. He took a few lessons; he didn't learn to read music. On the river boats which came to Davenport in summer he heard jazz. He bought a cornet and taught himself to play; his fingering was unorthodox; he developed a round, full tone which was a wonder and a delight to all who heard it.

For a brief period he attended Lake Forest Academy in Chicago; he won prizes in music and flunked everything else. He listened to the jazz bands in Chicago, and when the players knew him and had heard him they asked him to sit in. He jobbed around with small pickup bands through the Middle West until 1923, when Dick Voynow, a piano player, organized the Wolverines. They made records for Gennett, a small recording studio at Richmond, Indiana, owned by the Starr

102

Piano Company. Hoagy Carmichael heard Bix and brought the Wolverines to Indiana University in the spring of 1924; after eight return visits on eight successive week ends the Bix legend was begun. The Wolverines took their place as one of the great white jazz bands; their records were a sensation; Bix was on his way.

In Chicago young Condon and his friends played the records of the Wolverines and waited impatiently for Bix to hit town so they could hear him on the piano and take him to hear Bessie Smith. Bessie was Empress of the Blues. Ma Rainey, another great blues singer, discovered her in Tennessee, singing for $2.50 a week in tent shows. Bessie had a contralto voice of such power and range and tone, of such richness and adaptability, that there was no one to rival or imitate or follow her. She was unmatched; in the days before the depression Negroes stood in line all over the country to buy her records: Empty Bed Blues, Careless Love, Nobody Knows You When You're Down And Out, Young Woman's Blues. She sang many of the blues written by Clarence Williams, the New Orleans piano player who migrated to Chicago, opened a music shop on State Street, and became the publisher of his own songs.

State Street was lined with cafés and theaters where jazz bands played—the Elite, the Pekin, the Fiume, the Dreamland, the Panama, the Rose Garden, the Edelweiss and the Little Edelweiss, the Open Air Gardens, and the Vendome and Lincoln Theaters. There was also the New Orleans Babe's Saloon and Restaurant, and, near by on Wabash Avenue, the Dusty Bottom open air café. Wandering from saloon to saloon was a man named Jimmy Yancey, a piano player with a strong, rolling, rhythmic bass. Jimmy had been a vaudeville performer; now he was a favorite at rent parties. When things were low just before dawn he played his Five O'Clock Blues. Others picked up his style—Pine Top Smith, Albert Ammons, Meade Lux Lewis. It was given a name, boogie woogie.

Jazz was not considered a proper profession for well-bred young white men; band leaders who dispensed popular music were as disapproving as parents who revered Beethoven. The Austin High boys and their friends had to work in cabarets and speakeasies; Al Capone and his lieutenants replaced the madams of Storyville as sponsors for the new music. Playing in small groups, experimenting with techniques, the youngsters developed a style based upon but different from New Orleans jazz. The beat was pushed and nervous, the tympani had the urgent sound of Indian drums; there was tenseness, almost frenzy, in the solo flights of the horns; there was not the un-hurried, effortless, relaxed mood of Negro jazz.

Improvisation by adolescent white boys reared in polite homes was bound to be different from the conversational in-strumentation of colored men belonging to a minority of thirteen million submerged in the freest nation on earth. It was a fresh expression, a new voice; it was first heard outside its habitat when in 1928 Okeh released a record made by seven of the youngsters: Frank Teschmaker, Bud Freeman, Jimmy MacPartland, Joe Sullivan, Jim Lannigan, Gene Krupa, and Eddie Condon. Condon organized the band, Red McKenzie arranged the recording date.

McKenzie was an ex-jockey, born in Holy Name parish in St. Louis in 1899, the last of ten children, christened William. After breaking both arms in his chosen profession he retired and hopped bells at the Claridge Hotel in St. Louis. Standing on the sidewalk waiting for patrons to arrive he folded a piece of paper over a comb and blew tunes to amuse himself. Across the street a Negro bootblack played a phonograph and beat out the rhythm on his customers' shoes. A young clerk named Dick Slevin came out of Butler Brothers Store with a kazoo· and hummed along with the music. McKenzie crossed the street and joined in. Slevin knew a man named Jack Bland who played a banjo. Bland, Slevin, and McKenzie began playing together. They went to Chicago with Gene Rodemich's band as a novelty. Isham Jones got them a recording date with Brunswick. They played Arkansaw Blues and Blue Blues; the records sold more than a million copies. The Mound City Blue Blowers, as they called themselves, went on tour. In Atlantic City McKenzie met Eddie Lang, another banjo player. McKenzie persuaded him to take up the guitar and join the Blowers. It was Lang who so popularized the guitar that the banjo disappeared from jazz orchestras. Before that happened McKenzie met another banjo player in Chicago, took him into partnership, and brought him to New York.

CHICAGO—1924

IT WAS cold enough to keep the snow comfortable in Chicago Heights. Ma had suffered another stroke and was getting around again by wheel chair. I took her to church in the afternoons; at night I played club dates in Chicago. My union card was being transferred; ninety days had to pass before I could take a steady job in town. Husk O'Hare's office sent me on high school and college party dates, and to dances in different parts of the city.

One night I went to a part-time cabaret on the far north side called the Cascades. It was run by Palmer Katy, a well-dressed ragtime guy, slightly on the promotional side. "Katy likes your kind of music," I was told. "You'll get five dollars if there's a crowd." The Cascades was a moderate-sized upstairs place, bring your own bottles and buy setups. When I got there the other musicians had arrived. One of them, Squeak Buhl, was setting up drums. A good-looking kid was trying to get notes from a tenor saxophone which was green with corrosion. It sounded the way it looked. A blond, solidly built boy was watching him; he had a cornet. I introduced myself; the saxophone player shook hands with me. "My name is Bud Freeman," he said. "This is Jimmy MacPartland." We sat down and began to play. Freeman seemed to know only one tune; everything sounded vaguely like *China Boy*. MacPartland had a strong, rugged tone; he knew where he was going and

106

enjoyed the journey. Buhl set a good beat and we all pushed it a little. Now and then Freeman hit a note that sounded like music.

Between sets we gabbed and I discovered that MacPartland and Freeman were from the west side. They were about my age; they had been in Austin High School together and with some other students had formed a band. They talked about jazz as if it were a new religion just come from Jerusalem. When MacPartland mentioned King Oliver smoke came out of his eyes. "He's playing a fraternity dance at the Chez Paree tonight," Freeman said. "Let's go down there after we finish."

We arrived in time for the last set; the musicians were reassembling as we pushed our way to the stand. "That's Oliver," MacPartland said, pointing to a big, amiable looking Negro with a scar over one eye who stood in front of the band holding a cornet. Near him was a slightly smaller and much younger man, also holding a cornet. "That's Louis Armstrong," MacPartland said. He pointed to the others: Johnny Dodds on clarinet and his brother Baby on drums, Honoré Dutray at the trombone, Johnnie St. Cyr playing banjo, and Lillian Hardin at the piano. Oliver lifted his horn and the first blast of *Canal Street Blues* hit me. It was hypnosis at first hearing. Everyone was playing what he wanted to play and it was all mixed together as if someone had planned it with a set of micrometer calipers; notes I had never heard were peeling off the edges and dropping through the middle; there was a tone from the trumpets like warm rain on a cold day. Freeman and MacPartland and I were immobilized; the music poured into us like daylight running down a dark hole. The choruses rolled on like high tide, getting wilder and more wonderful. Armstrong seemed able to hear what Oliver was improvising and reproduce it himself at the same time. It seemed impossible, so I dismissed it; but it was true. Then the two wove around each other like suspicious women talking about the same man. When they finally finished MacPartland said, "How do you like it?" There was only one thing to say: "It doesn't bother me."

We listened until the last note; Armstrong was reaching, showing his high shoes and his white socks; Oliver was looking at him with a fatherly smile. We hit the cold air outside and Freeman said, "Let's go down to the Friars' Inn." It was a late place, open until the customers stopped buying or went home. I spotted a few changes when I got to the bandstand; Schoebel wasn't at the piano and Ben Pollack was playing drums. Rappolo, Mares, Brunies, Pettis, and the others, including Lew Black, were still setting fire to *Shimmy Shawabble*, *Angry*, *Sobbin' Blues*, *Sugarfoot Stomp*, and *Everybody Loves Somebody Blues*. What was left of our capacity for enjoyment we turned over to Rappolo. He played clarinet the way Shakespeare played English. It was afternoon when I got back to Chicago Heights.

At O'Hare's booking office I ran into a character who operated under the name of Murphy Podolsky; he played piano and had an inside track on school dance dates. He played a good opinion of himself straight for the amusement of his friends; he pretended to believe in his own greatness. But he pretended to nothing else; he would crawl on his hands and knees through a moving field of wild cats to needle a phony. Often we went window shopping together; I was saving my dough for some of the haberdashery in Dockstader-Sandberg's on Michigan Avenue, a store so high class it eventually soared out of business. One day I spotted a new style hat, with a high crown. That's for me, I thought, when I get enough paper. The next night I worked on a date at Northwestern University in Evanston, just over the line from Chicago. A gaunt, hollow-looking kid came in, dragging drums. Something about him seemed familiar. Then I spotted his hat—he had the pilgrim's model. Damn him, I thought, he got it before I did. He said his name was Dave Tough; he set up the drums and I wondered where he would find the strength to hit them. He was behind me when we started our first number; what he did to the drums nearly drove me through the opposite wall. I turned around and looked at him. He was possessed.

While we were having a drink between sets I said to him, "You sort of like this music, don't you?" He nodded gloomily. "I guess I do," he said. "My family doesn't understand what I'm doing. I can't get a job with a big band because they don't play this kind of stuff. I must be crazy to keep on playing it, but I do."

"Where do you live?" I asked.

"Oak Park," he said.

I knew he wasn't kidding about bucking his family; Oak Park, a suburb of Chicago, was credited with being the richest village in the world.

"Do you go to school?" I asked. I had a feeling he ought to be at Harvard; maybe he was being kept at Northwestern so his drumming could be watched for symptoms of violence.

"I go to Lewis Institute," he said. "It's a prep school for two kinds of people—those who can't go to the best schools and those who get thrown out of them. We have a dance there once a week, with a pickup band—this kind of music. Why don't you come and sit in?"

"Who plays?" I asked.

"Almost anybody. Some weeks we have all saxophones, some weeks we have all cornets, some weeks we have three sets of drums. Only two of us are regular, myself and a kid named Benny Goodman."

I knew Benny; we had met at union headquarters and played pool together until we discovered both of us were after the same thing, carfare and walk-around money. After that we took on separate opponents. I had been to Benny's home for dinner—a widowed mother, lots of kids, big bowls of good food, pitch until you win.

"So you know Benny," Tough said. "He and I joined the American Musicians Union the same day. We were both in short pants; I was thirteen, Benny was twelve. He's going to Lewis Institute now. I hope the education won't ruin his clarinet playing. We jazz players are supposed to be vulgarians beyond the moral as well as the musical pale; I guess we might as well live up to what is expected of us."

He looked at me.

"Do you expect to go on playing jazz?" he asked.

"While I'm eating meat*," I said.

"Then you are a no-good drunken. tramp and you'll never get anywhere," he said. "Come over to the Institute and play with us. Last week we had twelve trombones and a rhythm section."

When we finished and I was about to leave he said, "If you want to go to Lincoln Gardens ask Voltaire Defoe. He took me when I was small. He's a friend of mine."

"Thanks," I said. "I can usually get in by myself."

* while I'm alive

"Come to the Institute," Tough said. "We have never had twelve banjos."

A lot of older white kids had been enlisted from time to time to take youngsters to the Lincoln Gardens, the southside cabaret where King Oliver played. It was by and for Negroes, and the white kids in short pants who went there—some of them on bicycles—to hear the music had good reason to feel slightly uncomfortable until they had pushed their way close to the bandstand and been recognized by Oliver. A nod or a wave of his hand was all that was necessary; then the customers knew that the kids were all right. Night after night we made the trip.

In the cubicle outside where we paid admission the sound was loud; it came like a muscle flexing regularly, four to the bar. As the door opened the trumpets, King and Louis, one or both, soared above everything else. The whole joint was rocking. Tables, chairs, walls, people, moved with the rhythm. It was dark, smoky, gin-smelling. People in the balcony leaned over and their drinks spilled on the customers below. There was a false ceiling made of chicken wire covered with phony maple leaves; the real roof was twenty-five feet up. A round, glass bowl hung from the middle of the chicken wire; when the blues were played it turned slowly and a baby spotlight worked over it. There was a floor show and a master of ceremonies named King Jones. He would stand in front of Oliver and shout, "Oh! One more chorus, King!" Oliver and Louis, would roll on and on, piling up choruses, with the rhythm section building the beat until the whole thing got inside your head and blew your brains out. There was a place near the band reserved for musicians who came to listen and to learn; we sat there, stiff with education, joy, and a licorice-

111

tasting gin purchased from the waiters for two dollars a pint. You could bring your own but it didn't matter much; in the end the effect was the same—the band playing *Froggie Moore, Chimes Blues, Sweet Baby Doll, Jazzin' Babies' Blues, Mabel's Dream, Room Rent Blues, High Society Rag, Where Did You Stay Last Night, Working Man Blues,* and everything and everybody moving, sliding, tapping out the rhythm, inhaling the smoke, swallowing the gin.

After ninety days the union allowed me to take a steady job. I went to work at the Palace Gardens, a cabaret in the 600 block on North Clark Street, the heart of the tenderloin. There were five blocks almost solid with cabarets—The Derby, The Erie, Liberty Inn, 606, etc., *ad infinitum.* Most of them were like the Palace Gardens, which had a small band with hag singers going from table to table moaning gold-toothed ballads full of moons and Junes. Harry Greb, the fighter who trained in night clubs and was afraid of nobody, listened to them and melted. Babe Ruth was another customer; he would clout a few over the fence in Comiskey Park in the afternoon and listen to *When You Look In The Heart Of A Rose* at night.

Nobody went to bed; there must have been people who slept at night and who worked by day but I didn't see them during those months. Charlie Straight's orchestra played at the Rendezvous up the street until two o'clock, then an overtime band took up. It was a pickup outfit and it played jazz. One night it had a cornet player who sounded somewhat like King Oliver—a miraculous sense of time, pulling the whole band along with him, and a mellow tone, with drive. He had a face stuck together with shamrocks; he said his name was Muggsy Spanier and that he was a local boy, south side. "What do you do besides this?" I asked. "I'm at the Columbia Ballroom,"

112

he said. "I should have known," I said. The Columbia, also on North Clark Street, had the best dance band in town— Sig Myer's Druids. They played a Sunday matinee and I was there to hear Muggsy's cornet. "I was christened Francis," he told me, but my mother calls me Muggsy. I don't know whether to be a baseball player or a doctor." "What's the matter with music?" I asked. "It isn't hard to do," he said.

Spring hit the Palace Gardens and I was back at the union shooting pool. One day I missed the side pocket on an easy shot. "The hotter it gets the more often it will happen," Al Beller, a fiddle player, said. "By August you won't even be able to make your room rent at this racket. Why don't you take a resort job for the summer?" "My white flannels are packed," I said. "When do I leave and for where?" He made the shot I had missed. "There's a job at Lake Delavan with Wop Waller," he said. "He's been there for years. Right now he needs a banjo player." I missed another shot. "You don't have to stay if you don't like it," Al said. Again he made the shot I had missed. The word lake had shoved me off balance; I was thinking of canoes and red-headed girls. The next day I left for Delavan, Wisconsin.

The lake was three miles from town and Wop Waller was a drummer. He was playing at the Woodlawn Hotel with four pieces; I made five. We were housed in a bowling alley converted into a dormitory; I slept in alley 4. The food was good, the swimming was excellent, the canoes were seaworthy. "Where are the people?" I asked Wop. He swung his arm, indicating the shores of the lake. I could see spots of white and patterns of lawn, indicating that the Indians had been conquered. "Big houses," Wop said. "Things will pick up when the kids get home from college. Sidney Smith lives over

113

at Lake Geneva"—he pointed past my shoulder—"he's probably drawing Andy Gump right now." I was depressed. What was I doing here?

Monday night didn't encourage me. We could have discharged shotguns from the bandstand without hitting a dancer. Once in a while, out of the gloom, a couple appeared, passed, and disappeared. "Let's go play in the cemetery," I said to Wop, "where we'll have an audience." Just then a couple danced by and the girl turned her head and spoke to Wop. She was young and black-haired and beautiful. "Who is she?" I demanded. One woman can't save a season, but she can help. "Her name is Barbara," Wop said. "Her family are summer residents. Last year her older sister dated my banjo player. His name was Eddie, too."

The next time Barbara passed I got a smile. "Want to sing?" Wop said. I assaulted the air with *All Alone*. Barbara got the idea. She asked Wop for *What'll I Do?* After that I sang, *I Want To Be Happy*. Barbara asked Wop for *I'll See You In My Dreams*. I sang *June Night*. Barbara asked Wop for *When Day Is Done*. That did it.

She was a gold-coaster from Chicago; she attended a girls' school in Massachusetts and was staying at Delavan in a modest summer mansion with her family. She was seventeen; every night she came to dance; by day we swam, played tennis, canoed. Seeing her from the bandstand was easy and tantalizing. Meeting her otherwise was difficult. Her mother objected to me and I sympathized with the prejudice. Barbara's older sister, I discovered, had died as a result of an automobile accident the previous summer, while on a date with the other banjo player named Eddie. Barbara and I managed to get together, anyhow. We couldn't help it. The chauffeur conspired

114

with us; we rode around in one of the Packards, or in the family motorboat. When the coast was clear at the house we went there to play the phonograph and dance.

There was always a stack of new records by the machine. "Where do you get these?" I asked Barbara. "Oh," she said, "Tod Healy brings them from Chicago on week ends." She tossed her head. "He's an admirer of mine. He'll bring me anything I want." I found a pencil and a sheet of engraved note paper. On it I wrote: *Oh Baby, Copenhagen, Riverboat Shuffle, Susie, Sensation, Lazy Daddy*—Wolverines. "Give this to Tod and tell him you want these records," I said. Might as well make the guy work, I thought. Bix was with the Wolverines and they were making records for Gennett, in Richmond, Indiana. I wanted to hear that cornet again. He played it all wrong, so the experts said—he taught himself, and he couldn't read music—but it came out right.

Tod brought the records. "What kind of music is that?" Barbara wanted to know. "Are they aborigines?" She knew about paved streets so I told her about jazz. "I'd rather hear you sing *All Alone*," she said. I filled my pockets with chewing gum (her family was in the business) and left.

There was a lot of trump* at Delavan; I have seldom seen so many clean† people. One of my pals was Ray Whiting, a young fellow who stayed at the Highlands, a hotel not far from the Woodlawn. He was from Oak Park, was good-looking, and had a Wills St. Clair roadster with disc wheels and a mallard knob on the radiator. Another friend was Francis Garibaldi, son of a Chicago import-export family; he was a bachelor, an athlete, and he owned the fastest motorboat on the lake. There was also Ward Goslin, who now owns a string

* money   † wealthy

of mid-west hotels. His family had a private tennis court, and I played there when there was no excuse not to exercise.

We drove to town every day in the Wills St. Clair and checked our trap line for new girls—the post office and a drugstore operated by two youngsters named O'Neill and O'Brien were the liveliest spots. Coolidge was President but we still wore knickers; we drank ice cream sodas on the trap line and carried gin at night. I sang in the choir of the local Catholic church; it gave me an excellent view of the congregation; new and pretty girls were easy to spot.

From July 4th until Labor Day the crowds were large and loaded for fun; girls were now wearing knitted bathing suits. Sometimes after the dance we were invited to play for a boat party. In the middle of the lake we sang, played, danced and drank; fish have never been so bored. Next day Barbara would say to me, "You were out on the lake last night; I heard you playing." It always startled me that our music carried so far and so well over water. "Did you hear me play *It Had To Be You?*" I would ask. "Yes," she would answer, "and if you think I am going to believe what you are going to say your head was put together without a blueprint."

One day I walked to Lake Geneva, seven miles away, to buy the second record of the Mound City Blue Blowers, a trio with Red McKenzie blue-blowing on a comb, Dick Slevin playing a kazoo, and Jack Bland on banjo. The first record, *Arkansaw Blues* and *Blue Blues*, was a sensation. The second record, *San* and *Red Hot*, had Frankie Trumbauer added on C-melody saxophone. I wanted to get it and play it for Barbara, so she would know how real aborigines sounded. Suddenly as I walked a Cadillac touring car pulled into the road from a driveway ahead and passed almost over me at approximately ninety
116

miles an hour. I scarcely had time to notice that the girl at the wheel was blonde, young, beautiful, tastefully dressed, tanned, healthy, athletic, with short hair, wide eyes, and a wrist watch on her left hand. I managed to meet her the next Sunday at church. Her name was Grace and she developed into my next year's girl. There was no family opposition but I had to attend Mass every Sunday.

It was lazy through *Dinah* that summer. Wop and I committed a duet on *Too Tired*, but I never slept less and felt better. Some day a psychoanalyst is going to discover that I am still in a canoe at Lake Delavan, singing *Memory Lane* to Barbara or Grace. Nobody had any intention of moving a foot east or west of the resort until Labor Day, but all that summer everybody sang *California Here I Come*. The boys loved to get sad-eyed and wonder what had become of Sally, and they told the girls that, "You're *Nobody's Sweetheart Now*." When Barbara turned up with Tod I gave her *Everybody Loves My Baby* and *Why Did I Kiss That Girl?* One night late in August she spoke to Wop. When we finished the number he said, "All right, boys, *You Gotta See Mama Every Night*." As we played it Barbara danced by with her nose up and her eyes averted. "Then I *won't* see mama at all," I sang at her. I meant what I said, too. I was fifteen minutes late for my date next day.

EDUCATION AND
BIX AND BESSIE

AS I PACKED UP to leave Lake Delavan a new idea nudged me. The college kids I had met during the summer were like me but they had a different manner. "Who is Proust?" I asked Wop one day. "What does he play?" Wop said. That was it. Education was something you couldn't see but it was there, like being able to throw a curve. I decided to get some for myself. It doesn't come in bottles, I figured, so it can't do me any harm.

Back in Chicago I went to live with brothers John and Jim at the Allerton House, a hotel for men at 700 Michigan Avenue. John was working for our brother-in-law, Jack Dunn, Lucille's husband, who had a wholesale and retail jewelry business in the loop. Jim had succeeded in tuning his banjo and was playing club dates. We found two other banjo players and formed a quartet, doing specialty numbers with bands. One of the quartet was Herbie Kaumyer; later he changed his name to Herbie Kay, started an orchestra and married his singer, a girl named Dorothy Lamour.

My summer money went into a winter wardrobe. Now that I was going to get an education I had to be careful about the difference between a gentleman and a dude. A dude, I figured, is a fellow who makes a business of dressing correctly; a gentle-

118

man is a guy who can't help putting on the right clothes; he doesn't know any better.

My school was located on Catalpa Avenue on the north side. It was the home of Mrs. Reid, a retired Northwestern University professor, who occupied herself with tutoring and whose credits were accepted at Northwestern. She had half a dozen boys and girls in addition to myself; I was due at nine in the morning and I had to take a bus to get there. It was grim, but I had something to find out—who was Proust? I began with French, English, mathematics, and some other stuff. I never got time to do homework and I never got time to sleep. I arrived at nine o'clock with my eyelids taped. When the questions were asked and the other students began writing their answers I sneaked into the kitchen, lighted a cigarette on the pilot of the gas stove, and looked out of the window. What the hell am I doing here, I asked myself. I can stay home, get some sleep, and be just as stupid. This way I don't get any sleep and I'm still stupid. But I kept going. Somewhere ahead of me was Proust.

Barbara wrote to me from her school in Massachusetts. When she came to town for the Christmas holidays I swapped overcoats with Benny Goodman to take her on dates; Benny and I were the same size then and he had a new outdoor job. I told Barbara about my school work and she was very happy. About the time I got back my own coat I ran into Milton Mezzrow, who was addicted to the saxophone. Mezz knew the leader of the band at Ike Bloom's Rendezvous on Randolph Street, a fiddler named Irving Rothschild. He got jobs for both of us and we went to work with Rothschild and with Johnny Fortin on piano, Don Carter on drums, and Murphy Steinberg on trumpet. It was steady and pleasant work; by now the customers were providing most of the entertainment in night clubs and speakeasies. Everyone was friendly with the band and the band was friendly with everyone else. We did our best to help the tone of Mezzrow's saxophone. We put cigarette and cigar butts, ashtrays and damp paper napkins, into the bell, but they didn't help. Mezz had a couple of breaks to take on his tenor saxophone during *Eccentric*. Somehow he always got nervous and flubbed them. "This is a serious thing, Mezz," we told him. "Unless you break this fixation now it will ruin your career. We'll stick with you, no matter how long it takes." We kept playing *Eccentric* and Mezz kept flubbing his breaks. "Maybe we ought to forget it for a while," Mezz suggested. "No," we said, "you have got to break it now." But he didn't, although we played *Eccentric* all winter long.

Bix came to town that spring. He left the Wolverines when they went on the road; Jimmy MacPartland replaced him. Charlie Straight, at the other Chicago Rendezvous, on North Clark Street, wanted to hire him. The union pointed to its ninety-day clause. Straight made a statement which probably sums up what musicians thought of Bix; he said that Beiderbecke was a unique attraction, that he was not just a cornet player, and that if it were possible to find his equal anywhere in Chicago he, Straight, would hire the equal rather than Beiderbecke. The union agreed with him; Bix was allowed to take the job.

For the opening night I moved the population of the Allerton House to the Rendezvous. There was a floor show with dancing in between—tunes like *Alabamy Bound, Collegiate, If You Knew Susie,* and *Valencia*. All this was drool; we were waiting for Bix to cut loose. One of his Wolverine records for

Gennett was *Riverboat Shuffle*; on it Bix took a chorus and hit a high note that became famous. A hasty arrangement of the tune had been made for the Straight band. When Bix stood up to take his chorus we waited for the high note. It never came. That night Bix blew a clinker. But he made up for it later, when the floor shows were over and Straight let the band have its own way.

Bix stayed at the Rienzi Hotel, down the street from the Rendezvous. Often he came to the Allerton House and played the grand piano. Jim and I sat listening to him by the hour, as hopped up as if we had been blown through an opium pipe. My school books stayed on the table, unopened. One day Bix saw them. "What are these?" he asked. I explained that I was getting an education. He looked perplexed. "What are you going to do with it?" he said. "If you can't read music why do you want to read books?" He sat down at the piano. "By the way," I said, "who is Proust?" He hit a chord, listened to it, and then said, casually, "A French writer who lived in a cork-lined room. His stuff is no good in translation." I leaned over the piano. "How the hell did you find that out?" I demanded. He gave me the seven veils look. "I get around," he said.

First trumpet in Straight's band was played by Gene Caffarelli, a thorough musician. He interested Bix in the idea of reading music and began to teach him. It was a curious setup; Gene and the rest of the boys were contributing part of their salary to make up the fee Straight was paying Bix, the only member in the band who couldn't read music. Bix didn't know about this financial arrangement. When he found it out he quit and left town.

He was having the usual trouble with his pivot tooth; it was in front, upstairs, and it frequently dropped out, leaving Bix unable to blow a note. Wherever he worked it was customary to see the boys in the band down on the floor, looking for Bix's tooth. Once in Cincinnati at five o'clock in the morning while driving over a snow-covered street in a 1922 Essex with Wild Bill Davison and Carl Clove, Bix shouted, "Stop the car!" There was no speakeasy in sight. "What's the matter?" Davison asked. "I've lost my tooth," Bix said. They got out and carefully examined the fresh snow. After a long search Davison sighted a tiny hole; in it he found the tooth, quietly working its way down to the road. Bix restored it to his mouth and they went on to The Hole in the Wall, where they played every morning for pork chop sandwiches and gin. It was natural for Bix not to get the tooth permanently fastened; he couldn't be bothered going to the dentist.

He ran into some of Jean Goldkette's boys while he was at the Rendezvous. They were playing a prom date at Indiana University; Bix had a strong following there, led by a piano-playing student named Hoagy Carmichael. He was asked to go down and play the date with the band. He turned up at the Allerton House in the usual dilemma—no tuxedo. Jim and I put him together: Jim's jacket and trousers and shirt, my studs and tie. For good measure and the cool spring nights we gave him a topcoat and a hat. A few days later he returned and brought us the borrowed articles. There was a tuxedo, complete with studs, tie, and shirt. But the tuxedo was not Jim's, the shirt was not his, and the studs and tie were not mine. The topcoat and hat were also different from those we had given him. "Did you have a good time?" we asked politely. "I don't know," Bix said.

That spring Bessie Smith also came to town; we went to hear her at the Paradise, a battered joint with the buttons off at 35th and Calumet. The first night Bix turned his pockets inside out and put all his dough on the table to keep her singing. We had been raised on her records; we knew she was the greatest of all the blues singers; but she was better than any of us could possibly have anticipated. She had timing, resonance, volume, pitch, control, timbre, power—throw in the book and burn it; Bessie had everything. She was a likeable gal and a large piece of woman, with long, beautiful hands, and a thirty-six inch smile. The setting in which she worked didn't quite live up to its name. Rats as big as your arm prowled around casing the customers. Mitch, a hunchback, played cornet; he almost touched Oliver and Armstrong. Tubby Hall was on drums. The place was small, unventilated, gin-soaked, and had been slept in by everyone but George Washington. Bessie rocked it. We heard her sing *Baby Won't You Please Come Home?*, *Jailhouse Blues*, *I'm Goin' Back To My Used To Be*, *Downhearted Blues*, *Tain't Nobody's Business If I Do*, *Ticket Agent Ease Your Window Down*, *Nobody In Town Can Bake A Jelly Roll Like Mine*, *Careless Love*, *Gulf Coast Blues*, *Jazzbo Brown From Memphis Town*, *Empty Bed Blues*, *A Good Man Is Hard To Find*, *I Used To Be Your Sweet Mama*, *Nobody Knows You When You're Down And Out*. When they finally poured us into the street we could only mumble one thing, "Well, we've heard Bessie." We were back that night and every night thereafter, sitting and listening. Once I turned to Bix and said, "How do you think Bessie would sound in that cork-lined room of Proust's?" Bix didn't hear me. He was leaning on the table, eyes glazed, listening to Bessie.

Between midnight and dawn in those days you met all sorts of people in Chicago. You might be sitting quietly in a speakeasy and be informed that for the rest of the evening drinks were

123

on the house; Capone, the owner, had wandered in, ordered the doors closed, and settled down to enjoy himself. Once Dave Tough played in a cabaret which had a clientele composed almost exclusively of baseball players, gangsters, and detectives. It was managed by an ex-prize fighter named Jake, who weighed three hundred pounds and who had a little brother named Joe who weighed two hundred fifty pounds. Capone, of course, was the owner. Jake was bad-tempered and moody, particularly on rainy nights, when the weather got into his battered sinuses. Sometimes he would turn off the lights at midnight, order the customers out, and take the band into the bar to play for him. He had a passion for crossword puzzles, the easy ones in the Hearst papers. One night in the bar Dave helped him with a couple of words. From then on Jake grabbed him every night and asked him all the words. If Dave got stuck Jake would reach across the table, put his six-pound hand on Dave's shoulder, and say, "Come on, think!" So Dave worked the puzzles at home in the afternoon and went to work prepared; anything else for a drummer weighing 108 pounds would have been suicide.

One night after finishing the puzzle and grabbing a double rye at the bar Dave was hurrying to the bandstand. An inconspicuous-looking man standing in front of him didn't move. Dave put both hands against the man's shoulders. "Get the hell out of my way!" he said. One of the boys on the bandstand looked at Dave with admiration as he sat down at the drums. "I guess you don't care how long you live," he said. "Or aren't you afraid of Bottles Capone?" Bottles was Al's kid brother. Dave played the set involuntarily; he shook enough to beat the drums in perfect time. But Jake saved him; he couldn't afford to have his crossword puzzle expert damaged.

Once when Jim Lannigan was playing at the Friars' Inn after the New Orleans Rhythm Kings had left, some of the Capone mob came in and took the place over for the night. The other customers left and the doors were closed; the band played and the hoods drank. One of them noticed Jim's bass fiddle. The bulge on its underside caught the light and made an attractive target. The hood kept looking at it, measuring the distance and cocking one eye. Finally he took out a revolver and fired. The bullet hit the fiddle on the seam and the whole back opened up. The band kept on playing; the hood asked Jim how much the fiddle cost and stripped off enough from his roll to have it repaired.

In all of the joints the bands kept on playing no matter what happened, though sometimes the drummer would hold his bass drum over his head to keep it from being smashed. Muggsy Spanier saw two people killed in front of him one night; he kept on playing but he was so nervous that afterward he couldn't remember what tune it was. His clothes were so drenched with perspiration he had to change even his shoes. Customers often shoved five, ten, and even twenty dollar bills into Muggsy's horn. Sometimes he sat and played at their tables. There were no command performances for the gangsters, but sometimes the hoods took Muggsy with them from place to place. "We brought our own entertainment," they would say. They all liked jazz. "It's got guts and it don't make you slobber," one of them said.

All this was educational, but Northwestern did not accept such credits. When spring came and Bix arrived I got to Mrs. Reid's later and later, and finally I did not arrive at all. Next year, I said to myself, I will find out about Proust. I got out my knickers and flannels; we were to open at Delavan on Memorial Day.

Wop Waller was tied up at French Lick, Indiana, and couldn't get away for the opening. He wired me to organize the band and proceed without him. I got Murphy Podolsky to play the piano. Murphy mentioned that he could get a saxophone and clarinet team composed of Bud Freeman and Frank Teschmaker. I liked Bud but was leery of his corroded saxophone. I had never heard Teschmaker, nor did I know how much Bud had improved in a year. I let them go to Lost Lake on some board and room job and hired Bud Jacobson and Jimmy Vanderbosch on saxophone. Jimmy also played violin. Benny Goodman and Murphy Steinberg were playing at the Midway Gardens Ballroom on the south side. They came to watch me pack. I felt a slight sense of justification as they envied me the climate of Lake Delavan. Previously they had finagled me a job in the Midway; I opened and closed in one night, although I arrived on the job in what I considered to be a perfect state of equilibrium, half man and half alcohol. They still let me sit in once in a while. The Midway was the biggest dance hall on the south side until the Trianon was built. It had terraces and a balcony; the band sat in a shell on the balcony and poured it down on the people. One night after relieving the banjo player for a set I found I had a fan, a young drummer named George Wettling, who used to ride around the south side on his bicycle listening to jazz bands. "You were swell," George said when I met him at Feurs Restaurant. I was afraid of his judgment for years.

Dave Tough was at Lost Lake that summer. Wettling went to Lake James, Indiana. A young Chicago piano player I had met while jobbing, Joe Sullivan, was at Powers Lake, Wisconsin. Jim went out with Frank Barbino's band. At Delavan we had a little trouble with Podolsky. Murphy couldn't read music very well; at rehearsals we had to stop for him again and again. "The little round black things are the notes, Murphy," someone would say, and Murphy would be hurt. He looked like Groucho Marx and he had a frog voice; when he tried to appear sad and stabbed-in-the-back it didn't work. He would get up from the piano and say, "Why do I sacrifice myself for you peasants? Why do I bother with life at all, when it brings me nothing but misunderstanding of my talent?" Then he would leave the stand and walk straight down to the lake. Someone would holler, "Don't jump there, Murphy, it's too shallow!" Then we would play *Pal Of My Cradle Days, Oh How I Miss You Tonight,* and *Brown Eyes Why Are You Blue?* After a while Murphy would come back and sit down at the piano. Without a word he would begin to play *Because I Love You.*

Wop finally arrived and so did the crowd. While waiting for both, Bud Jacobson and I wrote a song; we worked it out during the dull days, thinking it might come in handy for romantic crises. It was called *Laughing At You,* and the music, curiously, wasn't bad. Later Carroll Dickerson's band in the Sunset Café played it, with Louis Armstrong on trumpet and Earl Hines at the piano. The lyrics, naturally, were awful. "You broke my heart but now I'm laughing at you," was the first line. We had our choice of true, blue, and new for rhymes, but we didn't want to be obvious. "There are some Indians named Sioux," Bud said. "Can we bring them in? Something like—so far as I am concerned you can go back to the Sioux?" I was fooling around with drew, flew, yew, and stew—you are just a carrot in my bowl of Irish stew. I forget what we decided but the last two lines were:

> Now that I've found somebody who is so true,
> I will be laughing, laughing at you.

When the girls arrived Murphy bought a Kissel Kar with wire wheels. He drove it in a slouched, tipped position with his left arm hanging over the side. No one could resist him, so he thought. He was right. Everyone laughed.

It was unnecessary to try *Laughing At You* on Grace. We got along well both in and out of canoes. At the dances she was content with *I Love My Baby*, *I'm Sitting On Top Of The World*, *Oh How I Miss You Tonight*, *Because I Love You*, *Who*, *Show Me The Way To Go Home*. "Why do people make such messes of their lives?" she used to say. "It's so easy to find happiness."

Jim wrote me from some lake where he was playing with Barbino. "My name has been changed," he said. "There were already five boys named Jim in the band when I arrived. Barbino refused to have another one. He said, 'You're Irish so your name is Pat.' I think I'll accept it; it sounds more like the way I feel. Our piano player is Mel Stitzel; you remember him. He has written a pretty good song, *Doodle-de-doo*. Art Kassel wrote the words. Mel is teaching me a lot about chords; I am thinking of learning to play the banjo. I am reading Dostoievski. It's an easy way to get an education. It won't get you into college but after the revolution there won't be any colleges."

"What is Dostoievski?" I asked Murphy.

"I think it is a kind of language, like Esperanto," Murphy said.

I decided against it. If I couldn't learn French what chance did I have with Dostoievski?

When I got back to Chicago Jim, now Pat, was still with Dostoievski. He showed me *The Brothers Karamazov*. I read a few pages and got interested in the story. "You must realize the difference between education and knowing something," Pat said. "When the revolution comes all those guys with college degrees will go down the drain. You had better stay away from Mrs. Reid. Sooner or later she will get you into Northwestern, even if you don't study." I decided he was right. I had gotten in my crack about Proust during the summer, anyhow. Right in the middle of a bunch of Harvards and Yales I had come up with, "What can you expect of a guy who lives in a cork-lined room? No wonder Proust isn't any good in translation." It was a success, but it brought me neither money nor friends. On the way home Grace said to me, "Who is Proust?" To hell with Mrs. Reid, I thought.

35th AND CALUMET

THERE'S a job at McVickers Theater for a banjo player," Pat said. "They want someone who can play a solo and accompany a girl singer. I think I'll take it." I was worried. "Are you sure you are ready for that?" I said. Pat smiled. "I can play *Doodle-de-doo* on the banjo better than anybody in the world," he said. "The composer spent all summer teaching me." "But you don't like work," I said. "You only like music, travel, and the revolution. What will you be doing in McVickers Theater behind a girl singer? That's work." Pat picked up his banjo. "It pays fifty dollars a week," he said. "At that rate playing the banjo is a pleasure."

He took the job and got away with it; McVickers even wanted more. "Next week there's a spot for two banjo players doing a duet in blackface," Pat said. "You're it." "What happened to the girl singer?" I asked. "She moved on," Pat said. "She was just a girl singing *It Had To Be You.* Somebody named Ruth Etting." We settled down to practice *Twelfth Street Rag*.

We found we were to be in quite a fancy scene. There were piles of cotton bales, draped with singers. We were to stand in front of them and do our duet. "Smile!" the bald-headed director in the pit said to us. "Smile! Remember you are supposed to be happy, carefree Negroes." I was late getting to the theater on the first day; I slapped my make-up on and rushed to the wings to meet Pat. "You're shaking and your hair is

130

sticking out from under your wig," he whispered. There was no time for adjustments; we were on. We played *Twelfth Street Rag*, shaking and without a smile. The director came backstage to tell us about it. When he was gone I had an idea. "We've got to laugh at something," I said to Pat. "How about that guy's bald head? We'll feed each other cracks about it." "Fine," Pat said. "It should be a perfect inspiration." "What's his name?" I asked. Pat thought for a moment. "It's a funny name," he said. "I never can remember without concentrating—H. Leopold Spitalny."

There was a job at the Merry Gardens for an alternate band. I went in with Art Grenwald, a pianist, Ralph Snyder on drums, Floyd O'Brien on trombone, and Bud Freeman and Frank Teschmaker on saxophones. As soon as I heard Bud and Tesch I groaned. They were wonderful, and I could have had them all summer. Our leader and trumpet player was from New Orleans and had one arm; his name was Joseph Wingston Mannone. Wingy wrote a song which we played. He sang the lyrics. It was about mosquitoes and its title was *I Wonder Where They Go When The Winter Winds Do Blow*. Wingy was articulate about practically everything. "Did I ever tell you about how it happens I have not got two right hands?" he would say. The correct answer was always no, because the story was never the same.

The Merry Gardens was one of the larger ballrooms and we had plenty of time to dish out our music. When work was done we went to the Dreamland, where Louis Armstrong, back in town after playing with Fletcher Henderson in New York, was performing with his wife Lil Hardin on the piano and Mitch the hunchback on second cornet. Teddy Weatherford, another piano player, later a voluntary exile to China, was the leader.

Louis was also appearing with Erskine Tate's orchestra at the Vendome Theater. There he began singing and "preaching" as the Reverend Satchelmouth. During the spring he went into the Sunset Café at 35th and Calumet, with Carroll Dickerson's band, which then had Earl Hines at the piano. About the same time King Oliver opened at the Plantation, just across the street. According to legend Oliver sent a note to Louis, saying, "Close those windows or I'll blow you off 35th Street." Louis kept right on blowing, and so did Joe. Muggsy Spanier used to drop in at the Sunset after work and sit in with Louis; Muggsy wanted to learn from the master. When the Sunset closed the musicians went across the street to the Nest, an upstairs place next to the Plantation. There they listened to Jimmy Noone do things with a clarinet which no one had considered even probable. Jimmy was a chubby, congenial, gentle Negro. He had gold keys on his clarinet and almost any morning after one o'clock the clarinet was pointed down at Teschmaker, who sat smack up against the bandstand, staring up at Jimmy. Benny Goodman was there often, too, and the nonclarinet playing Noone fans—Freeman, MacPartland, Lannigan, Tough, Wettling, Spanier, Mezzrow, and myself. We were the Nest's best customers. Often Jimmy Noone drove me home in the morning, then went to the links to play a round of golf before going to bed.

One night Arthur Kitti, flautist for the Chicago Symphony Orchestra, brought Maurice Ravel to hear Jimmy improvise endless choruses of *Four Or Five Times.* "Impossible!" Ravel muttered. Then he tried to write down some of the runs Jimmy was playing, but he quickly gave it up. After that he just sat back like the rest of us, listening and staring at the gold keys.

We went to the Nest at least five times a week. We left our golf clubs there, our instruments, our galoshes. The place made

132

no attempt at elegance; later, when there was some trouble, drapes were put up and it was called the Apex, with a Peacock Room on the side. There was vocal entertainment. One of the singers was Broadway Jimmy, a little fellow four feet high; another was Nora, straight from Paris, with the international touch. The drummer who alternated with Zutty Singleton was Johnny Wells, an official in the Negro Musicians Union. One night Johnny told us about a member who had so flagrantly violated a rule that he had to be punished. "What are you going to do to him, Johnny?" we asked. "I'm going to jack up the union and let it fall on him," Johnny said.

Thirty-fifth and Calumet was jacked up every night, with Louis and Oliver and Jimmy all playing within a hundred feet of each other; at dawn there fell a tremendous silence. Unless it happened in New Orleans I don't think so much good jazz was ever concentrated in so small an area. Around midnight you could hold an instrument in the middle of the street and the air would play it. That was music.

The job at the Merry Gardens didn't last long. Tesch and Bud went to station WHT—named for William Hale "Big Bill" Thompson, ex-mayor of Chicago—with their Blue Friars Band, including Dave Tough. They were studio musicians; when nothing else was available for broadcasting they played. Meanwhile they spent their time close by at Kelly's Stables, where Johnny and Baby Dodds were playing. It was really a barn; an old fellow led the customers upstairs by the light of a lantern. At night the Blue Friars would be grouped around the band, Tesch listening to Johnny Dodds on the clarinet, Tough watching Baby at the drums, when a messenger from WHT would rush in and call, "You're on!" The boys would run for it, shouting to each other about what they would play and how they would play it as they went down the stairs and raced along the street.

I took a job at the Columbia Ballroom on North Clark Street, playing with Bob Pacelli's orchestra. The Columbia was a barrel-house dance hall running four nights a week with four fights a night. Pacelli played trombone, Mel Stitzel was the pianist. The trumpeter's name was Pungui Altiere. He decided to get married. I offered to provide music for the wedding party; Tesch, MacPartland, Tough, and the other Blue Friars accepted an invitation. We met at the hotel where the reception was to be held and went to the bandstand in the ballroom. There was to be a march and we were to render *Here Comes The Bride*. We did. "Any man who plays the melody will have to leave the stand," were the orders. We gave it the straight jazz treatment and Pungui loved it. I don't know what the bride thought but she kept marching. After that the Italian cordials started flying and I don't remember a thing.

Murphy Podolsky's folks visited in Texas for the winter and I went to live in the family apartment with Murphy. Murphy also occupied, for the winter, a raccoon coat. He still had the Kissel Kar. One day as we drove toward the intersection of Wabash Avenue and Lake Street he said to me, "See this cop up here? He's my pal." He drove close to make the turn and greeted his friend. There was a slight miscalculation; one of the wheels of the Kissel ran over the cop's foot. After the air had cleared and we were on our way again I said, "Murphy, I don't think your pal recognized you." Murphy was undisturbed, though he had been hit with everything outside the dictionary. "New man on the beat," he said. "My friend was probably transferred for doing me favors."

Murphy had a succession of girls; he liked them not for what they were or for what they looked like, but for what other men they had been mixed up with. One of his dames was being courted by a judge. "She can have a member of the judiciary," Murphy would say, "but she prefers to go out with me." This fascinated him. Another doll had attained some temporary notoriety in connection with the Leopold-Loeb case. Murphy stared at her as if she had four heads. "A very interesting girl," he would say. "She has had a sorrowful past."

About twice a week we were practical. Cruising in the Kissel we scouted for girls with the rural look—good arms and a short, strong back. When we found two we asked them to take a ride; later we suggested a drink. At the apartment things were in a mess; we put on an act of being helpless, abandoned by Murphy's parents and unable to cope with the intricacies of housekeeping. Invariably the girls found aprons, mops, brushes, cleansing powder, etc., and in a few hours the place was shining. "How can we ever thank you?" we would say to the girls as we drove them home. "It was fun," they would reply. "We'd love to come and do it again."

That spring I worked briefly with a drummer named Johnny Constantine at a place called the Alcazar. Occasionally Capone, the owner, dropped in. Then the doors were shut, Al changed a few hundred dollar bills and distributed the paper among his pals, and the party was on. There was no shooting while I was there but I decided not to push my luck; I quit.

The weather was just getting warm when I got a call one night from Chicago Heights. Ma had suffered another stroke; this was the third. I grabbed the next train, an express headed for St. Louis. Its first stop was Chicago Heights. At a place called

Haney, about fifteen miles from Chicago, we slowed down and came to a halt. Twenty minutes passed while I paced the aisle. Then we started again. In a few minutes we pulled into Chicago Heights. When I walked into the house I knew it was all over. "How late am I?" I asked. "Twenty minutes," someone said.

PROSPERITY

THE WOLVERINES lost men until only Dick Voynow was left; Husk O'Hare reorganized the band with Teschmaker, Freeman, Tough, Lannigan, Floyd O'Brien, Mac-Partland, and Dave North. They opened at the ballroom in White City, a south side amusement park. Bix had been playing for almost a year with Frankie Trumbauer at the Arcadia Ballroom in St. Louis. Now he was at Hudson Lake, Indiana, with a combination of the best hot men from the Arcadia and Jean Goldkette's band at the Greystone in Detroit. The lake was an easy run of seventy-five miles from Chicago; we drove there frequently to hear the music and get cooled off. Sometimes I went with Mezzrow, sometimes with Tesch or Dave Tough or George Rilling, sometimes with my brother John. In addition to Bix and Trumbauer the St. Louis boys in the band were Itsy Riskin, piano; Sonny Lee, trombone; Dan Gabe, bass; Pee Wee Russell, clarinet; Dee Orr, drums. The band played six nights and a Sunday matinee, with Monday night off. Tesch and the boys sometimes drove down Saturday nights after White City closed, and heard the music on Sunday afternoons.

One Monday night we lost Bix in the revolving barrel at White City. Most of us had managed to crawl or roll or fall through it. "Watch me," Bix said. "I'll show you how to walk through it without even losing my balance." He plunged in and fell flat. We waited, but the more he rolled and crawled the less progress he made. Finally the attendant had to stop the machine and go in and drag him out. Undaunted, he went on to the roller coaster, the shooting gallery, and the ski ball. "This is one thing I can always beat," he said to me. "Remember how I learned in Syracuse?"

The band at Hudson Lake wore uniforms, with fancy two-tone shoes. Bix was the last to arrive on the job, naturally; he got the last uniform and the last pair of shoes. The uniform was too small for him and the shoes were too big. One night after the dance Pee Wee Russell and Bix went for a row on the lake; the boat upset and after that Bix's uniform was even smaller for him; the toes of his shoes curled up.

He and Pee Wee, a tall, mournful-looking kid, lived in a cottage near the lake with Riskin, Gabe, and Orr. There were three bedrooms, a kitchen, a living room, a tired grand piano, and no housekeeper. The place was always a shambles. The only commodity kept in sufficient stock was a local whiskey, purchased in large quantities for five dollars a gallon from three old-maid hillbillies who lived five miles away. Barefoot in a cabin with a brother they were all past sixty and asked no questions.

Bix and Pee Wee were without a car. It bothered them; they couldn't visit the old maids when they wanted to. One day, having received some pay—usually they owed it all—they went to LaPorte to buy an automobile. There were several secondhand Model T Fords available but Bix had notions of grandeur. He found a 1916 Buick which could be had for eighty dollars. It ran around the block well. "This is it," Bix said to Pee Wee. "Wait until the guys see us with this. We won't have to ride with them anymore, they'll be begging to ride with us." Pee Wee was dubious, but he agreed.

They drove back to the lake and hid the car in a side road.

138

Just before starting time that night they sneaked off, got into it, and drove to the pavilion. As they reached the entrance and caught the attention of the boys on the stand the motor stopped. It refused to start; the owners had to push it to the cottage. Next day they got it going and decided to visit the old maids. They took Charlie Horvath's wife with them—Charlie was managing the band for Goldkette. They got to the cabin, bought a jug, and started back. Half way home the Buick went dead. They had to find a farmer and hire him to tow it by horse to a garage. Sitting in the car they nibbled at the jug; they arrived at work, loaded, at eleven-thirty. A surprise awaited them. Goldkette was there; he had chosen this one night of the whole season to visit the band at Hudson Lake. "Is this the way things always go—the cornet and clarinet players drunk and mad and missing with your wife?" he asked Horvath. "It's their birthday," Horvath said. He could think of nothing else.

The car was delivered next day at the cottage. "Park it in the backyard," Bix said to the man who towed it from the garage. It never ran again. It had a fine mirror and the owners used that while shaving. Ten years later Pee Wee was driving to the coast with the Louis Prima band; he detoured to reminisce at Hudson Lake and found the cottage. The car was still in the backyard, on its wheels but groggy with rust. Pee Wee pointed it out to the Prima boys. "I own half of that," he said.

One Monday I drove down to the lake with George Rilling, a Chicago boy who played piano and composed. Bix entertained us at the piano; during the winter at the Arcadia ballroom he had completed a piano piece and later Tommy Satterfield wrote it out for him. It was called *In A Mist*. Bix played it for Rilling, who liked it so much he suggested we go to Detroit and celebrate with some real whiskey. We made the trip, slept three in a bed for a few hours, and raced back, trying to get Bix to the pavilion in time for the first set. We pulled up as the music started. Bix jumped out, ran to the stand, picked up his horn, and put it to his mouth just in time to take a chorus on *Sweet Georgia Brown*. We stayed to feed him between sets from the stock of ale and Scotch we had brought with us. The band had arrangements of all the new tunes: *Tonight You Belong To Me*, *Always*, *Yes Sir That's My Baby*, *In A Little Spanish Town*, *Black Bottom*, *Remember*, *Horses*, *When The Red Red Robin Comes Bob-Bob-Bobbin' Along*, *After I Say I'm Sorry*, *Where Do You Work-A John?*, *Bye Bye Blackbird*, *Let A Smile Be Your Umbrella*, *Crazy Words*. Bix was featured. When the dancing was finished we went to the cottage and he sat down at the piano. Sleep, food, and women, were things he never allowed to interfere with music.

Late that summer I went to work at the Vanity Fair, a café at Broadway and Grace Street, complete with floor show, dance teams, singers, funny men, lines of girls, and plenty of customers. The band leader was Art Cope, a violinist. Jack Gardner, who had just written a hit song, *Bye Bye Pretty Baby*, played piano. Teddy Arnold was the drummer. When I went to work the first night I saw a bass fiddle resting in the corner. While I was tuning my banjo a beautiful girl walked in. She kept coming toward me, stepped up on the bandstand, and went to the fiddle. "Nice to see you," she said to me casually. "I'm the bass player." Her name was Thelma Coombs, and she had been held over from the previous band. When I heard her behind me in the first number I knew she was a musician. This, I thought, is wonderful—a beautiful blonde in the rhythm section, a first class café, and good pay. Wonderful was the right word. The job lasted ten months. I made well over a hundred dollars each week, and all that winter Thelma was my date. She was a guy's girl; I never had to worry about her no matter where we were, and we were in some curious places. Often we cabareted on the south side until seven or eight o'clock in the morning. It never bothered Thelma; if she got tired or bored she got up quietly and went home by herself.

As a gentleman with an established income I opened a checking account. I wore twenty-dollar English hats, thirty-dollar shoes, and bench-made suits. I even took out an insurance policy. "In ten years, Eddie, you'll be on easy street," the salesman said. "You'll be thirty-one years old and you'll have ten thousand dollars." After losing a considerable amount of money over a period of years on this proposition, I finally managed to sell the policy back to the company for four hundred and fifty dollars.

The trouble with the checking account was that after a night of cabareting I usually found a number of stubs in my book with nothing written on them. I never quite knew whether I had money in the bank or whether I didn't. Once I asked a friend's father to get me two tickets to the Notre Dame-Army football game in New York. I wanted them for Frank Dodds, a fellow who was moaning about the impossibility of getting a seat in the Yankee Stadium for less than a scalper's price of a hundred dollars. "I'll get them for you," I said. My other friend's father was president of a large industrial concern; he could have managed admission to the St. Valentine's Day massacre. I went to his office to pick up the tickets; with a flourish I wrote out a check for the price, six dollars. I gave the envelope to my other friend, accepted six dollars in cash, and forgot about the deal. He went to New York and enjoyed the game; I went cabareting. Tuesday I received a call from the gentleman to whom I had given my check. He asked me to come to his office.

As soon as I saw him I knew what had happened; the check had bounced.

"Sit down," he said. "I'm sure it's something you're good at."

I sat. He was a nice-looking, prosperous, intelligent, obviously talented man.

"What sort of young men exist now in this country?" he asked me. "So far as I can discern there is not a shred of responsibility in all of your generation. You seem obsessed with a single desire—to compress as much uninhibited pleasure into as many ungodly hours as it is possible for human ingenuity, physical stamina, and moral disintegration to accommodate. I have never observed as many healthy and well-bred young people engaged in such utter waste of time, talent, and intelligence. You are as determined to be irresponsible as you are to be happy. You are engaged in the destruction of yourselves and the society in which you are allowed, by some gruesome mistake of nature, to dwell. I hope the enjoyment you insist upon drawing from this carnage is worth the consequences you some day shall be called upon to meet. My opinion of you is this."

He tore up the check.

"Good day."

As I recall it Notre Dame lost the game.

Work at the Vanity Fair was pleasant. Cope, Gardner, and I formed a singing trio in which I was the baritone. We had two styles of singing, through the nose and through the mouth. Cope, who was smaller than I, had a ventilator large enough for eight people. Even so, he never got the Calvin Coolidge tone, even on *Thinking Of You*; only Rudy Vallee had that, and he used a megaphone.

142

We had a lot of steady customers. One of them, a profes-sional football player named George, liked to stand on a table and jump off, landing on his hands. One night another customer, a former all-American halfback named Harold, challenged George to a real exhibition of strength. "Jumping off tables is for kids," Harold said. "Let's go outside and have some grown-up fun. I'll knock your block off."

George declined and left. After closing we went with Harold to Ike Bloom's Frolics on Twenty-second Street, to see the Williams sisters, Hannah and Dorothy. There was George, sitting at a table with some girls. Harold went downstairs and found an ice truck somewhere in the street. He bought a large cake, carried it upstairs, staggered across the dance floor, and placed it in the center of the table at which George was sitting. Then he stood and waited. George remained sitting. The ice melted. The girls got up and excused themselves. Water began running off the table into George's lap. Finally Harold, tired of standing, turned and staggered away.

Bix was at the Greystone in Detroit with Goldkette's band, which now had Jimmy Dorsey, Don Murray, Frankie Trum-bauer, and Chauncey Moorehouse. One Sunday night Mezzrow and I drove down, hoping to spend the next day with Bix, since the band didn't work Monday. We found Bix in his room at the Billinghurst Hotel, brooding over a fancy-dress costume. "We've got to work tonight," he said. "It's the Scarab Ball. You can't get in for a million dollars. Charlie Horvath can't even get his wife in." That settled it. "We've got to get in," I said. Bix agreed. "You go and get some costumes," he said, "and I'll see what I can figure out."

We drank a few bottles of ale to settle the pact and set off. At the costumer's we got ourselves into some medieval armor.

It may have been the right thing for fighting but it was obviously impractical for drinking; we needed something less rigid, something which would give a little as the night wore on. Besides, we might have to climb through a window, and however we got in, it would be necessary to make as little noise as possible. Finally we settled for clown suits. "You will be completely anonymous," the costumer said sadly. He liked us in the armor. Back at the hotel Bix had a plan. He had discovered a coal chute leading from a window at the rear of the Greystone. At a fixed time, between sets, he would go down into the cellar and open the window. We would slide down the coal chute and he would lead us upstairs. We had a few more bottles of ale to seal the agreement.

The dance started. In our clown suits we waited in Bix's room. Outside the snow was high; we didn't want to wait at the window any longer than was necessary. Suddenly the door opened and Bix walked in. "Look what I've got!" he hollered. It was a card, signed by the president of the Scarab Ball, stating that Mr. Condon and Mr. Mezzrow were to be admitted to the ball as guests. We grabbed it and ran to the Greystone. The gendarmes at the door looked at it and tore a wall down getting us in. Ten minutes later I was in the middle of a champagne party; my hostess was a middle-aged woman in a Chinese costume who was without an escort for the grand ball. She chose me. I stomped around with her, crisscrossing and countermarching, while Bix and the boys played and the newsreel cameras ground away. At one of the turns my hard-heeled shoes kept going the other way and I did a prattfall, almost fracturing my partner. A few weeks later in Chicago a friend stopped me on the street. "I saw you in a newsreel in Detroit," he said. "There

144

was a wonderful closeup of you lying on the floor at the Scarab Ball. I didn't know you were in society."

In the spring of 1927 the Vanity Fair job ended. Thelma went with the Music Corporation of America, which organized a band for her, changed her last name to Terry, and sent her on tour. Jack Gardner landed a job for a pit band in a neighborhood movie house on the far south side, the Commercial Theater. He hired Dave Tough, Bud Freeman, a trumpet player named Roy Peach, and a violinist named Carl Kitti, young brother of Arthur Kitti, the flautist. We played between shows and during the newsreel; on Saturday and Sunday there was a vaudeville bill. Gardner, Kitti, and I formed a trio. Kitti, who sang tenor, had almost platinum hair—it had all fallen out once after he fell asleep on the top shelf of a Finnish bath; he wasn't found for hours.

For convenience we took an apartment near the theater. Our neighbors were railroad workers, many of them Mexicans. When the wind was right we got perfume from the stockyards. One night Mezzrow dropped in and rubbed limburger cheese on Bud Freeman's pillow. All night Bud moaned and complained about the odor from the stockyards. Teschmaker came to live with us; he was playing at the Midway Gardens. Tesch was studious, solemn, with a ruddy Dutch complexion, mousy hair, and large, horn-rimmed glasses. Freeman at that period looked a little like John Gilbert, the movie lover. Bud was a friend of culture, averse to violence. One night between sessions at the theater he said to me, "Let's go across the street to the drugstore for a chocolate malted." We walked up the aisle and into the lobby. It was full of Mexicans and they all looked at Bud, slender and handsome in his tuxedo. Bud stopped. "I don't think I'm really thirsty," he said. "Let's go back."

145

Actually the customers were afraid of us. They didn't know what we were doing when we broke into *Jazz Me Blues* or *Fidgety Feet.* We were supposed to watch the newsreel and play appropriate accompaniment; we seldom did. One night in the middle of *Clarinet Marmalade* I looked up and saw a French general placing a wreath on the tomb of the Unknown Soldier. Just then Dave Tough went into an explosion on the drums. Things like that confused the Mexicans. Later that year we discovered that a south side kid was sitting through two shows every night and three on Saturday to hear Tough on the drums. His name was Gene Krupa.

At the apartment we played records and analyzed them, drank Italian wine, talked music, and played it together. We knew what we wanted to do and we tried to make sounds that represented it. Tesch was mastering the clarinet, Bud was getting better and better on the tenor saxophone, Tough was a murderous drummer with a miraculous sense of time.

Summer kept coming and the stockyards become more fragrant. The band was cut down at the theater and I was free to run for President. Roy Peach went to work at the College Inn in the Sherman House. I ran into Johnny Constantine and agreed to work for him three nights a week at a pavilion in McHenry, Illinois. One night Mezzrow, Tesch, and I walked out of the Southmoor Hotel after listening to Ben Pollack's band and looked up at a full moon. "Let's go to Detroit and see Bix," Mezz said. I had to work the next night, so I called Dick MacPartland, Jimmy's young brother, and asked him to substitute for me. He agreed and Mezz, Tesch, and I went to Detroit. The Goldkette band was preparing to move to Cincinnati; after that they were going to New York. We heard the music, promised to visit Bix in Cincinnati, and drove back to

146

Chicago. Constantine was raising hell; he called me up at the union for sending a substitute without notifying the leader of the band. I was fined and I was mad. "How about working with me at the College Inn?" Roy Peach said. "Morrie Sherman is looking for a banjo player who can sing. I'll fix an audition." I was wise to my singing by this time but I wanted to get away from Constantine. I auditioned, defaced a few songs, and got the job. It was almost too good to be true. The College Inn, later the Panther Room, did not open at night during the summer. We played for tea dancing from three to five-thirty in the afternoon and for dinner from six to eight. That was all; we were through in time to go to a prize fight, a movie, or even a late dinner date. On Saturdays and Sundays we played for dancing on the roof of the Parkway Hotel from eight-thirty until one. For this week's work I received $145. I moved into the Lincoln Park West Hotel. It had a swimming pool, and late at night I was permitted to borrow the key. By that time bathing suits were being made of silk. At last I was living; Lindbergh had flown the Atlantic and I was singing at the College Inn: *Girl Of My Dreams, My Special Friend Is Back In Town,* and the good old *Milneberg Joys*—"Rock my soul with the Milneberg Joys." I decided to study music.

All my life I had wanted to be a pianist; anything I knew on the banjo I could chord on the piano in the key of F, but I couldn't read music and my hands were small. I went to a teacher named Rex Keyes, who was also a theosophist. "I'll teach you to read music," he said, "and stretch your hands so you will be able to play anything." "I want to play like Fats Waller," I said —I had heard Waller's records. "I will stretch your hands," Keyes said, "this much—" he indicated almost an inch. I began two kinds of exercises, one on the piano, one on my hands. The

147

webbing between my fingers had to be stretched; then I would be able to play a tenth—reach ten notes—without rolling. I didn't want to roll; girl players did that. I stuck to the exercises for six months; I bought an upright piano for forty dollars from one of the guests at the hotel and practiced every day. While walking or riding in taxis I stretched my fingers. I learned to read music. Still I couldn't reach a tenth. Waller's records sounded better and better. Louis Panico offered me a job playing at Guyon's Paradise, a ballroom on the west side. I went to work and found Mel Stitzel playing piano. He left shortly and Joe Sullivan took his place; Mel had big hands, Joe had big hands—he could play a tenth and reach for a drink at the same time; he had studied piano for twelve years, including a stretch at the Chicago Conservatory of Music. Oh hell, I thought, after listening to Mel and then Joe, I didn't want to play the piano anyhow. I quit.

THE THREE DEUCES

THE GOLDKETTE BAND broke up in New York. Some of the boys, including Bix, went with Paul Whiteman, who had an outfit as massive as himself. Late in the fall they hit the Balaban-Katz circuit, opening at the Chicago Theater for a week. Bix arrived in the usual predicament—no tuxedo. Jimmy MacPartland contributed the jacket and pants; I dug up the fixtures: studs, shirt, and tie. When Bix stood up to take his chorus on *Sugar*, Jimmy's pants hit him halfway to the knees. He was wearing white socks.

The show had everything but a slack wire juggler. The Rhythm Boys sang, one of the trombone players did a number on a bicycle pump, and Henry Busse, who wrote *Hot Lips*, soloed on *When Day Is Done*. Whiteman, always a gag man, announced that Henry would hit a note never before played on a trumpet. When the moment came Busse held the trumpet to his lips and closed his eyes in rapture. The note soared away and hung in the air. After a while Busse got tired and lowered his horn, but the note kept going. Then a spotlight picked up the clarinet player standing behind him, still blowing. Ferde Grofé did the scoring for the band; there was a hot group in which Bix performed. With him were both Dorseys. Jimmy got married during that first week in Chicago, to the Miss Detroit of that year.

After the show I met Bix and took him to a speakeasy around

the corner at 222 North State Street. It was a no-knock place, just walk in, with a lot of five- and ten-cent bums, Burnett's White Satin gin, and a cellar with cement walls and an upright piano. About two o'clock we took our drinks downstairs and Bix played. Some of the other Whiteman boys followed us. Suddenly everybody was there and everybody was playing along with Bix. Some singers arrived but they kept quiet and listened. They were the Rhythm Boys—Al Rinker, Harry Barris, Bing Crosby—sharp-looking lads, slightly young.

We played until dawn; I bought a quart of milk off the wagon on my way home. The next night we were back again; Bud Freeman dropped in, the Dorsey brothers were there, Harry Gale and Ben Pollack played drums. At half past seven the following morning Bix was playing *In A Mist* and Joe Sullivan was sitting next to him, hypnotized. The room was getting crowded; customers were coming down to listen—the Whiteman players and their wives were enough to put the place on a paying basis. Tesch and MacPartland showed up; George Wettling and young Gene Krupa helped out on the drums. There was a lot of music, a lot of gin, and a lot of talk. It was noon before I got home. Without pre-arrangement we all turned up again twelve hours later in the cellar.

One night I called for Bix backstage and he said, "We are going to a party out in Cicero. Some guy has invited Crosby. He is going to send a car." The three of us stood outside the theater and waited. Crosby was slim, dapper, casual, and full of laryngitis. "It's the water in Chicago," Bix explained. "It's full of germs." I asked Crosby who the friend was who had invited him to Cicero. Cicero, a suburban district of Chicago, had a not too fragrant reputation at the time. "Some big shot,"

Crosby said. "He's throwing a party at a place called the Greyhound."

A long, black car drove up to the curb and we were told to get into the back seat. At the Greyhound we were greeted with open arms and bulging hips. There was a lot of drinking and talking and pretty soon Bix was at the piano and Crosby was trying to sing through his laryngitis. About the time I began to worry about internal drowning, the long black car returned and we were put into the back seat again. The guests waved us off with the same open arms and bulging hips.

As we drove along Bix said drowsily, "Lovely party."

"Lovely people," Crosby croaked.

After a while I said to Bix, "Remember the guy you kept telling to shut up?"

"Sure," Bix said. "Why didn't I knock him down? I'm too good-natured."

"I thought you'd like to know his name," I said.

"The hell with his name," Bix said.

"His name is Capone," I said. "Bottles Capone."

"Lovely people," Crosby croaked.

Poor Bottles! He was always getting pushed around.

After the Whiteman band left town we continued to gather at 222 North State Street. Naturally we called it the Three Deuces, since Capone had a place called the Four Deuces, on Wabash Avenue. The Four Deuces had no music. One night Red McKenzie, the St. Louis ex-jockey, dropped in at the Three Deuces. He was in town scouting talent for the Mound City Blue Blowers. They had toured the country and been to England since making their first hit record in 1924. Red was still singing and blowing through a comb. He listened to our conversation for a while, then turned to me. He looked like a mad bartender.

"Say, boy," he said, "you're running down some pretty good guys—Red Nichols and his Five Pennies. Do you pop off for exercise or does it help you to breathe?"

"We're talking about music," I said, "not about guys. We don't care who the player is, it's what he plays."

"What's the matter with those Nichols' records?"

"The music is planned," I said. "Jazz can't be scored."

Red lowered one eye. "You talk big," he said. "What do you do?"

"I play the banjo and mind my own business. Why don't you try it?"

"You can't be doing so good, not with those funny clothes you're wearing. Where did you catch them, on the other side of the wringer?"

"I'm playing with Louis Panico. When I have to ride a horse I'll dress like you."

"So you don't like that music Nichols plays. Do you know anybody who can play half as good?"

"I know a dozen guys who can play twice as good. If you don't agree when you hear them play I'll shut up and buy you a horse so you won't look so silly walking around in that suit."

"Where can I hear them?"

"At my apartment in the Lincoln Park West Hotel tomorrow afternoon."

"The Lincoln Park West Hotel? So you're a Gold Coaster! Does your old man let you clip your own coupons?"

"I'll expect you at five o'clock. Come formal. Wear shoes."

I rounded up Tesch, Bud, Jimmy MacPartland, Lannigan, Sullivan, and Gene Krupa. The next afternoon McKenzie heard us drop a rock on *Nobody's Sweetheart*.

"You win," he said. "I'm going to get you a record date

152

with Tommy Rockwell of Okeh. He's in town for two weeks. I'll see him tomorrow. This band is as hot as a cheap sidewalk on August 15th."

"You know Rockwell?" I said.

"Who do you suppose pulled Bix and Frankie Trumbauer out of Goldkette's band in New York to make those Okeh records?"

"Red Nichols?"

"McKenzie. I'll call you tomorrow. Try to learn English in case you meet Rockwell."

He left. The guys in the band blinked and looked at me. "Is he on the level?" Bud asked. "I don't know," I said. "He's a gruff mick but he knows music—he liked us. Maybe he'll do something." Tesch got dreamy-eyed. "Gee," he said, "maybe we'll get on records. Then we'll be famous." "Let's practice some numbers," Jimmy MacPartland suggested, "in case we get a date."

What McKenzie told Rockwell I'll never know, but it worked. In New York Bix had made some records for Okeh— *Clarinet Marmalade* and *Singin' The Blues*. McKenzie had sold the idea to Rockwell; the men were hand picked—Bill Rank on trombone, Don Murray on clarinet, Adrian Rollini on bass saxophone, Frankie Signorelli on piano, Howdy Quicksell on banjo, and Chauncey Moorehouse on drums. The records, to Rockwell's surprise, were successful. "I told him you guys were just like that mob in New York," McKenzie said when he called up. "Here's the date—he had to cancel something else to put it in so be there on time and be good— December 9th at ten in the morning. What's the name of the band?"

"It hasn't any name," I said. "The only time it ever played together was for you."

"Then it's your band. Stick your name on it."

"No, it's your band," I said. "I got it together so you could listen."

There was a moment of silence, indicating thought.

"The McKenzie-Condon Chicagoans," McKenzie said.

"Fine," I said. "Tell that to Rockwell. We'll be there at ten o'clock next Friday."

We decided on our numbers—China Boy and Sugar, the latter in honor of Bix and also for Ethel Waters, who had made a record of it which I played for breakfast. We arrived on time at the Okeh studio, a barnlike place at the corner of Washington and Wells. McKenzie brought Tommy Rockwell to meet us. Rockwell was polite but dubious. Except for Jim Lannigan I was the oldest member of the band, and I had just turned twenty-two. Mezzrow was helping Krupa set up his drums. "What are you going to do with those?" Rockwell asked. "Play them," Krupa said simply. Rockwell shook his head. "You can't do that," he said. "You'll ruin our equipment. All we've ever used on records are snare drums and cymbals." Krupa, who had been practicing every day at home, looked crushed. "How about letting us try them?" I asked. "The drums are the backbone of the band. They hold us up." I could see that Rockwell was leery of the whole business; drums or no drums, I figured, we are probably going to get tossed out. "Let the kids try it," McKenzie said. "If they go wrong I'll take the rap." I didn't know until long afterward that Red had guaranteed our pay for the job. "All right," Rockwell said, "but I'm afraid the bass drum and those tom-toms will knock the needle off the wax and out into the street."

154

The rules and regulations were explained to us; one white light—get ready, one red light—play. We were to run through the numbers and hear them played back to us so we could iron out the rough spots; then the master records would be cut. We warmed up and told the engineer we were ready. Rockwell and McKenzie went into the control room. I could hear the boys fidgeting behind me. Someone muttered, "Damn!" Somebody else whispered, "Where did you put the bottle?" The white light flashed. I swallowed. The red light came on. I gave the boys the beat and we jumped into *China Boy*. We opened on the nose, all playing, with everyone knitting from his own ball of yarn. The nights and years of playing in cellars and saloons and ballrooms, of practicing separately and together, of listening to Louis and Joe Oliver and Jimmy Noone and Leon Rappolo, of losing sleep and breathing bad air and drinking licorice gin, paid off. We were together and apart at the same time, tying up a package with six different strings. Krupa's drums went through us like a triple bourbon. Joe Sullivan took a chorus and all the good things he had learned from Earl Hines came out in his left hand. MacPartland followed him for half a chorus. Tesch finished it; then we went into ensemble, followed by Bud on tenor saxophone. Lannigan took a release of eight bars and we finished on an ensemble, with the tom-toms coming through strong.

Quietly we waited for the playback. When it came, pounding out through the big speaker, we listened stiffly for a moment. We had never been an audience for ourselves. Then Joe's piano chorus started and smiles began to sprout. MacPartland, Tesch, Bud, Lannigan—as each heard himself he relaxed. At the finish we were all laughing and pounding each other on the back. We were the happiest kids since the founding of Fort Dearborn. Rockwell came out of the control room smiling. "We'll have to get some more of this," he said. "Can you boys come again next week?" "We could come tomorrow," I said. "How were the drums?" Rockwell nodded toward Krupa. "Didn't bother the equipment at all," he said. "I think we've got something."

We tried Sugar then, a lazy rhythm. Tesch had rigged a brief three horn introduction for himself, MacPartland, and Bud. After that we rolled along from horn solos to ensemble; Rockwell was more than satisfied. Finally we began to cut the masters, and right in the middle of China Boy Bud laughed and ruined it. He was taking his solo when suddenly joy overcame him. He was so happy he leaned back and guffawed. We tried again and this time I was so excited I played along with Jim Lannigan for a bar before I remembered that he was supposed to be on his own. Rockwell had a luncheon date and came to say good-by to us. "How about the 19th, same time?" he said. We agreed without reluctance.

When it was over we stood around trying to realize what we had done. "You're in," McKenzie said. "Now all you've got to do is learn to blow your nose by yourself and you can hit Broadway." Bud began to laugh again. He couldn't stand the excitement. We packed our instruments and headed for the Three Deuces.

It was bad economics to expose a bottle of gin in the cellar of the Three Deuces; between the time you uncorked it and the moment it touched your lips the contents were apt to disappear—it was polite to offer your friends a drink before imbibing yourself. During our celebration Dick Slevin, the kazoo player of the Mound City Blue Blowers, went behind the piano to sneak a nibble at a pint he had hidden in an inside pocket.

He crouched, uncorked, lifted the bottle, and threw back his head quickly. His skull hit the cement wall, his teeth hit the bottle, and McKenzie had to drag him from behind the piano. "What are you trying to do," Red demanded, "drink yourself to death?"

For our second date we decided on *Nobody's Sweetheart* and *Liza*, the latter a lazy-through-Dixie tune which George Rilling and I had put together. Tesch organized a three horn introduction for both numbers and again we used a full set of drums. Mezzrow was useful on this date; one of Gene's tom-toms broke loose and Mezz held it. When we walked out of the studio that day and headed for the Three Deuces we weren't even close to the sidewalk; everybody wanted to buy the first drink. "Wait until the records come out and people hear them," we kept telling each other. "It'll be the end of Wayne King." We were convinced that if the public was given a chance to hear our music it would like it and understand what we were trying to do. We were young, very young.

McKenzie left town with the Mound City Blue Blowers, taking Dick MacPartland as an addition to the outfit. Christmas came and Guyon's sent each member of the band a bottle of whiskey. I was lounging at the desk in the hotel lobby on Christmas Eve, fondling my package from Guyon's and waiting for the boys to assemble for a trip to the Nest, now re-named the Apex, when the most beautiful woman I had ever seen walked by and got into a self-service elevator. She didn't know how to start it. I went to her assistance. We rode up and down a few times and she decided to join us at the Apex; her name, she said, was Jessie Reed. I sucked in my breath—Jessie Reed, the great Follies beauty, heroine of a dozen romances with men who could buy me with ash from their cigars. Well, hell, I

157

thought, I've got a checking account and I'm on records, or I will be soon. Why shouldn't I be the poor man in her life? I was, though I was dead that first night; she went for Kit Carson, one of my pals. But Kit didn't live in the same hotel; I did.

It was probably a cold winter but I wouldn't know. With the records coming out and Jessie in the building I ran a permanent temperature. One night when I couldn't find the manager I walked down the hotel alley through two feet of snow wearing a silk bathing suit, to jimmy a window and get into the swimming pool. It didn't even lower my body heat to normal.

The records sold well and the drums were a sensation among musicians. In New York Wingy Mannone got Vic Berton out of bed—Vic had been king of the dance-band drummers for years—and played a side for him. "Man," Wingy said, "that's the way drums ought to sound." Later, when Vic heard Krupa play in New York, he stuck out his hand and said, "Shake, kid; you're the champ." Joe Sullivan's piano solo caused excitement, too, and nobody believed that Tesch had been playing the clarinet for only two years. On the strength of his performance on the tenor saxophone Bud Freeman got a job with Ben Pollack, who already had Jimmy MacPartland. Pollack was playing then at Pershing Palace, a residential hotel on the south side; he had, in addition to MacPartland and Freeman, Benny Goodman and a trombone player from Denver named Glenn Miller.

With McKenzie absent I went to see Joe Lyons at Brunswick and tried to sell him a record date. He listened to what we had done for Okeh and shook his head; it was too rough, he said; it was unsalable. Shortly thereafter I received a call from Jack Kapp, who said he was at Brunswick and wanted us for a date. He explained that Lyons was now at Paramount and that he,

Kapp, had seen McKenzie in New Orleans. "Red played your Okeh records for me," Kapp explained. "I think we ought to have some of that music on Brunswick."

We set a date and decided to play *I've Found A New Baby* and *There'll Be Some Changes Made*. Pollack's band had gone to New York to play at the Little Club, so we used Muggsy Spanier in MacPartland's place and Mezzrow on the tenor saxophone. McKenzie arrived at the studio just in time to sing the vocal on *Changes*, having come straight from the train. The next day he went to Paramount and sold Lyons a date for us. What Red was doing in music when there were pipe organs and steam locomotives to be sold I don't know. He could sell hell to a bishop.

One mistake was made on a second Brunswick date. We did all right with *Jazz Me Blues*. Then we tried *Baby Won't You Please Come Home*, and I sang the vocal. I couldn't have lured a baby bull home; the record was never released. Some years later a jazz historian dug up the master and my sin hit me in my good ear. I'm sorry. What more can I say?

McKenzie had another band he wanted to sell Brunswick. One night he slugged Jack Kapp into meeting us at the Apex at one o'clock. When he arrived we were sitting near the bandstand enjoying Earl Hines at the piano and watching Johnny Wells at the drums and Jimmy fingering the keys of his clarinet. It must have seemed like a waterfront clipjoint to Kapp; he looked as if he wished he had left his watch at home. But after a few drinks and a dozen choruses of Jimmy's *Four Or Five Times* he was reassured. He agreed with McKenzie. "We've got to have some of this," he said, and set a date. Jimmy Noone was disinterested. "How can I play music at ten o'clock in the morning?" he asked. "That's my bedtime." Kapp and McKenzie convinced him that for the sake of art he ought to stay up another few hours.

But in the bright light of ten o'clock in the morning a week later it was Kapp who weakened. McKenzie and I were with him in the control room when Jimmy and the boys broke into *I Know That You Know*. Hines was never better at the piano; Jimmy was doing impossible things with his clarinet. Kapp looked perplexed. "What are they doing?" he asked. "Where is the melody?" McKenzie looked at him in scorn. I tried to explain. "Anybody can play the melody," I said. "These boys are doing better than that." Kapp still looked dubious. "What are we supposed to be making," Red said finally, "a Q.R.S. piano roll?" Kapp, listening to the music, began to feel it again. By the time masters had been made of *I Know That You Know* and *Sweet Sue*, he was enthusiastic. The record, when it came out, upheld his judgment. It sold amazingly, and Jimmy stayed up other mornings and made more: *Four Or Five Times, Every Evening, Apex Blues, Sweet Lorraine, Oh Sister Ain't That Hot? Blues.*

Between numbers that first morning I talked to Earl Hines. "You're not bothering anybody with that piano," I said. Earl smiled. "If you want to hear the real master you'll have to go to New York and get hold of Fats Waller," he said. "Man, he's really got it." After a while he said, "You know, I started to learn the cornet once, back in Pittsburgh. Just when I was fooling around good I heard Louis Armstrong. I went right back to the piano."

A few days later McKenzie said, "Well, we've got some money. Why don't you come to New York with me for a couple of weeks while I run it into a million? You can hear Fats Waller, see the ocean, and ride on a train. I'll teach you how

160

to act." I spoke to Louis Panico, a very amiable boss. "Why not?" he said. "You've got to learn about life some time." I got my brother Pat, formerly Jim, to take my place. McKenzie and I hit the plush. "Can you breathe in New York without straining the air?" I asked Red. "People in New York don't inhale," he said, "they just exhale."

UNTIL it reached New York jazz was required neither to meet critical standards nor to make a lot of money. It worked for its keep and was content. Along the Mississippi River people in the towns and cities liked it, danced to it, and accepted it as one of the natural riches of a land drowning in bounty. To the Negroes of the south side of Chicago it was their own music, a modest cultural possession; the white musicians who went to the Lincoln Gardens, the Sunset Café, and the Nest, knew that however long they tried they would never more than imitate what they heard. But they felt the sting of an art form which transformed interpreters into composers, made creators from copyists. "The Negro is born with rhythm," Eddie Condon said. "We've got to learn it. The rhythm section is the spine of a jazz band. It holds the music together." He exemplified his theory; the small orchestras with which he played had unity. "Condon has a miraculous sense of time," Red McKenzie said to the boys at the Three Deuces. "He doesn't make much sound by himself in a band but he makes a lot of difference in how the whole band sounds. He knows music."

It was natural for McKenzie and Condon to set out for New York in 1928; anybody with a rag of talent went to the Big Town; Manhattan was the place where things happened; it was the world's great caravan city, the office where accomplishments were assayed according to man's standards of worth. Jazz had been in and out of New York for years before the Chicagoans arrived; it was considered of no value. It could not be used in trade; its appeal was special and its margin of profit narrow. It had not come from Europe and it therefore could not be imposed upon the public as something the public ought to hear; the people to whose culture it belonged could not support it in the concert halls nor offer it with pride as the expression of a civilization superior to that of America's. It went to Harlem and remained there. When the visiting Chicagoans wanted to hear it they journeyed north from Times Square to Pod's and Jerry's, Connie's Inn, the Cotton Club, Small's Paradise, the Savoy Ballroom, or one of the numberless speakeasies offering a pianist or a trio along with the customary gin and fried chicken.

One colored orchestra played downtown; it was led by Fletcher Henderson, a pianist. It was Henderson who first expanded the jazz band, multiplying the brass and reed sections and writing "hot" arrangements which simulated improvisation. He was the son of a Georgia schoolteacher; he took his first band into the Roseland Ballroom in 1919. Meanwhile Paul Whiteman was building the first symphonic jazz band; he came to New York from Atlantic City and played for three years at the Palais Royal. His records sold prodigiously, and eventually he became, like Buddy Bolden and Joe Oliver, a king, the "King of Jazz." In 1924 he gave a concert at Carnegie Hall; George Gershwin wrote a tune for it: Rhapsody In Blue.

That same year Edward Kennedy Ellington, a duke in the royal family of jazz, came up with a band from his native Washington, D.C., and opened at the Kentucky Club. Later he moved to the Cotton Club, the most publicized and popular of the Harlem spots. Ellington was a composer of imagination and resource; his was the first large "hot" band to attract attention; through the years it remained the most persistently successful. In 1929 Luis Russell's band was at the Saratoga Club in

163

Harlem; Russell had reached New York by way of New Orleans and Chicago. His was also a large group; with Henderson and Ellington he set a pattern which later was copied by white band leaders of the late thirties—Goodman, the Dorsey brothers, Krupa, etc. It was slick, commercial, arranged music; it was successful; it paid the rent. Late at night, when the business of making a living was finished, the men in the big bands sat around in small groups playing music the way they wanted to play it, improvising, creating. Jazz was for them a luxury, something to be enjoyed on their own time at their own expense. Frank Teschmaker had often said, "You can't play it hot and make a living out of it."

Occasionally small groups were assembled for recording dates. For a while Red Nichols, a cornet player from Utah, had almost a monopoly in this field; he used various men for the personnel of his Five Pennies. The Nichols records are not collector's items; the music on them, though not scored or arranged, was planned. It was Red McKenzie who began breaking the Nichols monopoly; when the Goldkette band reached New York in 1927 McKenzie extracted a group which included Bix Beiderbecke and Frankie Trumbauer and sold it to Okeh. The McKenzie-Condon records were another blow at the monopoly. In New York Condon by instinct and interest became a free lance jazz missionary; he talked executives of recording companies into dates; he selected and rehearsed the musicians himself and played with them. He was responsible for the first recording by a mixed group of white and Negro musicians; he knew Harlem as he knew the south side of Chicago—he listened particularly to the Negro pianists, James P. Johnson, Willie the Lion Smith, and Thomas Fats Waller, the minister's son who was a composer and organist at the age of ten, and who said to a lady who

164

asked him to explain rhythm, "Lady, if you got to ask you ain't got it." Condon was unswervingly devoted to jazz; with quiet, stubborn fanaticism he proselyted for it. He stayed away from the contamination of big bands; sometimes he made a living, sometimes he didn't. "We bled to death," he once said of those years. "We gnawed at each other's wrists."

Prostitution mothered jazz in New Orleans; prohibition fostered it in Chicago and New York; repeal threw it into the street—Fifty-second Street. Its name was changed; it was called swing, a term used by jazz musicians to describe the growing pattern of intercommunicative, interdependent, spontaneously created music which builds as a band improvises chorus after chorus on the basic chordal structure of a standard tune or theme; when the pattern is clear and exciting the band is swinging. Swing was played on Fifty-second Street in small, dark basements for people who drank watered whiskey, inhaled stale air, and considered themselves the patrons of a fresh fad. It began in Adrian Rollini's taproom on Forty-eighth Street near Eighth Avenue, where Wingy Mannone played. It spread to the Onyx on Fifty-second Street, where the Spirits of Rhythm and Stuff Smith played, and where the ropes had to be put up when Maxine Sullivan moved in and began to sing Loch Lomond. Louis Prima opened at the Famous Door, across the street from the Onyx, with Pee Wee Russell and George Brunies; later Count Basie came to town. Then swing hit the entire nation; it was a fad, it could be exploited.

The bands got bigger and bigger, the music was more carefully arranged, more mechanically "hot." Jazz was more forgotten, more neglected, more a luxury for those who liked to play it than ever before. It was then that Eddie Condon began to work seriously and persistently for the music in which he be-

165

lieved. With the help of a few friends he set out to win recognition and respectability for jazz. He succeeded. He talked, he argued, he pleaded, he demonstrated; he organized, rehearsed, and led some of the finest white jazz groups ever heard. He won serious critical acclaim for the music; he built a concert audience for it; he labored patiently and constantly for it; he even gave his identity to it. People referred to him as "Mr. Jazz."

"THE POOREST 7-PIECE
ORCHESTRA ON EARTH"

WE CHECKED IN at the Forrest Hotel on
Forty-ninth Street west of Broadway. It was a Sunday night
in May, 1928. McKenzie took me to the window and pointed to
St. Malachy's Church across the street. "A very historical place,"
he said. "They held the Rudolph Valentino funeral there." I
was impressed, but I wanted to see Fifth Avenue. "It's folded
until tomorrow," McKenzie explained. "It hasn't any joints; just
stores." I made him take me anyhow, and we looked at St.
Patrick's Cathedral. McKenzie regarded it with awe. "That's
Saks Fifth Avenue," he said, pointing to a building on the
next corner. "It's a clipjoint for dames."

On the way back we stopped at a speakeasy. "Pick any
place without lights and knock at the door," McKenzie said.
"It's a saloon." I was surprised when the bartender put the
bottle on the bar and walked away. "Are we allowed to pour
our own?" I said. In Chicago under the Capone system the
bartenders and waiters did the pouring. "This is a gentleman's
town," McKenzie said. "Very honorable."

Next morning I noticed garbage cans on the street; Red explained that New York has no alleys. "Everything is right out
in front, very honorable, like I said. In Chicago all this stuff
is put in the alleys. You never know what kind of a town

you are living in." We walked up to the Mayflower at Sixtieth Street and Central Park West to see Jimmy MacPartland and Bud Freeman. They were surprised to see us, and glad. Their unpaid rent was up to their ears; Pollack's band was idle, waiting to open at a Brooklyn theater with Bee Palmer, the singer, and her husband, Al Siegel. The Whiteman band was in Brooklyn at the moment; we jumped in a subway—it was my first ride in a sewer—and went to visit Bix. We found him in his dressing room. Three hundred dollars a week hadn't changed him; he still needed a suit that would fit him. We had a few drinks and played a little—Bix found a saxophone for Bud and a cornet for Jimmy; I played drums on the dressing table with two empty pint bottles until one of them exploded. "That was a wonderful effect," Bix said.

We went back again to Brooklyn to hear Pollack and the boys with Bee Palmer. "She's heard our records," Bud told us. "She thinks they're sensational. She wants us to work with her." Bee was a Chicago girl; I had met her at the College Inn. She was a beautiful blonde, sang superbly, and had the advantage of a husband who was not only an accompanist but a fine vocal coach. Backstage we talked with her; she had a plan.

"Lou Schwartz is opening a new night club," she said. "He wants me to go into it. I'd like to take your band with me. I'll introduce you to the audience and explain your music. Once people hear it they'll like it."

That night she took the four of us—McKenzie, MacPartland, Bud, and myself—to the Club Richman. We sat around a table and watched Schwartz become aware that he wasn't going to get Bee without accepting us. Everytime he talked about the new club, the Chateau Madrid, Bee countered with a eulogy of our records. George Olsen's band played background music while she talked. "You've heard these records?" she said. "Yes," Schwartz said, as if admitting he had beaten his wife. "Aren't they wonderful?" she demanded. "Wonderful," Schwartz said sadly. "You see," Bee said, turning to us.

The deal was set. Freeman and MacPartland left on tour with Pollack, prepared to return to New York in time for the opening. We were to use a New York bass player; I went to Chicago to get Teschmaker, Sullivan, and Krupa; McKenzie went to St. Louis to see his wife and son. Panico was amiable when I asked him for Sullivan without the customary two weeks notice. Nothing had bothered Louis since he learned to play the cornet in Italy. His instructor held needles against his cheeks; if they puffed out as Louis blew, the needles went into them. "Those needles hurt like hell," he told me once. "Naturally I learned to blow the right way."

"So you want my piano player too?" he said, when I turned up unprepared to return to work. "Have you got a brother to replace him?"

"I'll send one of my sisters," I said. "Can Joe leave right away, without notice?"

Louis waved his hand toward the band. "Take as many as you like," he said.

Teschmaker was working at the Triangle Club with Floyd Towne's band, which included Muggsy Spanier and George Wettling. The Triangle boss was Mickey Rafferty, who used to stand by the rail in front of the stand and do a dance. Once Mickey wanted Muggsy and Wettling to take a rest without pay. They protested mildly, so Mickey took them for a ride in his automobile, closed the windows, and exploded a teargas gun—a small weapon disguised as a fountain pen. After

169

that the boys needed a rest, and they didn't care whether they got paid or not. Towne was as amiable as Panico; he agreed to let Tesch go without notice. Krupa was working at the Wilshire Dance Pavilion with Eddie Neibauer's Seattle Harmony Kings; I got him off too. Then I heard the news. Al Siegel had left Bee Palmer and joined the De Marcos, a dance team, as accompanist. He was in Chicago with them, at the Palace Theater. Bee was also in town at the Sherman House, visiting her mother and obviously hoping for a reconciliation with her husband.

The Palmer-Siegel marriage and business partnership had been through separations and reconciliations before; there had even been a divorce and a re-marriage. With four tickets to New York in my pocket I found myself backstage at the Palace pleading with Siegel to talk to Bee. The De Marcos were opposed to the idea, naturally, but I managed to persuade Al and between shows we went to the Sherman House. Bee was cordial and things went smoothly. At what I considered the psychological moment I withdrew and rounded up the boys. "Everything is set," I said. "They'll be in New York in a week." I wired McKenzie in St. Louis that we were leaving for New York. We stayed up all night at the Fullerton Plaza Hotel, packing, talking, and celebrating our success. In the morning we took the train. In New York we registered at the Cumberland Hotel, across the street from the Chateau Madrid on Fifty-fourth Street, just off Broadway. McKenzie came back from St. Louis. MacPartland and Freeman called us long distance from some road stop to ask how things were going.

"We're ready," I told them. "Come on in."

"Fine," Bud said. "By the way, would you like to hear the greatest trombone player in the world?"

"Put him on," I said. "What's his name?"

"Jack Teagarden," Bud said. "He's from Texas. Wait until we get some blues going; then Jack will play for you."

I listened for a while, then handed the phone to McKenzie. He passed it on to Tesch. Tesch gave it to Krupa. When we had all listened and Bud was back on the other end of the wire I gave him the consensus. "He doesn't bother us," I said. "Put a brand on his stomach and bring him in." "I can't get him now," Bud said, "but we'll snatch him later."

In a few days Bee arrived in town. Siegel was still in Chicago with the De Marcos. The panic was on again. "I'll show him," Bee said. "I've signed up Frankie Signorelli." Signorelli was a fine accompanist and we all felt better. He went to the May-flower, where Bee was staying, and rehearsed with her. Every day before leaving our hotel we looked across the street at the Chateau Madrid, which was being decorated for the opening. We felt that we ought to talk to Schwartz but our orders were specific—stay away and let Bee do the negotiating. Then one day she said, "I'll show him"—she still meant Siegel—"I won't open without him."

We were sunk, but at least there was no reason now for us to stay away from Schwartz. We walked across the street and asked him if he would listen to the band. "Why not?" he said gloomily. He knew what he wanted, and it wasn't us. The plumbers, carpenters, and decorators were hard at work when we set up our instruments. "He'll have to admit we're good," Bud said hopefully. "It's a free country," McKenzie said. "He can like Leo Reisman."

Schwartz sat at a table and listened. We played *Clarinet Marmalade*, *Jazz Me Blues*, and *Nobody's Sweetheart*. The noises of the carpenters and plumbers didn't help. We could see Schwartz hadn't the slightest idea what we were doing. He didn't have to tell us we weren't hired; we knew it. The Chateau Madrid opened with a fiddle outfit and was a success. We sat in the Cumberland and watched the crowd go in on opening night.

We didn't realize then how little chance we had in New York. Violins and soft saxophones were the fashion. Leo Reisman, Emil Coleman, Pancho, Meyer Davis, Mike Markel—these were the prosperous band leaders. The only place we could play was in our rooms, at our own request. Krupa set up his drums and we played every night until the complaints began. Don Voorhees had a big band down the street at station WOR; many of his men dropped in to see us and to hear us play. They liked our music. One of them was Vic Berton, the drummer. Red Nichols was another. When we saw Vic listening with admiration to Krupa, our faith in our future rose. If musicians agreed we were good how could the public resist? Something would break soon; Bee Palmer was sending us to agent after agent—one of them was certain to get us a job. Bee was also taking us to parties, where we were introduced as celebrities from Chicago. "But we're still loafing," McKenzie muttered. "How long can we live like gentlemen and work like bums? Breakfast at Dave's Blue Room for two dollars! We're nuts!"

One day Pancho called and said he was sending Jolly Coburn to interview us about a job. McKenzie was worried. "What does Pancho want with us?" he wondered. "What will we do in the middle of those fiddles and accordions?" Coburn arrived and seemed glad to see us.

"Pancho is going to Newport to play for the debut of Princess Miguel de Briganza's daughter," he said. "He'd like you to

172

come along as an alternate band; he thinks it would be an interesting novelty."

"I think it will," McKenzie said. "It will be the most interesting novelty Newport has ever had."

The eastern seaboard must have been drained of blue blood for the Briganza party. Every name was a foot long; I was surprised that anyone ate with his own hands. The affair was held in the country club; the only common things there were champagne, caviar, and musicians. Even the servants were pedigreed. "Well," McKenzie said, "what are you guys looking at? Those mugs have five fingers on each hand and one head apiece, haven't they?"

I remembered the out-of-town doctors at Mayo's in Rochester. The Briganza guests were all out-of-towners; those born in the United States were pretending it was a sordid mistake, an unhappy mischance. The musicians were supposed to help the pretence with Viennese waltzes. I looked around; Krupa was adjusting a tom-tom. The artillery was ready. "Well," I said, "let's give out with some of that old world atmosphere— *Clarinet Marmalade.*"

Eight seconds later everyone in the room was staring at us. Pancho was smiling; he liked it. So did his boys. The guests automatically began drinking more champagne. They couldn't talk because we were playing too loud; between sets we pushed them out of the way to get at the champagne. "Extraordinary demonstration of the freed libido," I heard one matron mutter. "Lady," I said, "will you hold this glass while I get some caviar?" "Extraordinary creature!" she said, but she took the glass and held it while I got some eggs.

After the party a truck was sent from the hotel to pick up the instruments. I was placed on top of them and driven to the

173

Viking Hotel. Next day I met Pancho in the lobby. "How did we do?" I asked. "You were a hit," he said. Then he smiled. "One of the ladies told me it was just like having the Indians in town again.

"She was old enough to know what she was talking about," he added.

Back in New York our money ran out. Musicians came to see us and brought liquor but never food. It was then I discovered a simple truth about modern society; you can drink yourself to death on your friends except for one thing—you'll die of malnutrition first. When you're broke you can get all the whiskey you want almost anywhere you go, but don't ask for a sandwich; it lowers the social tone of friendship. The important thing is to have enough money to buy a can of tomatoes the next morning; they feed the body and break the hangover.

We discovered the automat. We walked up and down Broadway, listening to the music coming from commercial bands in dime-a-dance halls. We went to see more agents. We lived on the olives from Martinis and cherries from Manhattans at the cocktail parties to which we were invited. We opened a charge account at a delicatessen for canned tomatoes, to be kept on ice until we called for them in the morning—or in the afternoon. We heard from Pancho again. Barbara Bennett had just left Maurice, her dancing partner, and was forming a new team with Charles Sabin. Sabin was from society; his mother was fighting prohibition. The team was scheduled to go into the Palace, and Pancho recommended us for background music. We auditioned for Barbara and she offered us the job. "Are you sure you know what you're doing?" I asked. "Is this the kind of music you want for your class act?"

"It will be something new," she said. "I'm delighted. We'll start rehearsals tomorrow at Steinway Hall."

By then it was July. We rehearsed for ten days in heat that melted everything but our hunger. One of the dance numbers, a waltz, required a fiddle in the orchestra. Tesch had begun his career on the violin; we borrowed an instrument from Joe Venuti and handed it to him. After one rehearsal we took it away from him and gave it back to Venuti. We got a violinist from the Meyer Davis office, a nice guy named Charlie Miller. Then MacPartland and Freeman were offered a job on the *Ile de France*. They considered taking it.

"You mean you would rather play on a frog ferry than at the Palace?" McKenzie said. He was incredulous. "Thousands of men and women have died of old age on the road trying to make the Palace, and you guys want to sell your chance for a doily and a *crêpe suzette!*" he roared.

MacPartland fidgeted. "I was only thinking about it," he said. "I'll stay."

"So will I," Freeman said, but he looked unhappy. Bud loved culture.

We opened at the Palace on the 16th of July. We were nervous and hot; the fiddle sounded strange and embarrassed in the middle of our mob. When Barbara and Charles ended their waltz they stepped back and bowed; Barbara's legs were shaking worse than mine. Here we go, I thought, she's going to fall on her face—what are we doing here anyhow? While the team was changing costumes we played *I Must Have That Man*. When we finished there was silence. Then two, three, and finally four people applauded. "Musicians," Tesch whispered. At the end of the act the dancers got a good hand.

Barbara and Charles waited impatiently for the reviews to

175

appear in Variety and Billboard. We didn't care if we never saw them. When they appeared Barbara was ecstatic. In Variety she was chosen as the "best dressed woman of the week" by The Skirt, Jr. The Skirt described in detail the clothes worn during the act. Barbara read the piece to us. . . . "She appears again in a stunning orange chiffon gown with ragged hem reaching to the floor on one side with a huge spray of coque feathers on the other side and on one shoulder. This is for a weak blackbottom. After a pause in which their rather dreadful orchestra plays an off-key selection. . . ."

She stopped. "Don't mind us," I said. "Go right ahead."

"I'm sure that's just meanness," she said. "There's a review here of the show itself, not of my clothes. Let's see what it says."

It was bad for all of us: "The class act was Charles Sabin and Barbara Bennett, nite club dancers. The nite club they were in may have had a steady trade of 750 people. Of these 600 are now out of town. And of the 600 not 50 would care to see either of the dancers anywhere other than at their homes or in a club ballroom. . . . The couple are no stage dancers of any kind, with the poorest 7-piece orchestra on earth. . . . As a side remark, Mr. Sabin and Miss Bennett neglected to bow to their musicians when exiting. No one could blame them, but it is customary."

"That does it," Tesch said.

"Local boys make good in big city in large way," Joe Sullivan said. "I can see the headlines in the Chicago Tribune."

"Well, at last I've played the Palace," I said. "Now I owe Cliff for my banjo."

The next day Krupa turned up with a copy of Billboard.

"Look at this," he said. "Maybe we're not as much a failure as we think."

The review said: "Charles Sabin and Barbara Bennett closed the first half in an exhibition of ballroom dancing, assisted by a commendable 7-piece musical unit . . . the act was heavily applauded but the hurrahs were not for the terpsichorean talents. They are both graceful, but far removed from being world beaters."

"Who wrote that?" Tesch asked. "The man is a genius." Krupa read out the name—Elias E. Sugarman. "He'll go down in history," Tesch said.

At least the musicians were with us. Johnny Powell, the drummer, went twice a day every day during the week; in the general applause we spotted isolated patches of enthusiasm for our numbers. But we were about as far from being a popular success as it was possible to be. Jazz was still a special taste.

In the middle of the week Bud announced that he was going to take the job on the *Ile de France*. It was sailing the next day. McKenzie was in favor of violence. I told Bud that if he went we would collect his pay at the end of the week and split it among ourselves.

"I don't care," he said. "I'm going to France."

"I will also not pay you that fifty dollars I owe you," I said.

"I still don't care," he said, and he went.

When we finished the run Sabin refused to pay us for Freeman, contending that Bud had forfeited his salary by deserting the act.

"I have had enough trouble, Charles," McKenzie said, "but if necessary I will make some more, all by myself, and give it to you. If you don't pay Freeman's salary I will really louse you up at the union—remember we rehearsed with you for ten days without pay."

"Oh, Charles, shut up!" Barbara said. "Let's not quarrel about trifles." She reached into her stocking, took out a roll of bills, and handed McKenzie Bud's money. We used it to cut down the bill at the Cumberland. McKenzie went to St. Louis to see his family again.

There were five of us now in the two rooms; Mezzrow and Josh Billings, a jazz fan, had come in from Chicago. Very quickly we were back on the olive and cherry diet, with canned tomatoes for breakfast. One day the clerk handed me our bill and added a meaningful look. We owed an interesting sum, ninety-nine dollars. We had to do something.

The Jimmy Noone records were out under Brunswick's Vocalian label and were selling well. I took one of them and went to see Tommy Rockwell at Okeh.

"See how you like this small ensemble group," I said. "I can get you one like it—Teschmaker, Krupa, and Sullivan."

Rockwell listened to the record and nodded agreeably. "Let's make a date," he said.

"Let's make it for tomorrow morning," I said.

"I think we ought to have a vocal on one side," Rockwell said.

I swallowed hard. "I'll sing," I said.

We were at the studio ahead of time. We set up and made Oh Baby, from "Rain or Shine." The second side was Back Home In Indiana, and I sang a chorus. Before the wax was cool on the master I was in Rockwell's office.

"Tommy," I said, "do something about this."

I gave him the hotel bill.

"Why didn't you say something about it before?" he said.

178

He took a wallet from his pocket and handed me two fifty dollar bills.

"There will be fifty dollars more," he said. "I'll send it to you."

I walked out of the room eighty pounds lighter than when I went in. Back at the hotel I paid the bill. The clerk gave me a dollar.

"What shall we buy with it?" I asked the boys. The vote was unanimous—canned tomatoes.

HANDFUL
OF HARLEM

GERALD GILLIS and Johnny Powell, both drummers, were among the few who realized we had to eat as well as drink. They fed us often, and one night Johnny brought good news along with some sandwiches. He had a job for Mezzrow and me in Valley Stream, Long Island. It was after Labor Day and two of the musicians at the Castillian Gardens had come into town to work.

"It's a duck dinner joint run by Chick Goldman," Johnny explained. "I know some of the boys in the band—Sidney Jacobs is the drummer and Max Ceppos is the fiddler. They'll send a car in to take you out."

The additional fifty dollars from Okeh got us out of the hotel. Soon after we reached Valley Stream Krupa got a call from Chicago; his mother was ill. We took him to the station; his mother died while he was en route.

We took room and board with an old lady who boasted of her piety and her cooking; her pies were so bad we hid our pieces under our coats and threw them into the garbage; when she thought we weren't around she cursed like a piccolo. Billings, a natural prowler, discovered a hoard of wine in the cellar and tapped it. The old lady put locks on the cellar doors. Billings, who could open a bank vault with the hairspring of a watch, picked them with a nail file. The old lady bought a police dog. The dog slept with Billings. Finally we tired of malnutrition and moved to the home of a Jewish lady. She fed us herring for breakfast. It gave us such a thirst we went straight from the table to a grocery store run by an Italian named Joe; for the rest of the day we drank red wine and ate Roquefort cheese. Mezzrow decided this was an ideal diet; he added white grapes, which were in season, and charcoal tablets, which he considered the secret of health. There was no limit to Mezzrow's genius. When a table lamp in our room refused to light and the landlady wanted to send for an electrician Mezz stayed her hand. "I'll fix it," he said, "and it won't cost you a cent." He blew out all the lights in the block.

Dave Tough came to see us; he was playing with the band on the *Ile de France*, which had docked that day. Sidney Jacobs asked him to sit in with us. We played *Sugar*. The customers stood up and the help came out of the kitchen: it was the first time any of them had heard a set of drums really played. When we finished work Dave, Sullivan, and I drove to town and went to Harlem. Some time before I had stumbled on a place called Pod's and Jerry's, a speakeasy at 133rd Street and Seventh Avenue which specialized in fried chicken and piano players. There were also a couple of girl singers, Big Red and Mary Stafford; there was also Jazzbo Jimmy, a tall midget who reminded us of the Nest's Broadway Jimmy.

"Just like home," Tough said. "Who's the piano player?"

"Joe Sullivan," I said. Our Joe Sullivan, sitting between us, looked innocently at Tough. Tough patted his arm. "Every light has its shadow," he said. "I like both."

The Negro Joe Sullivan had a powerful, unique style. After

his night's work at the Cotton Club was done Duke Ellington dropped in to hear him. James P. Johnson was often in the place, eating fried chicken, listening and beating time. It was a "cutting" joint—by five o'clock in the morning pianists from all over town were taking turns at the keyboard, each trying to outplay the others. Willie the Lion Smith, who replaced Joe Sullivan, would come to our table and say, "Man, the tiger was here last night trying to claw the lion; he got a little blood." The only white pianist Willie respected was Arthur Schutt, who had big hands and a powerful style. It was nine or ten in the morning before everyone left; hitting daylight then, after hours of smoke and gin and music, was like walking into a truck. Frequently I went broke in the place and had to ride the subway home. If I had a job I would be in working clothes—tuxedo—and the honest johns on their way to day labor gave me hard looks.

When Tough and Sullivan and I left it was well after breakfast. "Come home with me," Dave said. "I want to show you what a real ocean liner is like." We rode in a taxi to the *Ile de France* and Tough led us aboard. The musicians were asleep—they were all French—but Dave woke them up and introduced us. Then he took us on a tour of the boat, bringing us finally to the main saloon, where Sullivan spotted a birds-eye maple grand piano. He sat down and began to play. "Day has replaced night," Tough said, "but it's still Joe Sullivan." He made a speech about it in French to some deck hands who came in to listen. "What are you telling them?" I asked. "I am explaining that there is no difference between night and day, between black and white," Dave said. "Either way it is Joe Sullivan and it is wonderful."

More deck hands and sailors came in to listen; bottles of wine appeared and were opened and handed to us. After a while we realized that Tough had disappeared. We tried to ask our audience where he was but none of them spoke English; at that point we spoke very little of it ourselves. We made gestures of drum playing; we said "moosick" again and again. The sailors laughed, nodded, and passed us more wine. We left the saloon and tried to find our way off the ship, but the longer we walked the more confused we became. Every time we met a sailor we said "moosick" and made motions of violin playing. Finally one of them got the idea and led us to the musicians' quarters. Tough was asleep in his bunk. We woke him up and made him lead us off the boat.

Business got slowly worse at the Castillian Gardens. One night a large party came in and drinks were sent to us by the skinny man who was acting as its host. I found myself mixing with his guests. The prettiest girl at the table was none too good for me. I danced with her, sat with her, and held her hand. As I passed the bandstand with her, dancing to *I Can't Give You Anything But Love, Baby,* I threw the boys a superior smile. Sidney Jacobs gave me an imploring look and beckoned with both hands. Nuts, I thought, the job is folding anyhow; why go back to the stand when this romance is ripening up like an apple in the sun? When the music stopped I went back to the table. Sidney sent a waiter after me. "Excuse me," I said to the romance. "I've got to resign from an unimportant position. I'll be right back." I went to the stand and started to tell Sidney what I thought of the Castillian Gardens, duck dinners, and fifteen requests every night for *Ramona.* Sidney grabbed me and pulled me behind the piano.

"Chicago or no Chicago," he said, "lay off that dame. Her

183

name is Kiki Roberts and she belongs to the guy who's giving the party—"

"The skinny guy? Hell, I can—"

"No, you can't. His name is Legs Diamond. He eats six guys a week. Don't be the seventh."

"Who is Diamond?" I demanded. "What's he ever done?"

Sidney told me. After a ten-minute recitation of Diamond's career as a New York gangster I changed my point of view. After all, a dame is only a dame; she can be duplicated.

We lost Sullivan; he got a job in New York. "What's the name of the place?" I asked. "Don't hit me," he said. "It's the Chateau Madrid." I shook my head. What was that thing I had heard Mrs. Reid talking about back in Chicago one morning? "Divide and conquer," I said. "I guess they've got us licked." One jazz player in an orthodox band is like a jigger of whiskey in a bottle of milk; you can't feel him.

Billings one night decided to be a good Samaritan and drive a drunk's car home to Jamaica. When it was done the grateful drunk said, "I'm all right now. I'll drive you to the bus stop." Billings surrendered the wheel. Before they were out of second gear the car hit an El post and Josh was thrown through the windshield. He went to the hospital in an ambulance with a maternity case; both patients made it in time. Billings arrived home for breakfast; the only parts visible on him were his nostrils and one eye. The owner of the car was an insurance man; Billings collected some money—he wouldn't tell us how much—and went into town. He registered at the Pennsylvania Hotel and gave Harlem hell.

In the end we were playing tired tunes to an empty house. The management paid us off in ducks from the icebox and we went back to Broadway. Joe Sullivan and I moved into the

184

Grencourt Apartments on Fiftieth Street between Seventh Avenue and Broadway, the crummiest block in the city—taffy joints, hamburger stands, popcorn stalls, and a subway entrance. The apartment building was four stories high, with signs all the way up. No light from the outside got into any of the rooms; all the windows opened on billboards. We lived behind a loaf of Bond Bread, in a two-room suite the size of a single-jointed peanut.

Johnny Powell got a job for Mezzrow, Sullivan, and myself at the Pelham Heath Inn. Johnny lived in a basement room at the Mansfield Hotel; musicians leaving town always left their belongings there; it was called Johnny's Storehouse. Johnny walked over trunks and skirted drums and bass fiddles to get to his bed; he was too good-natured to resist the imposition. He even worried about keeping the instruments in good condition.

We were due at seven o'clock in Pelham. That meant diving into the sewer at five-thirty, taking a local to Seventy-second Street, changing there to an express, riding to the end of the line, and then mounting a bus. The pushing and shoving in the subway made Sullivan furious; every night he fought back; by the time he got to work he was exhausted. "You might as well get used to it," I said. "It's part of the job." Joe shook his head. "I wouldn't get used to it for a million dollars," he said. "In fact if I didn't need the money I wouldn't even do it and not get used to it."

I was the first to be fired. I ate Thanksgiving dinner alone in the Brass Rail on Forty-ninth Street; my heart was tying my shoelaces until a waiter came up and spoke to me. "Remember me, Eddie?" he said. "I used to work at the Three Deuces in Chicago." I felt better; I knew somebody in the place

185

besides the turkey. A few weeks later I met George Rilling, the composer; he was living in a penthouse at Riverside Towers, on Eightieth Street at Riverside Drive. Farther down in the building Sullivan and I found two small rooms with a connecting shower for fifteen dollars a week each; just before New Year's Eve we moved in. I was playing club dates again.

Five nights a week I went to Harlem, early or late, whether I was working or loafing. At Small's Paradise on 135th Street I heard Charlie Johnson's band, with Leonard Davis on trumpet, Happy Cauldwell on tenor saxophone, and George Stafford on drums. Somebody, I thought, ought to put this music on records; it's too good to miss. I went to Ralph Peer, of the Southern Music Company, a subsidiary of Victor. He looked dubious when I outlined my idea. "I want to use Davis, Cauldwell, and Stafford," I said, "with some friends of mine—Jack Teagarden, Joe Sullivan, and Mezzrow." After listening to me talk for twenty minutes about the music which would come out of such a combination Peer gave in and set a date. "This will be for Victor," he said. "I hope it's good."

It was, though Mezzrow and I played too. We made *I'm Gonna Stomp Mr. Henry Lee* and *That's A Serious Thing*. The Negro Joe Sullivan supplied us with some special introductory chords for *That's A Serious Thing*. When the masters were cut Mr. Peer congratulated me. "You were right about the music," he said. "It is excellent. All in all I should say this has been an interesting experiment." It wasn't until I got out in the street that I realized what he meant. I made some inquiries: so far as I could discover we had made the first mixed recording date on any national label, using both white and Negro musicians. I thought it had been done long before.

186

Shortly afterward Mr. Peer called me to his office and introduced me to Mr. Adams. Mr. Adams had a mustache and a problem. The problem was Fats Waller, my favorite piano player. The Southern Music Company had an interest and an investment in Fats; Fats, who was having alimony trouble, had become indifferent to his Victor recording dates—he didn't get what he earned so he didn't care. Either he didn't keep the appointments or he arrived with a band which was unrehearsed. The Southern Music Company was disturbed, Mr. Adams said. It had advanced Fats some money.

"Mr. Peer has recommended you as a reliable and enterprising young man," he went on. "We would like you to undertake the task of finding Waller and delivering him to the studio on time and with a well-rehearsed band."

It sounded difficult. I hadn't yet met Waller; why should he let me discipline him for the sake of the Southern Music Company?

"We'll pay you seventy-five dollars if you can do it," Mr. Adams said.

At the moment I would have attempted to produce Herbert Hoover in a soft collar.

"I'll try," I said.

"Fine," Mr. Adams said. "We know where you can locate Waller. He's at Connie's Inn in Harlem rehearsing a new floor show. You can find him there this afternoon. The date is four days from now; that will give you time to assemble a band and rehearse it."

Connie's Inn was at 131st Street and Seventh Avenue, a corner inhabited also by the Lafayette Theater and by the Wishing Tree, a sidewalk totem pole which entertainers stroked for good luck. There were also an all-night barbershop,

187

a rib joint,* and, above Connie's Inn, a barrel-house café called the Performers and Entertainers Club. Waller was at Connie's Inn as predicted; the floor show, "Hot Chocolates," was being rehearsed. The score was by Fats and Andy Razaf, and included *Ain't Misbehavin'* and *Black And Blue*. Later it went downtown to Broadway, with Waller and Louis Armstrong in the cast.

I waited for a pause in the rehearsal; then I introduced myself to Fats. "Earl Hines told me to look you up," I explained.

"Ol' Earl?" Fats said. "Well, that's fine. How's ol' Earl? I'm so glad to hear about him. Sit down and let me get a little gin for you. We'll have a talk about Earl."

He was so amiable, so agreeable, so good-natured, that I felt almost ashamed of my mission; but I performed it; I asked Fats about making a record. A recording date? He'd be delighted, he'd be proud; just any time. In four days? Fine. At Liederkranz Hall? Wonderful. At noon? Perfect.

I telephoned Mr. Adams.

"Very good," he said. "We shall expect you at noon on Friday. You had better stay close to Waller."

I did, but every time I opened my mouth to say something about getting the band together or discussing the numbers to be played, Fats said, "Fine! Wonderful! Perfect!" and handed me another belt of gin. We were in perfect accord on everything. Nothing happened.

At the end of the first day I was not overly worried except in the matter of my capacity for gin. Obviously it was suicide to match Fats drink for drink. I began to duck and sidestep. All during the second day and the second night I kept trying.

* restaurant specializing in barbecued spareribs

"Fine! Wonderful! Perfect!" Fats said whenever I mentioned the recording date. "Now let's have a little gin and talk about it." The third day I was desperate; as night came on I kept talking and Fats kept handing me drinks. There was still no band. "After we get the band together what shall we play?" I asked. "Why, we'll play music," Fats said. "Now let's have a little drink and talk about it."

Things grew faint and finally dark. When I awoke I was lying on the wall cushions at Connie's Inn, fully dressed. It was half past ten in the morning. On another cushion Fats was curled up, also fully dressed, asleep. I staggered over to him. He opened his eyes and smiled.

"It's half past ten," I croaked. "We're due at the studio at noon."

He sat up, stretched, and yawned.

"That's fine! That's wonderful! That's perfect!" he said. "Now we've got to see about that band. Look around for some nickels so I can make that telephone go."

He went to the phone booth and made three calls. By the time we finished washing and straightening our clothes three musicians had arrived: Charlie Gains, a trumpet player; Charlie Irvis, a trombonist; and Arville Harris, who played clarinet and alto saxophone.

"What are you going to play?" I asked, though by now I figured it didn't matter. Mr. Adams would throw me out after the first note.

"You mean what are we going to play?" Fats said. "Man, you're with us. Where's your banjo?"

"But I'm not supposed to play with you," I said. "I only came to make the date and help you get the band together."

189

Fats looked hurt. "You mean you don't want to play with us?" he said.

"I would love to play with you," I said. "My banjo is at the Riverside Towers."

"We'll stop and get it," Fats said. "Charlie, get a taxi."

We piled into a taxi and headed down Seventh Avenue.

"Now here is what we are going to play," Fats said suddenly. He hummed a simple, basic pattern of rhythm and melody, a blues in a minor key. When we had it memorized he explained what each of us was to do. "You got that, Charlie?" he said.

Both Charlies said yes. They had it.

We stopped at the Riverside Towers and I got my banjo. At ten minutes before twelve we walked into Liederkranz Hall at Fifty-eighth Street and Lexington Avenue. Mr. Adams was waiting for us.

"I see you are punctual," he said to me. "Congratulations." To Fats he said, "Well, Mr. Waller, what is it to be this morning?"

"Well, Mr. Adams," Fats said, "this morning I think we'll start with a little thing we call *The Minor Drag*. It's a slow number. Then we got a little ol' thing for the other side we call"—he hesitated—"*Harlem Fuss*."

"Excellent," Mr. Adams said. "Let's begin with *The Minor Drag*."

We set up our instruments and Fats repeated his instructions. He played the theme for us; as soon as I heard him I knew why we didn't need drums—his left hand would take care of the bass. "Ready?" Fats said.

"Let's go," one of the Charlies said.

The warning lights flashed and we took off, every man for

himself, with Fats holding us together. When we finished Mr. Adams came out of the control room. He didn't say anything. We listened to the playback.

I had a difficult time believing what I heard because it sounded wonderful. I looked at Mr. Adams. He was smiling.

"You see," he said to me, "what careful rehearsal will do? You have performed your job excellently."

I walked over to Fats. "What are we going to play for the other side?" I whispered. "What is *Harlem Fuss?*"

"It's just a little blues in a major key," he said.

We made it. When the master was cut Mr. Adams was delighted.

"I wonder, Mr. Waller," he said, "if we could have some piano solos now?"

"Wonderful!" Fats said. "Perfect! We'll have some piano solos." Without moving from the bench he made *Handful Of Keys* and *Numb Fumblin'*. *Handful Of Keys* turned out to be the most popular of all his recorded piano solos.

"We must have some more of these dates," Mr. Adams said. "This is an excellent example of the wisdom of planning and preparation."

After that the Southern Music Company, with careful planning and preparation, brought out the record on a Victor Label with the titles reversed: *Harlem Fuss* was called *The Minor Drag* and *The Minor Drag* was called *Harlem Fuss*. I got my seventy-five dollars.

THE BLUE BLOWERS

THE PANIC was on for us early in 1929. You could make a million dollars in anything but jazz that spring. We ate from hand to mouth and it was somebody else's hand. I even sang again, on a recording date for Okeh. Mac-Partland, Teagarden, Sullivan, Mezzrow, and Krupa were along, plus a bass player named Artie Miller. The song I mangled was *I'm Sorry I Made You Cry* and I'm sorry I did it. For the other side we played *Makin' Friends*. Teagarden took the vocal and he meant it.

> I'd rather drink muddy water, Lord, sleep in a hollow log,
> I'd rather drink muddy water, Lord, sleep in a hollow log,
> Than to be up here in New York, treated like a dirty dog.

Mezzrow, who had been quietly playing clarinet, rushed to the microphone and acted as a Texas cheering section for Jack. "Sing it, Jack!" he hollered. "Man, you got it! Man, that's the stuff! Man, that's how we feel!"

There was nothing you could do about Mezz, who was from the west side of Chicago; when he fell through the Mason-Dixon Line he just kept going. About that time he decided to go to Europe to join Dave Tough. They passed each other in mid-ocean; Tough arrived in town looking for Mezz.

Red Nichols dropped in at the Riverside Towers and said he wanted to take a band on tour through New England during the summer. Would we be it? We said we would; Red couldn't spoil our music all by himself, and he was going to pay us $125 a week. Red got Bud Freeman in from Chicago and Pee Wee Russell from St. Louis. Tough agreed to play the drums. MacPartland and Teagarden were with Ben Pollack. We got Max Kaminsky of Boston on cornet. While we were rehearsing, Bert Lown, who had an agency in partnership with Rudy Vallee, asked us to play a club date at the Gedney Farms Country Club in Westchester.

"Are you sure you want us?" I asked. "This is a hot band; we don't play society slop."

"They'll love it," Lown said. "It will be a novelty."

The day of the date we spent the afternoon at an impromptu party in George Rilling's penthouse at the Riverside Towers: Dave, Max, Pee Wee, Joe, and myself. Fats Waller dropped in and began playing. We kept him company. One of the guests sent for her twelve-year-old son's junior drum set and Tough was able to join the band. Suddenly I looked at somebody's watch.

"Fats," I said, "you're my nemesis. We've missed the last train to Gedney Farms."

We piled into two taxicabs, picked up Tough's drums, and eighteen dollars later by the meters arrived at our destination. We were an hour late and in bad shape. The entertainment committee met us and escorted us to the locker room. We were supposed to be dressed in tuxedos and we were, technically. Kaminsky wore white socks; all of us were dishevelled. Nobody had a drink and none was offered us. We were beginning to shake. Tough went to the entertainment committee.

"I'm sorry to tell you this," he said, "but unless we have a drink we cannot go on. We have had a harrowing experience; our lives were nearly lost while coming here."

193

Without a word the chairman of the committee went to a locker, took out a bottle of gin, and handed it to Dave.

"Thank you," Tough said, "your kindness will not go unrewarded."

We ducked behind the lockers and gulped. Then we went upstairs and played. The complaints began almost immediately. There were three generations of Westchesterites present: the kids wanted *Tiger Rag*, the middle-aged group wanted *Alice Blue Gown*, the old folks asked for Strauss waltzes. The entertainment chairman came up and said, "I used to play drums at Yale. Trouble with your man is he doesn't syncopate enough." "He didn't go to Yale," I said.

Nothing pleased anybody—the music was too fast, too loud, too slow, and where was the melody? Finally we decided to turn our backs on the audience and enjoy ourselves. We took off on *Jazz Me Blues, I Wish I Could Shimmy Like My Sister Kate, I Ain't Gonna Give You None Of My Jelly Roll, Royal Garden Blues,* and *Clarinet Marmalade.* Now and then I took a quick look at the dancers; they were shocked, disgusted, irritated, bored, and mad.

McKenzie and Billings were with us, sitting on the stand. We began playing the blues. Billings picked up a megaphone and sang, improvising as he went along. It was a final insult to the audience:

I came up to this party thinkin' I would have a good time,
I came up to this party thinkin' I would have a good time,
I'd sell it for a nickel and a high price would be a dime.
I'd rather take a baby out for a moonlight walk,
I'd rather take a baby out for a moonlight walk,
I'd make her happy and she wouldn't even have to talk.

194

Oh, why don't someone give me a little of the lovin' I crave?
Oh, why don't someone give me a little of the lovin' I crave?
If I can be so weak why can't one of you girls be so brave?

We finished and went back to New York by train. I waited a few days before calling at the Lown-Vallee office to collect our money. I figured there had been complaints and I wanted to give Lown a chance to consider them objectively. Finally I walked in and asked his secretary to announce me. Lown started talking as I entered his office. I managed to sneak in a word about pay.

"Go to the union and try to get it!" he yelled.

I reminded him quietly that we were a jazz band and that I had explained this to him before accepting the job.

"You are a gang of hoodlums!" he shouted. "You have no relationship whatever to music! No band in history has ever drawn so many complaints! You insulted every decent person in Westchester! What's more, you lost the account for us!"

"We played for dancing," I said. "That's what we were asked to do. We insulted nobody."

"Your appearance was an insult—and while we're on the subject, who were the two Chicago gangsters you brought with you?"

I left and went to Plunkett's, a speakeasy on West Fifty-third Street. McKenzie was there.

"Lown won't pay us," I said to him. "We lost the contract for him. Besides, he says we brought two Chicago gangsters with us."

Red put down his drink and stared at me.

"You and Billings," I explained.

"Wait for me," Red said, "I'll be right back."

I followed him into the street. "You don't know where the office is!" I hollered.

He stopped and waited for me.

"Point for me," he said. "Just point."

I led him to the office. He walked past the receptionist, found Lown, and made a lunge for him.

"Who am I?" Red yelled.

Lown retreated. "I don't know," he said nervously. "I never saw you before."

"Then how do you know I'm a Chicago gangster, you mango-head?" McKenzie screamed.

Lown tried to say something but McKenzie hit him with two hundred words a minute. He ran the total into four figures, ending with, "and the next time you call somebody a Chicago gangster get it straight! I'm from St. Louis!"

We were all the way back to Plunkett's before we realized we still hadn't collected any money for our work at Gedney Farms, not even the eighteen dollars I spent for taxi fare.

"I guess people just don't like jazz music," I said.

"Don't worry," Jimmy Plunkett said. "Look what happened to water. For thousands of years people wouldn't drink it for fear of getting poisoned. Now they drink so much of it they think they can get along without whiskey."

"Who thinks that?" McKenzie said. He was still looking for a fight.

"The people who voted for prohibition," Jimmy said.

Plunkett's was at 205½ West Fifty-third Street, under the elevated, which ran down the street to get from Sixth Avenue to Ninth Avenue. The place had a glass front door painted black; the floor was cement; something called decoration had been done to the walls by a utility employee named Three-Star

Hennessy. The room was sixteen feet long; the bar was two feet shorter. There was a small backroom with a few chairs and tables; off it was a stand-up icebox in which I often changed my clothes. It was already a musicians' hangout when Tommy Dorsey first took me there. In the telephone book it was listed as the Trombone Club, in honor of Tommy.

The original Plunkett died soon after I met him; his son Jimmy took over the business with Gene O'Byrne as partner. Gene had been at college with John McCormack in Dublin; he gave the place a classic touch. There were a good many Irish among the customers, a scattering of newspapermen, and clerks from the near-by magistrates' court. The majority of the clientele were musicians—the Whiteman boys, the Dorseys, Russ Morgan, Eddy Duchin, Glenn Miller, Tony Pastor, and any of our mob who were in town and ambulatory.

All sorts of business was transacted at Plunkett's; the telephone rang constantly, bands were organized at the bar, and everybody drank. Those who were working bought drinks for those who were not working. This was a communal arrangement; you might be buying drinks today and you might need to have drinks bought for you tomorrow. You might be standing at the bar with fifteen cents in your pocket and the man next to you might have fifteen radio programs. He would pay for your drinks.

One day Tommy Dorsey came in during the afternoon. He had a radio program in half an hour.

"I'll have to drink in a hurry," he said to Jimmy. "I need a shave."

"Maybe you need a drink more than you need a shave," Jimmy suggested. He was a practical man, a non-drinker.

197

Tommy looked in the mirror. "I need a shave," he said. "I'll have to skip to the barbershop."

Standing quietly down the bar was Tommy O'Connor, a former wrestler with gnarled fingers and an eighteen-and-a-half-inch neck. He was from the Dorsey home town in Pennsylvania.

"Nothing of the sort, Tommy," he said. "You'll not have to stir from this place."

"I need that shave," Dorsey said.

"It so happens that I myself am now in the profession you intend to patronize," O'Connor said. "I am a barber."

He reached into a vest pocket and took out a straight razor.

"It will take but a minute," he said. "Jimmy, run some of that draught beer."

Jimmy ran some beer and O'Connor shook some salt into it. A fine head of suds formed. O'Connor scooped the suds off and put them on Dorsey's face.

"Put that bar rag around his neck, Jimmy," he said to Plunkett. "I don't want to soil his shirt. Now, Tommy, just lay your head back and relax."

In a few minutes it was over and Dorsey, stunned, bleeding, but shaved, was standing upright with another drink in his hand.

"Just one more thing, Tommy," O'Connor said. "Give me a shot of that gin, Jimmy." He poured the gin over his hands and rubbed Tommy's face.

"Finest after-shave lotion in the world," he said.

Dorsey finished his drink, had time for another, and left for Radio City in excellent condition.

Chelsea Queely, a steady patron, came in one night with two black eyes. Jack Bland studied them for a while; then he said, "Chelsea, what you need are some leeches. I'll get them for you at the drugstore." He went out and was gone for a while and we forgot about him. Chelsea had a few drinks and felt better. Then Bland turned up with a large smile and a small box.

"Everything is set, Chelsea," Jack said. "I've got them right here in this pill box—two of them. Just lean your head back against the wall and I'll put one on each eye." Chelsea was sitting in a straight-backed chair. He tipped it backward. Jack took a leech from the box and dropped it on Chelsea's right eye. There must have been a lot of poison in the lid because the leech wanted no part of the job. It wriggled and squirmed and started down Chelsea's face. Chelsea suddenly looked scared. He tried to move but Jack jammed his head against the wall. "Just hold it a minute, Chelsea!" he said. "Everything will be all right!"

He put the leech back on the eye and reached for the other one. Chelsea tried to move. Jack kept him against the wall. Chelsea opened his mouth to holler.

At this point Jack dropped the other leech. He miscalculated. It fell in Chelsea's mouth.

"Spit it out before it dies, Chelsea!" he said.

Chelsea treated his eyes for the rest of the evening with alcohol.

Louis Armstrong came on from Chicago that spring for a one night stand at the Savoy Ballroom in Harlem with Luis Russell's orchestra. Afterward an impromptu banquet was staged in his honor. I looked around the table and shook my head; I had never seen so many good musicians, white and colored, in one place at the same time.

"You ought to make a record while Louis is here," I said to Tommy Rockwell, Armstrong's adviser at the time.

He looked uneasy. "I don't know about using a mixed group," he said.

"If Victor can do it Okeh can do it," I said. I told him about what we had done with *I'm Gonna Stomp Mr. Henry Lee* and *That's A Serious Thing.*

"That's good news," he said. "I'm glad to hear it."

He looked around the table. "I've got a date at nine this morning with the Luis Russell band. I'll put it back to this afternoon. Get your boys together and I'll speak to Louis."

It was then four o'clock. At nine I reported at the Okeh studio with Jack Teagarden and Joe Sullivan. The colored musicians who joined us were, in addition to Louis, Kaiser Marshall, a drummer, and Happy Cauldwell, who played tenor saxophone. Eddie Lang, the guitarist, had been scheduled to play with the Russell band; no one had been able to reach him and he was on hand. He took my place and the group made *Knockin' A Jug* and *I'm Gonna Stomp Mr. Henry Lee.* I stayed for the afternoon date, when Louis and the Russell men made *I Can't Give You Anything But Love* and *Mahogany Hall Stomp.* Backing up Louis' trumpet were J. C. Higginbotham on trombone, Lonnie Johnson on guitar, Pops Foster on bass, Luis Russell on piano, Paul Barbarin on drums, and Charlie Holmes, Albert Nicholas, and Teddy Hill on saxophones. They let me sit in a corner and hold my banjo.

In June we went on the road with Nichols. For three dreary weeks we toured New England and New York State, then returned to New York. There was no doubt about it, the East was not ready for jazz. We took up the study of beans again, particularly automat beans, which cost ten cents a pot. One night walking out of Bickford's at Broadway and Eightieth Street someone tapped me on the shoulder. It was John Bright, a young Chicago reporter. With him was Jack Glassman, also of Chicago. They were eating beans too. Bright had finished a book about Big Bill Thompson, called *Hizzoner the Mayor*, and he had a movie script finished.

"It's about the hoodlums back home," he said. "I call it *Public Enemy*."

"Too bad you can't sell it," I said. "I guess that gangster stuff is like jazz; nobody is interested in it."

Red Nichols said he would have a job for us in the fall. He promised to take us to Chicago, to the Drake Hotel, the finest spot in town. It would be a triumphant homecoming.

"Didn't I tell you?" Joe Sullivan said. "They can't keep us down!"

"But we still haven't licked New York," I said. "We're walking around here on our knees. Nobody knows what we're doing and nobody cares—the poorest 7-piece band on earth."

"Never mind that," Joe said. "Some day the whole world will listen to our music and tell us it makes sense."

"How much money have you got?" I asked.

"A nickel," Joe said.

"Let's buy a glass of milk and split it," I suggested.

"All right," Joe said, "but remember what I said. Some day they will have to admit we're good. They can't stay tone deaf forever."

Again we rehearsed for Nichols; everyone packed for the trip to Chicago. The day before we were to leave, Red called.

"Be at the Hollywood Restaurant at nine o'clock tonight," he said. "We open there tomorrow with a floor show."

That was the way things were with Nichols. We went to the Hollywood, the first big night club to run without cover charge. We rehearsed until seven o'clock in the morning with a line of

N.T.G. girls, a team of Greek adagio dancers, and some other acts. We took a quick nap, got our tuxedos pressed, and returned to the Hollywood at six-thirty. We were tired, not too well acquainted with the music we were to play, and the Greeks were dependent upon our cues for the success of their dancing. They threw a girl back and forth between them; I heard Pee Wee's clarinet quaver as she sailed through the air; we all had the feeling that if we missed a cue she would either keep on going or fall on her face. The N.T.G. girls, led by their master, Nils T. Granlund, came out wearing shoes, earrings, and gloves. Pee Wee tried to ask me a question but only succeeded in stuttering.

"Just like the Drake Hotel," I said to Nichols.

"If any of you boys want to leave I'm sure I can replace you," he said.

He was paying us $125 a week but even at that Pee Wee couldn't stand it; he left. John Bright dropped in one night and said he and Glassman were going to Hollywood, California. Why not go with them?

"We're going to write for the movies," Bright said. "Maybe we can work you in as a gagman."

I shook my head.

"I'd be three thousand miles away, in a place with the same name as this club, and out of a job," I said. "I'll stay here."

But I didn't. One night Jimmy Dorsey came in with a party and sent a request to Nichols for Nobody's Sweetheart. We had played it nine or ten times that night already. Since recording it in Chicago we had not been able to get away from it.

"Nobody's Sweetheart," Nichols said. "Let's go."

I looked at him pleadingly.

"Oh, no, Red!" I said. "Not again!"

"You're fired!" he said.

And I was. It was early in November, 1929. The stock market had fallen down a rabbit hole. Bright and Glassman were in California, where Bright sold his *Public Enemy* for $750 and Glassman changed his name to Kubec Glasmon. Both boys were successful. I was broke.

I ran into McKenzie.

"Well," he said, "you're carrying the burlap again."

"I didn't lose any money in Wall Street," I said.

"Let's get a drink," he said. "I have plans."

We went to the nearest speakeasy, eight feet away.

"Bland wants to play parties and saloons," Red said. "I think it's undignified."

"Is it undignified to make a living?" I asked.

Red tasted his drink. "Would you wear a jersey and a cap and play for Mrs. Vanderbilt's dinner parties?"

"I'd rather play in a jazz band."

"Jazz is a luxury. Too bad it's such good music. The poor man likes it but only the rich man can afford it."

"I guess I wouldn't mind a cap. Bix used to wear one."

"A jersey and a cap. The jersey has horizontal stripes. I hate them but the society folks think they are cute. They won't let you play at parties without them. So you'll do it. Good! We're all set," Red said.

"I thought you said you wouldn't play at parties. Aren't they too undignified?"

"Mind your own business. Bland will play the guitar; you'll louse up the banjo; Billings will play the suitcase."

"At last I've reached the gutter. I'd never have known it except for the company."

"Blow your nose and order another drink. How about getting

a couple of those lutes for you and Bland? Maybe Mrs. Vanderbilt will dance for us." He grinned. "We're going to play jazz. It'll be disguised so the people won't know it, but it'll be jazz."

Rome had a fiddler while it was burning. New York in 1929 had the Mound City Blue Blowers. We played for cocktail parties, dinner parties, parties at night, and parties in the early morning. Our hosts were Jimmy Cromwell, Mary Brown Warburton, Mrs. Graham Fair Vanderbilt, Larry Doyle, George Preston Marshall, Mrs. Woolworth Donahue, the various Munn families, Billy Leeds, Marjorie Oelrichs, and a lot of week-end millionaires who were broke or dead a year later. Nobody thought the stock market crash was serious, or that the panic would last. Only the Blue Blowers were having a hard time, though as usual we drank well. Billings had a phrase for his diary which covered our daily life: panic, parties, and pollution.

Billings had finally contrived a place for himself in music. In Chicago in a hotel room during a jam session involving a comb and a banjo he had rigged a suitcase to act as a drum. For soft effects he covered the case with wrapping paper, which he wrinkled and then stroked with whisk brooms. For bass effects he kicked the suitcase with his heel. McKenzie, dubious but intrigued, let him try the trick with the Blowers on a party job. It was a success; Billings was a Blue Blower.

At parties everyone wanted to play the suitcase, and sooner or later everyone did, even Mrs. Vanderbilt. Mrs. Vanderbilt was our favorite hostess; she was a horse owner and had a soft spot for McKenzie, whom she considered an occupational casualty of the race track. During the 1929 Christmas holidays we played at her town house for a dinner party. In our caps and

204

jerseys we sat in a corner of the dining room playing while the guests ate from gold service. It was the first time I had seen this type of crockery. The food was normal—automat fare with French sauce and a lot of wine on the side.

We weren't getting any drinks that night. Mrs. Vanderbilt's head butler loathed us; he considered that we were hired hands and resented any favors we received from his mistress. When the guests broke for coffee, cigars, and cognac Mrs. Vanderbilt came over and spoke to us.

"Are you getting enough to drink, Red?" she asked.

"I am not getting anything to drink at all," Red said. He pointed to the head butler. "I am sorry to report it but I do not think that man wants us to have a drink."

"I will see to it myself," Mrs. Vanderbilt said.

We got prewar champagne. The head butler went to the cellar, brought it up, and served it himself, hating every drop we drank.

"Let this be a lesson to you," McKenzie said to him. "Remember the Emancipation Proclamation—all men are created free and equal and are entitled to champagne."

A few nights later we played for a party at Mary Brown Warburton's, on Madison Avenue across the street from the rear of St. Patrick's Cathedral. An orthodox musician· was at the piano.

"Mary," McKenzie said to the hostess, "would you like to hear somebody really play that instrument?"

"Isn't he playing it?" Mary asked, looking at the pianist.

"I'll prove to you that he isn't," McKenzie said.

He called Joe Sullivan at Riverside Towers.

"I can't come," Joe said. "I haven't subway fare."

"Jump in a taxi and we'll meet you outside," Red said.

Thirty minutes later McKenzie lifted the incumbent from the piano stool and Joe sat down. He went into *Sweet Lorraine*.

"You're right," Mary said to Red. "Where did this man come from?"

"I made him up," Red said.

The guests gave Joe an ovation and crowded around the piano. Billings took the opportunity to snatch a few bottles of champagne. He walked across the street to the rear of the cathedral and hid them behind the wall which runs between the Cardinal's residence and the rectory. McKenzie was horror-stricken.

"How could you do such a sacrilegious thing?" he said to Billings. "Don't you realize that is sacred property over there? What do you want to do, get all of us sent to hell? Are you an agent of the devil?"

Billings was shaken. When we left the party he retrieved the bottles from behind the wall. I thought McKenzie was going to break them in the street but he didn't. In the taxicab he gave Billings another tongue-lashing. I have never heard such language. Billings began to weep. By the time we reached Riverside Towers he was on a crying jag. He went to his room, sobbing and muttering repentance.

"I don't know what the world is coming to," McKenzie said, opening one of the bottles of champagne and pouring himself a drink. "People have no respect for sacred things any more. Imagine stealing champagne and hiding it behind a cathedral!"

He drained his glass and filled it again.

"This is the best wine I ever tasted," he said.

After the holidays our clients went to Florida. We followed them, minus Billings, who returned to Chicago for a rest. The suitcase was taken over by Gordon Means, of the Oklahoma Means. Gordon was a pretty good suitcase player. We broke

206

our trip at Winston-Salem, North Carolina, for a party at Reynolda. Nancy Reynolds, one of the cigarette heiresses, was having an engagement party in the family mansion. We were met at the station and driven to the estate in a limousine.

The Negro servants treated us civilly until they saw us in our jerseys and caps. Then they froze. We knew how they felt. We loathed the rigs, which were used by the Blowers originally for a Bowery scene in the musical comedy "City Chap."

"We've got to soften these boys up if we want any drinks," McKenzie said. "Let's fly."

The servants watched us while we got ready for our first number.

"Here we go," McKenzie said.

We broke into St. Louis Blues.

The servants smiled and relaxed. Before we finished one of them came over with a tray of drinks. Later they even gave us food.

In Florida we were scheduled to work on a gambling ship, but the ship never sailed. The stock market hadn't recovered. We found ourselves stranded in Miami.

"This is getting serious," McKenzie said. "It's a good thing we're accustomed to being poor."

"I was reading the paper," I said. "Jimmy Cromwell is in Palm Beach."

McKenzie called him. "Jimmy, are there any parties going on?" he asked. "We're open for engagements. We could stand one."

"If there aren't," Jimmy said, "there soon will be."

Cromwell loved parties and he knew how to organize and operate them; he kept us out of hock all that winter, and sometimes it seemed as if he arranged parties just so we could work.

207

Money was still fairly loose; only the little fellows were diving from high buildings.

We returned to New York in the early spring and opened at Shanley's, a place on West Ninety-sixth Street operated by Hal Hixon. Gordon Means had returned to Oklahoma, and McKenzie wired Billings in Chicago to come on immediately. Billings walked into Riverside Tower two days later and tried to say hello.

"My God!" McKenzie said. "He hasn't any teeth!"

Billings tried to explain himself but could only mumble and drool. Finally he sat down and wrote us a note: "Trouble with teeth from accident in Jamaica. Had to have them all pulled. New ones not ready when I left. Coming by mail."

We opened at Shanley's without Billings' teeth. They arrived the next day. In a few weeks we closed and went back to panic, parties, and pollution.

Once we went to the Otto Kahn estate at Cold Spring Harbor, Long Island, to play for a house party given by Gilbert, the older Kahn son. The others in the family were away— Roger, Gilbert's brother, was on his honeymoon, having married the singer, Hannah Williams. A limousine picked us up at Plunkett's; we took Frankie Signorelli along to play piano.

The estate contained a fraction under a thousand acres; it had an eighteen-hole golf course with hand-stitched fairways, caddies of all sizes, and a pro. In the garage were twenty-two automobiles, including a selection of foreign models and several midget racing cars. In the house we were shown to rooms containing fireplaces and canopied beds. McKenzie and I shared one, Bland and Billings took another, and Frankie went by himself to a third. We put on our jerseys and caps and played for the guests. Everyone wanted to play the suitcase.

208

When the party was finished we went to our rooms. Billings, relaxing in a canopied bed, noticed a small cloisonné clock on the mantel. Bland was sitting quietly by the fireplace, admiring the room.

"Jack," Billings said, "I know a girl who would like that clock."

Bland jumped up and went to the bed.

"If you even tell time by that clock, Josh," he said, "I'll break it over your head! Don't touch anything in this house! It's too nice a palace."

We were invited to stay over and play some golf in the morning. Frankie had to go back to town for a radio rehearsal and Billings went with him. McKenzie, Bland, and I went to the course after breakfast and began to play. At the third hole Bland teed up his ball and addressed it. Suddenly he dropped his club and stared past us, a look of fright on his face.

"Oh, Lord!" he said.

Then he ran back to the house. We watched him. The guests were gradually assembling to lounge on the lawn. Jack went through them like a broken-field runner, jumping over chairs, and disappeared into the house.

McKenzie and I sat down and waited. In a few minutes we saw him reappear, walking. He threaded his way through the guests again, then stopped and shouted to us.

"It's all right!" he yelled. "It's still there!"

Ann Pennington signed us to work with her in a vaudeville act. We opened in Paterson, New Jersey. Ray Goetz came out from New York and offered Ann a spot in "The New Yorkers," a musical comedy he was about to produce.

"I hate to leave you boys," she said, "but I can't turn this down. I have an idea. Go to see John Perona at the Bath Club.

He has just opened the highest-class speakeasy in town. It's just the spot for you."

The Bath Club was at 35 West Fifty-third Street. It had a doorman named Barry, who was harder to get by than a saloon on Saturday night. How to get in and buy a drink was difficult enough; interviewing Perona, who lived in the upper floors of the club, seemed impossible. We sent Bland, who had plenty of courage and who was physically formidable; it would be hard to throw him out and it wouldn't hurt him much. He returned and said Perona would give us an audition right after lunch the next day.

"How did you get in?" I asked.

"I told Barry I had a date with his boss but couldn't remember his name," Bland said. "It was such an old gag he'd forgotten it. He let me in and sent for Perona."

Only one party was left in the dining room when we arrived and prepared to audition. Perona stood by a table, stone-faced, staring at the suitcase. We had put on our jerseys and caps. He isn't going to like this, I thought; we'll be in the gutter at half-past three. A man from the remaining luncheon party came up to McKenzie and said, "I want you to play the Coronation March."

"Sure," McKenzie said. "Here we go."

We played Sweet Georgia Brown, I Got Rhythm, and Sweet Lorraine. A waiter came up with a twenty-dollar bill. "From Mr. Neely," he said, indicating the man in the luncheon party, who was now earnestly talking to Perona and pointing toward us. Perona came over and smiled.

"You seem to have taken the fancy of Mr. Neely," he said. "I think you might be an interesting novelty in the bar. When can you start?"

"Tonight," McKenzie said.

"Be here at ten o'clock," Perona said.

"Who is Mr. Neely?" Red asked.

"He owns the Nedick's stands," Perona said.

"Glad to hear it," McKenzie said. "It's nice to know that this is where he spends our money. We've been eating at his hot dog stands for months."

With the twenty dollars we got our trousers pressed, our hair cut, and bought dinner. At ten o'clock we opened in the Bath Club. We ran for nine months. It was the easiest job I ever had, with the least work, the most fun, and the highest income.

For fifteen minutes of each hour from ten o'clock at night until two in the morning we performed in the bar on the second floor. Perona didn't want much music. "Let them drink and talk," he said. "They will listen to you attentively for fifteen minutes; if you play longer it will be an annoyance." During the forty-five minute intermissions we amused ourselves with the house commodity and played ping-pong in the game room on the third floor. We gave one of the bus boys five dollars a week to bring us the best food in the house. Perona said, "If you want a drink go to the bar and get it." We did, but when the next inventory was taken such an alarming leakage was discovered that we were asked to sign a check each time we ordered liquor. We expected to be charged at a moderate rate and at the end of the first week asked for our bill. "Don't bother about it," Perona said. "We'll settle it later." On the last night of our run he called us to his office and showed us a stack of stubs four feet high.

"The signatures on these checks are as follows—William McKenzie, J. Billings, J. Bland, and Eddie Condon," he said.

211

"Oh, Lord!" McKenzie moaned. "We'll have to work three months for nothing!"

The cheapest drink in the club was gin and water. It cost a dollar, and we never ordered it.

Perona looked at us solemnly and waited for someone to speak. Finally, in a weak voice, Red said, "Could you tell us the total?"

Perona leaned back and laughed. Then he pushed the checks off the desk into a wastebasket.

"I just wanted to see you fellows look responsible once before leaving here," he said. "The drinks were on the house. You don't owe me a cent."

We were an unqualified success in the bar. Everybody wanted to play the suitcase and people stared at our lutes as if hypnotized. They were only four-string guitars made in the shape of a lute and tuned like a banjo, but in combination with the jerseys and caps, the suitcase, and McKenzie's comb, they were what one customer described as "cunningly anachronistic."

"Be careful what you say about these boys," McKenzie said. "They're sensitive."

"I was speaking of surrealism," the man said. "I have been painting such scenes in the belief that they existed only in my mind. Now I see one of them before me. It is amazing and gratifying. Is it the work of your own creative faculties?"

McKenzie turned on his heel and walked away. "If this wasn't such a good job I'd punch that guy right in the nose," he muttered.

McKenzie used up a lot of paper while blowing through his comb. Every day he cut part of the *Evening World* into strips, which he then put in various pockets. The texture of the *World*, he discovered, was just right for blue blowing. One night a customer asked what special paper he used to get such amazing sounds from a comb.

"I use the *Evening World*," McKenzie said. "It has a certain texture."

The customer looked concerned. "The *World* is being sold," he said. "It's going over to the *Telegram*. What are you going to do then?"

"I'm going over with it," McKenzie said.

One night Perona asked us to go into the dining room to play for a particular friend of his. She was a lady with lavender hair. "Exquisite!" she murmured after we gave her some blues. "You like it?" McKenzie said. He was obviously doubtful. "It's divine!" she exclaimed. "If you ever come to Paris I hope you will allow me to be the first to introduce you to Parisian society." She turned to a young man sitting with her. "My secretary will give you my address," she said. The secretary handed Red a card. "Lady Mendl will be pleased to receive you at any time," he said. McKenzie bowed. "We shall no doubt be in Paris this summer," he said. "I shall call and present myself."

Among the suitcase players were Earl Carroll, Gloria Swanson, and Billy Leeds. Leeds was a drum nut; he had a complete set of them in his triplex apartment. Once when we finished at two o'clock he took us there to play until dawn. There was a gymnasium in the place, a Hawaiian trainer, and an ex-prize fighter named Jack Renault who acted as sparring partner for Billy and his friends. Perona came over to use the gymnasium. He kept himself in excellent physical condition; his forty suits weren't padded anywhere. Normally he was reserved and quiet, but no one could resist the suitcase. He took a crack at it one night, doing his best to juggle the whisk brooms in imitation of Billings. Billings had a trick of flicking a tip—usually a five dol-

213

lar bill—off the suitcase and catching it under his armpit, so that it seemed to disappear. He kicked suitcases to pieces pretty fast. I went with him to the luggage shops to watch the proprietors when Billings tried out their wares.

"I'd like a suitcase," Billings would say. "I prefer one made of fiber."

The man would bring several. "This is our best," he would say, pointing to a particular one.

"A very nice bag," Billings would say. Then he would kick it. The proprietors never said anything—this was during the depression—but as Billings tapped, slapped, and kicked the bags, listening and muttering to himself, I had the pleasure of observing the effect on a man's face of the gradual discovery that he is dealing with a dangerous lunatic.

"He's harmless," I whispered to one luggage man who seemed really frightened. "He just likes to kick suitcases." The luggage man was willing to be sympathetic. "Maybe his wife ran away with a salesman," he suggested.

McKenzie often worked overtime to cover up the fact that he was a good boss and a sentimental guy; he would ignore our serious offences, then hit us with abuse for being five minutes late for work. Once in the game room I found Billings in tears. "What's the matter?" I asked. "Oh," he blubbered, "you know how McKenzie is. When in Rome you've got to do as they do in St. Louis."

Perona refused to let his customers take us out. If they wanted us for personal minstrels they had to wait until we finished work. The only person who broke him down on this point was Peggy Hopkins Joyce. She came in one night with a newspaper publisher and decided to take us with her to the Backgammon Club. She worked on Perona and he melted. At the Backgammon Club we met Jimmy Altemus and Mildred Patrick. They offered me a drink.

"I'm on the wagon," I said.

Mildred smiled. "I know just the thing for you," she said. "Absinthe. It's mild and soothing—just the thing to stay sober on."

"Are you sure?" I said. "As I recall it has other properties."

I knew she was lying, but she was beautiful. I drank absinthe all night, and I found out about it. Somebody got me home and somebody got me up in time to go to work the next night. I forgave Mildred; she was still beautiful.

George Rilling had given up his penthouse at Riverside Towers and rented a maisonette studio apartment in the rear of the Buchanan Apartments at 145 East Forty-seventh Street. It was owned by Richard Davis, a sculptor, whose father had built the Buchanan, an enormous building occupying the entire block from Forty-seventh Street to Forty-eighth Street. The studio, complete with skylight, custom-built furniture, indirect lighting, a living room thirty-seven feet square, and a Steinway grand piano, was in the backyard. Rilling asked me to move in with him; I was there most of the time anyhow. In the room set aside for clay and other art materials we had an L-shaped bar made by the same Spanish cabinetmaker who was responsible for the furniture. There was also a liquor cabinet, which Rilling kept filled and locked. We were seldom lonely. Once George went to Atlantic City for a week end.

"You might as well have a party while I'm gone," he said. "I've put some liquor out and locked the cabinet. I'm taking the key with me."

"George," I said, "don't you trust our friends?"

"They are musicians," he said.

The first night was quiet. I called Krupa and Sullivan and we got some girls and sat around talking and drinking. By the next night the news had gotten around; Bix came in, and he and Sullivan began playing duets on the piano. Krupa set up the telephone directories and used them for drums. It was hot and the windows were open. Some other guests arrived and the liquor ran out.

"There's more in the cabinet," I said, "but Rilling has the key."

"I know how to handle that," Ray Ludwig, an ex-Goldkette man, said. "I'll get the liquor out without touching the lock."

He went to work on the hinges, took them off, and we helped ourselves.

"Now I'll put the hinges back on," Ray said, "and Rilling will never know the difference."

By that time the population of Plunkett's had moved in on us. Since the courtyard of the Buchanan faced our windows I was pretty sure we were keeping some people awake, but I decided not to worry about it.

The next afternoon Rilling returned. He looked around the living room, inhaled the stale cigarette smoke, then went to the liquor cabinet and put his key in the lock. The door fell off and hit him on the head.

The next day he received twenty-seven separate formal complaints from residents of the Buchanan. Each one threatened legal action.

Bix was living at the Fourty-fourth Street Hotel. He wasn't being good to himself; he was cheating the cure he had taken. His feet were swollen and dragged when he walked; his thoughts were often muddled. He went to Harlem with us and sat quietly at Pod's and Jerry's listening to Willie the Lion Smith

216

play the piano. He came to the studio and sat for hours at the piano. I never let him ask for a drink; I offered it to him. It hurt me all over—in my eyes, in my brain, in my stomach, in my heart, but I knew nothing could help him. I suppose a guy gets closer to you when he is hurting himself and all you can do is watch. He was still shy, and the shyness was all the more evident now that he was getting mixed up about things. One day he walked in while Hal Skelly and Louise Groody were running through a dance in an act Rilling had written. He walked across the room to the bar before he realized what was going on. When the rehearsal was over he went to Louise and said, "Excuse me for interrupting you, Miss Brodie."

"You are a prophet," I told him later. "The act did a Brodie.*"

He couldn't go back to Whiteman; he didn't have the stamina for the job, or the ability to concentrate. He played college dates and made a few records: one day he ruined twenty-eight masters trying to get a solo right. Joe Sullivan was in the band; he almost cried when he told me about it.

But when I heard Bix at the piano nothing seemed changed; he played with the same effortless, unbelievable imagination. It was only when I looked at his face and saw the absence there that things got cold and tight around me and I stiffened my drink.

On the seventh of August—it was now 1931—Rilling and I got up in the early afternoon and moped around the living room. I was reading a newspaper; George was riffling a magazine.

"Hey, Slick," he said. "Come here."

Automatically I answered to my old nickname. He pointed

* took a dive, flopped (after Steve Brodie, a saloonkeeper who jumped off the Brooklyn Bridge on a bet and lived to collect it)

217

to an advertisement; a young man was staring up from it, wearing the proper kind of collar.

"Who is it?" he asked.

"Beiderbecke," I said. "It looks just like him."

The telephone rang. It was McKenzie, calling from Plunkett's.

"Eddie?" McKenzie's tone was gruffer than usual. We've been fired, I thought.

"Hello, Willie," I said. Sometimes he warmed up to his Christian name.

"Brace yourself," he said.

"I'm braced."

"Your boy did it."

"Did what?"

"He died this morning."

I didn't want to say it. I waited. McKenzie was making noises. "Bix?"

"Yes. Pneumonia. He was out on Long Island, living with some bass player. I'd better come over and tell you about it."

I hung up.

No more Bix.

George looked idly at the magazine again, then closed it.

A BIRTHDAY
FOR JOE

THE BATH CLUB was a mansion; the Stork Club was an old brownstone on West Fifty-eighth Street just west of Sixth Avenue. Prices in both clubs were on a level—three dollars for Napoleon brandy in a swizzle glass. In order to enter the Bath Club you had to be sober, rich, and somebody; you came out somebody. You had only to be sober and rich to get into the Stork Club, and you came out neither. We went to work there in the fall of 1931; we hadn't met the owner when we reported at ten o'clock and played our first set in the bar on the ground floor. When it was finished McKenzie went to the vestibule and paced the floor. He needed five hundred dollars to save an insurance policy and he didn't know where to get it.

As he walked and smoked he became aware that someone was watching him, a man dressed like an Oklahoma horse trader.

"Do you like this place?" the man asked. He was leaning against the wall, holding his chin in his right hand, squinting a little.

"How could I like this dump full of broads and booze when I can't get enough dough to keep an insurance policy that will take care of my family in case someone hates my singing and puts a hole in my head?" Red said bitterly.

Suddenly he stopped and looked at the man.

"Boy," he said, "what are you doing in here? You can't wear clothes like that inside a house."

"How much do you need?" the man asked.

"Five hundred dollars." McKenzie said. "Do you sing here too?"

The man reached into his pocket and took out a wad of bills. Red stared. The roll was two stories deep.

"Take a thousand," the man said, handing him the roll. "You may need it."

Red began to sweat. He peeled off a hundred-dollar bill. Below it was another, then another, then another. He took ten and put them in his pocket.

"That's a lot of dough to be carrying around," he said shakily. "If the guys who run this joint see it you may have to leave it behind when you go."

"I think I'll stay," the man said. "I own the place. My name is Billingsley. I hope you'll be happy here; the customers seem to enjoy your music."

McKenzie was a different man when he came back to the stand. "I just met the most wonderful guy in the world," he said. "His name is Sherman Billingsley. He's our boss and I want you lousy bums to treat him with respect."

For the Stork engagement the Blue Blowers expanded slightly; Joe Sullivan was added on piano. Billings went back to Chicago again and Slim Kurtzmann replaced him on the suitcase, which still attracted the customers. Our stand was surrounded by a brass rail which Earl Carroll hurdled three times a week to get at the whisk brooms. One night a man introduced himself to me; he was Harry Frazee, Jr., whose father made all of Boston sad by selling Babe Ruth to the New York Yankees. Young

Harry had been road secretary for his father's team, the Red Sox; one night he brought his mother in to hear Joe Sullivan. Joe played her requests—*I Want To Be Happy* and *Tea For Two.* Mrs. Frazee began to cry. "What's the matter with her?" I asked Harry. "Nothing," he said. "She's just enjoying herself. Those tunes are from 'No, No Nanette.' We produced it." I was disillusioned. I thought she was blubbering because her husband sold Babe Ruth. I figured it ought to be a family sorrow.

Billingsley wandered around with his chin on his hand, keeping his squint on things. The first two floors were for customers; we played on both floors, alternating with a Hawaiian group and a trio. On the third floor we ate. One night we were tearing into some pheasant when Billingsley wandered in and out; a few minutes later one of the waiters came up with two bottles of champagne and served them to us.

"Do you realize," McKenzie said, "that we are the only guys playing jazz south of Harlem who wear firsthand pants and sit down to eat?"

"I would like it better if I didn't have to dress like a convict, act like an idiot, and play a lute," I said. But I was almost happy.

The waiters were mostly Greeks and Albanians, some of them without citizenship papers. Their sense of humor was ideal for appreciating the Blue Blowers. They were fond of a certain song we played, *Stick Out Your Can, Here Comes The Garbage Man.* Billingsley instructed them to bring us brandy every time we played it. We played it a lot. We opened on our instruments, then in unison we sang, *Stick Out Your Can, Here Comes The Brandy Man.* The waiters raced each other trying to get to the stand first with a tray of drinks.

Billingsley allowed us to take out brandy in bottles for two dollars a pint. We drank nothing else. I began waking up in the

221

middle of the day with a pounding heart. It worried me a little; a guy doesn't have too many chances. I spoke about it to a suit-case-playing customer who had confessed to being a doctor.

"I go home half loaded," I said, "and I figure I ought to sleep like a guy with a tomahawk in his head. Instead I wake up and my heart is knocking down the walls."

"What are you drinking?" the doctor asked.

"Just what I have in my hand," I said. "Brandy."

"Nothing else?"

"Not a drop," I said. "So it can't be from liquor."

"It is," the doc said, and he told me the facts of life about brandy. They impressed me. All during prohibition we were taught that the illegal stuff we drank was dangerous—bathtub gin, alcohol mixed with soda pop, needled beer, New Jersey Scotch. Anything legitimate, we figured, was as safe as mother's milk.

"Your supposition is correct," the doc said. "The point is that you have been educated to drink in quantity, in order to prove that nobody can pass a law ordering you not to hit yourself over the head with a baseball bat. Brandy isn't meant for that sort of work. It's like sacramental wine; before dinner a gentle-man gives thanks; after dinner he drinks brandy."

One night a young man with no hat, a low hairline, and an air of authority walked in. His arms were full of books and magazines—New Republic, The Nation, The New Masses. He introduced himself as John Henry Hammond, Jr. "I have been told that I can hear some interesting piano playing in this place," he said. He sat down at a table and began reading one of his magazines. When Joe Sullivan played he listened. When the Blue Blowers performed he read. He ordered a single drink and sat with it for hours. He came night after night, stayed

222

three or four hours each time, and once in a while ordered two drinks. The waiters were mystified.

"What does he do, this Mr. Hammond?" one of the Greeks asked me. "He does not drink enough. He does not bring a girl. He does not play the suitcase. He reads magazines."

"He listens to our piano player," I said. "He likes jazz."

The Greek shook his head. But one night he came running to me in joy. "Mr. Hammond has ordered a third pony of brandy!" he said.

After a while Hammond came over to the stand and said, "I'd like to take you boys to Harlem tonight to hear a piano player. We'll go in my car."

We went to Harlem almost every night; there were hundreds of buffet flats in the district, each with liquor and music; we knew them all.

"Don't let on you've even been up there," McKenzie said. "This guy's a gentleman; let him show us around."

Hammond drove us to an ordinary speakeasy. A young Negro wearing a white turtle-neck sweater was playing in a light, unimpressive style. We had some drinks and waited patiently. Finally McKenzie said, "Mr. Hammond, when does this piano player you want us to hear show up?" Hammond pointed to the performer in the turtle-neck sweater. "That's he," he said. Red banged his glass on the table.

"Order some more whiskey and get that bum off the stool!" he bellowed. "Joe, go over and straighten him out!"

Joe went to the piano. In ten minutes the place was rocking and the customers were stamping and whistling. Hammond sat quietly, listening.

"I thought we were going to keep quiet and let him show us around?" I said to McKenzie.

"Blow your nose and go home!" Red muttered.

Joe and I lived in a two-room garden apartment at the rear of a building on Fifty-fourth Street between Park and Lexington. We realized that our birthdays were in the same section of November. We decided to celebrate them with parties; Joe's was first.

"We can begin at half-past two, right after we finish work," I said. "We'll gradually siphon in a lot of liquor. We can probably get forty people in here."

"We need a piano," Joe said. "I can't have a birthday party without a piano."

We tried to rent one but there were too many arrangements to make, too many papers to sign. We looked in the newspapers and found an upright for sale. The address was West Fifty-ninth Street. On the morning before the party we got up at nine o'clock and went to it. It was on the fourth floor; the piano was old, battered, and parched; the price was ten dollars. We went to a garage near Plunkett's and hired three Negroes with a truck. I telephoned a piano tuner and asked him to be ready to administer to a sick instrument. We bought a few bottles at Plunkett's and poured them into the boys on the truck—taking a piano down four flights of dark tenement stairs requires loyalty and courage. When it was done we gave them the rest of the whiskey and drove to the apartment. There we had no steps at all, but by that time the boys were drunk and it took them a long time to get through the narrow hallway.

The piano tuner was waiting. He took the front off the upright and worked for hours. It was so old and so dry that he was afraid to bring it up to standard pitch for fear it would explode, but when he finished it was in tune and Joe was satisfied. Meanwhile Slim Kurtzmann called and asked me whether I had a date for the party. I hadn't, so he promised to bring a girl for me, a pretty thing, so he said, from Little Rock, Arkansas.

"Remember not to worry about the wine," he said. "I've got dozens and dozens of bottles for you—Moselle, Burgundy, anything you want."

"That's nice of you, Slim," I said. "Where did you steal it?"

"Nothing is too good for Joe," he said.

The guests were on time; it was easy not to be late at two-thirty in the morning. I was taking care of coats and hats, filling the bathtub with ice, and helping Slim arrange the bottles of wine for chilling. Every now and then I noticed Sullivan talking to the girl who had come to be my date; he was bending over her like a man trying to light a cigarette in a high wind. Since it was Joe's party several of the guests were pianists; they took turns at the upright. Later Fats Waller dropped in; for a while he and Joe alternated at the keyboard. When the wine was cold I called a pause and brought out a dozen bottles.

It was the high point of the morning. Joe pulled the corks. They didn't pop. He poured the wine and we sipped it. It was the most gruesome beverage I have ever had gnawing at my taste buds. I looked at Slim.

"I thought you were a friend," I said.

He confessed. He had taken empty bottles and old corks from the Stork Club, purchased wine bricks, and cooked the Burgundy and Sauterne and Chianti at home. Wine bricks were the great flop of prohibition: the essence of the grape was compressed for you in a package no bigger than a bar of soap; you took it home and made yourself the worst drink in the world.

We toasted the first day of Joe's twenty-sixth year with Billingsley's brandy. After that I remember little except that I never got acquainted with the girl who came to be my date. It

225

didn't matter, because afterward Joe married her and wrote his first piano composition, *Little Rock Getaway*, in honor of the wedding.

Our guests finally left and we went to bed. We woke up in time to get dressed and go to work. I walked into the living room. There had not been much disorder and some of the girls had cleared away the glasses and emptied the ash trays. But something had happened which now slowly I recalled. The best hot piano players in town had been banging on the upright for five continuous hours, with the front off to get volume. I remembered a piano hammer sailing past my head while Fats was playing, and another landing in my lap. They had snapped off under the impact of his left hand. Now I saw piano hammers all over the floor, and on the chairs and in the sofa. One of them was hanging from a picture. The boys had literally beaten the upright to death. I walked over and looked at the corpse. Some of the hammers were hanging out, broken but not snapped off. Others were still intact. I tried the keyboard. There weren't enough notes left to play an octave.

On the night of December twenty-first Joe and I went to Harlem as usual. We got home at a decent hour, ten o'clock in the morning. After a quick nap we went to a party in the east Seventies where some former college musicians we knew were auditioning for a job on a cruise ship. Gin began to flow and time went with it. Suddenly it was twenty minutes of ten.

"McKenzie will cut out our tongues and eat them!" Joe said. "Come on!"

We grabbed a cab and headed for the Stork Club. We feared McKenzie's verbal abuse more than a blowtorch on our fingers.

"Don't circle the block," Joe said to the driver. "Let us off at the corner of Fifty-eighth Street and Sixth Avenue."

226

We paid our fare while the cab was in motion, jumped out at the corner, and raced down the eastbound street. I turned into the Stork at top speed and ran into an enormous man.

"Where do you think you're going?" he roared down at me.

"I'm going in here," I said. "I work here and I'm late. Get out of my way."

He laughed and stayed where he was. By now Joe was also trying to get by him.

"You're not late, you don't work here, and you're not going in," the man said. "Come over here."

He led us to the front door, where several other men were standing. "Look inside," he said.

It was a shambles. Men with axes were hacking up the bar, smashing the glassware, breaking the tables, and shattering the mirrors. The federal prohibition agents were staging a raid. I looked curiously at the argus glass. Customers looking into it saw their reflections; the doorman standing behind it saw the customers. It had always amused me; it gave the real spy touch to prohibition.

"Thanks for the Christmas present," I said to the agent.

"No trouble at all," he said. "Glad to oblige."

"Let's go back to the party," Joe said.

The next day we sent Bland, the ferret, to see about getting our instruments out. The place was padlocked but somehow he got in and brought out the lutes and the suitcase. I never knew how he accomplished such things; it took more than strength, of which he had plenty. At the Bath Club he gave Barry, the doorman, an inferiority complex by beating him at Indian wrestling. Barry considered himself the best rough-and-tumble man in town. "I don't mind being bested," he said, "but a musician has no right doing it. People who play instruments are

227

weak characters and they ought to stay that way. You fellows upset my theory."

"We play jazz," McKenzie said.

"That explains it," Barry said. "You're not musicians."

We spent New Year's Eve at the Napoleon Club on West Fifty-sixth Street, another town house, with a spiral staircase and wrought iron grillwork. Everyone was puzzled about the Stork Club raid. Billingsley had the only first-class speakeasy which had heretofore never been bothered. For three weeks before the agents arrived he had been giving a bottle of wine to each woman customer for Christmas; the news got around and business boomed. Apparently it was too much like the old days; Billingsley was impersonating an honest saloonkeeper. The government couldn't allow it.

Tesch died that January. He was working in Chicago with Wild Bill Davison. They were driving to work in Davison's open car, which had no top. Tesch was sitting with his hands in the pockets of his overcoat. A taxicab without lights hit them broadside in front of a drugstore at Magnolia and Wilson. Tesch was thrown over the hood and struck his head on the curb. He was killed instantly. Davison went to the police station to answer questions. He kept asking a question: "Where will we ever get another saxophone player like Tesch?"

In a few weeks a new Stork Club was opened at Fifty-first Street and Park Avenue and we went into it. We worked until spring, when McKenzie got restless. He had made a record, *Just Friends*, which was popular despite the fact that radio had made the phonograph almost extinct. Whiteman heard it and offered Red a job. Red joined the band in Cleveland; he stayed with it a year.

Meanwhile I sat around New York with my teeth in my

228

mouth, playing parties and club dates, making an occasional record, changing my clothes in Plunkett's icebox, keeping alive on free steaks at Joe Helbock's Onyx, a walk-up speakeasy on the north side of Fifty-second Street which served as a rich man's Plunkett's for musicians. Helbock, who liked jazz, hired Sullivan to play the piano.

The communal system of drinking prevailed at the Onyx as it did at Plunkett's. I might not be making enough to have my shoes half-soled, but I never suffered from thirst. One night I walked in and found Jimmy Dorsey and Jerry Colonna at the bar; Helbock was mixing drinks for them.

"We'd like to ask you to join us, Eddie," Dorsey said solemnly, "but we just decided on a new system. Each night one person will buy all the drinks; tonight that person is you."

"Fine," I said. I turned to Helbock. "Joe," I said, "ask the boys how they'll have their water, hot or cold."

Between sessions at the piano Sullivan used to sit and talk with me. "Eddie," he said one night, "do you think the public will ever make an honest woman out of jazz?"

I was feeling bitter; my rent was due.

"There is no such thing as an honest woman," I said. "There are just women who get higher prices than other women. Jazz is in the lower brackets."

In the spring of 1933 McKenzie left Whiteman; the Mound City Blue Blowers reorganized and returned to the Stork Club. In November repeal came and we were out of a job again.

"Prohibition put my father out of business," I said to McKenzie. "Now the country goes wet and I get fired."

"You shouldn't match nickels with a guy who uses a two-headed coin," Red said.

The speakeasies unlocked their doors and fresh air hit the

229

customers for the first time in thirteen years. The first flood of legal liquor was so bad everyone wished prohibition was back. Night clubs opened on Fifty-second Street like popcorn. The Onyx went across the street. Leon and Eddie's, Tony's, 21, 18, and Reilly's took off the locks and showed lights. Prices went down, musicians were out of work, and the weather turned cold. Max Kaminsky and I were living at the Lismore Hotel on West Seventy-third Street, just off Broadway. The rent climbed up on us like water from a broken dam. One afternoon in February we went around the corner to a Child's restaurant and sat with Bud Bohn, a Chicago boy who had moved to Brooklyn and opened a used car business. Bud had money and wanted company, so we drank and talked. The theme of our conversation was simple—some day we would have a jazz band and it would be appreciated and we would not be out of work every time the wind changed. Three shifts of waitresses came and went; at four o'clock in the morning the bar closed. We saw Bud to the subway, thanked him, and walked around the corner to our hotel.

"Does it seem cold to you?" Maxie said.

We stopped and looked at a drugstore thermometer. It was fourteen degrees below zero.

At the hotel the night clerk smiled but didn't hand us the key to our room.

"It's no use in going up, boys," he said. "The door is locked."

We owed fifty-five dollars. We had enough money for breakfast.

"It's twenty minutes after four," I said to the clerk. "Can't you let us lie down in the room until people start getting up? We can't raise the money now and we can't find a place to sleep."

"I'm sorry," he said. He smiled again; the look in his eyes was considerably below the temperature outside.

Maxie was at the telephone booth. "Artie Shaw has an apartment on Fifty-seventh Street," he said. "There may not be an extra bed but he'll give us floor space."

Shaw had offered us a job in a band he was planning to take to South America; we didn't think he would care if we joined up early. Maxie called him.

"I'll make it short, Artie," he said. "It's fourteen below and we're in it. Have you got some unused floor?"

I watched Maxie's face as he listened; it went slowly through disillusion, irritation, and disgust. "Aw, forget it!" he said suddenly, and hung up.

We stood without saying anything, trying to think. Finally I caught a name which had been eluding me.

"Landseer Apartments!" I said. "Krupa opened tonight at the Paradise with Buddy Rogers. He's staying at the Landseer."

I called him; I didn't tell Maxie that Krupa had just been married and was on his honeymoon. I was afraid he wouldn't let me ask if he knew it.

"Sorry to bother you, Gene," I said, "but Maxie and I have just been locked out of the Lismore and we wondered—"

Krupa interrupted me. "Come right down," he said. "I'm sorry I haven't a better place but this was all we could find. I'll fix the daybed for you in the living room and leave the door open."

He waited up for us, gave us a drink, and tucked us in. Later that morning I went to a delicatessen on Eighth Avenue to buy some ingredients for breakfast. The store was empty. I rapped on one of the cases. The icebox opened and a man came out.

"It's warmer in there than out here in the store," he said. "I was getting thawed out. This is the coldest day I have ever known in my life."

That afternoon Maxie got a job with Joe Venuti, who was opening in a basement club on Broadway. Joe gave him an advance and Maxie got his clothes and his instrument out of hock at the Lismore. It was more than a year before I went back to get my trunk; the manager told me it had been sold at auction for $1.35.

The panic was still on when I moved to the Elk Hotel next to Plunkett's on Fifty-third Street. One Wednesday George Carhart, a banjo player, came to see me.

"Get your summer clothes ready," he said. "You're leaving for South America on the *American Legion*. You're a member of the crew and you're in the band."

George was a Yale boy who liked to travel; when he wanted to take a cruise he exercised his connections with one of the steamship lines, organized an orchestra, stuffed it with his friends, and sailed. He had been to Europe twenty-four times and around the world twice in this fashion.

"You can't use two banjos," I said. "What are you going to do with me?"

"You're going to play the piano," he said.

"In the key of F?"

"What's the difference? It's only for fourteen thousand miles, down to Buenos Aires and back."

At sailing time on Saturday I stood by the gangplank on the dock, waiting for a signal. A professional pianist was performing the bon voyage music. Just as the ship was about to sail he sneaked down the gangplank and I sneaked up. As we pulled away from the dock into the river I stood at the rail with Art

Freeman, Bud's brother. Art, who had never played professionally, was our drummer.

"Well, Eddie," he said, "they're stuck with us now."

In addition to Carhart, Freeman, and myself we had a fiddle player who hardly took his instrument out of its case during the entire voyage. We had one real musician, Morrie Rosenbloom, who played the flute, clarinet, and saxophone. He saved us.

We played for luncheon, for dinner, and for deck dancing at night. We tried everything, even Victor Herbert. Rosenbloom was in front with the melody; we set the beat behind him. On songs which changed key at the release, such as *Smoke Gets In Your Eyes* and *China Boy*, there was nothing for me to do but take cover. "Heavy on the drums!" I yelled to Art, and he blocked me out. I played an oompah bass, keeping my left hand in the same position. One day a small boy stood and watched me, just as the officers came by for inspection. "You play the piano funny," he said. "That's not the way my sister does it." I began to sweat. "Step aside, sonny," I said. "You're annoying the artists."

As crew members we were not allowed in the bar. From the promenade deck we stared gloomily through a small window at the steward, who was mixing drinks. He was sympathetic, but he couldn't get a shot glass through the small space between the grillwork which covered the opening.

"Have you any straws?" George Carhart asked.

That did it. The steward put the drinks on a ledge inside the window, gave us straws, and we drank and sunned ourselves at the same time. We stopped at Bermuda, Rio de Janeiro, Santos, Montevideo, and Buenos Aires. All this time we had with us two Hindu boys from Trinidad, where we were to stop on our way back. They had been rejected at Ellis Island for some tech-

233

nical reason; their families owned large rice plantations on Trinidad. They explained to us how rice fields are inundated during the rainy season, and how crawfish, coming in with the water, damage the crop by snapping off the young plants.

"Why do they do that?" I asked one of the boys, Gamandhi.

"The sun shines on the still water in the fields and makes it very hot," he said. "When the temperature of the water is high the crawfish become very vexed and cut the young plants. It is, of course, a lack of self-control. In a higher animal it would be unforgivable; in a crawfish it is understandable."

In Trinidad we said good-by to Gamandhi. As we walked down the street a prostitute pursued us on a bicycle. "Lack of self-control," George Carhart said. "In a higher animal it would be unforgivable. In a woman it is understandable."

Back at New York we docked in Brooklyn and I left the boys; they may still be in the key of F. I got lost in the subway, wound up in Jamaica, and at midnight staggered into the Onyx. Fidgy McGrath, a professional pianist, introduced me to the customers. "Ladies and gentlemen," he said, "I want you to meet one of the world's most sensational piano players, Eddie Condon. He makes the piano talk—it says, 'Please let me alone!' "

I sat down and had a drink with McKenzie.

"How long does it take for a musician to be a success?" I asked.

"You're nuts from the heat," Red said. "A musician is a man who enjoys his work. How can he be a success?"

Early in June we saw some men who were successful. We played at Princeton for the fifth anniversary of Squirrel Ashcraft's class. Squirrel is a Chicago lawyer who likes jazz and plays the piano.

"There are a lot of guys here who have made a go of their lives, and they seem happy," I said to McKenzie.

"They're happy because they're listening to this music," he answered. "They won't be happy when they go back to their jelly factories and their cement yards and their cotton mills."

I didn't believe him.

PANIC AND
PANCREATITIS

SOUTH OF HARLEM the headquarters of jazz was a store nine feet six inches wide at 144 East Forty-second Street. It sold sporting goods, radios, and records, and was called the Commodore Music Shop. To attract customers the proprietor, Milton Gabler, kept a phonograph going; to please himself he played records he liked. Passersby heard jazz classics from morning until night; record collectors discovered the shop. Gabler, they found, either had what they wanted or could get it. The Commodore became a meeting place for jazz enthusiasts. One of these was Paul Smith, an illustrator, art director, aviator, advertising executive, and amateur guitarist. He was from Minneapolis; one day he passed by the Commodore while Gabler was playing a Wolverines' record of *When My Sugar Walks Down The Street*. He went inside.

"That isn't Bix," he said to Gabler.

Gabler's brown eyes shone and he smiled.

"You're right," he said. "That one was made just after Bix left the band. Jimmy MacPartland played cornet."

Smith joined the informal Commodore jazz club, which by now included John Henry Hammond, Jr., Richard Edes Harrison, and Wilder Hobson. I also joined; sometimes Gabler asked me to assist him in identifying the performers on a cer-

236

tain record. Discography, the history of records, was becoming an important study. In Europe, where the only jazz available was on records, it was already a full-grown scholastic enterprise.

No company ever bothered to list the personnel on a popular or jazz record; the only way to identify the performers was to ask a musician who had been on the date. After long study men like Gabler were able to spot certain performers by their style, but the task of discovering the names of all the players on all the great jazz records was staggering. Still, it was wonderful for me to know that it was being done. I listened to Gabler talk about the greatness of jazz, its recognition as an art by the people of Europe, and its future in America.

"Do you think it will be recognized here before we die?" I asked him one day.

He shrugged his shoulders and smiled; his eyes had the look of a kid sunk in a dream.

"It's recognized now," he said. "It's just a matter of spreading it to a larger number of people. Over here we never think anything is recognized until the entire population takes it up; then we get tired of it and call it common and look for something else. You can't do that with an art; in fact I don't think an art is ever popular; there aren't enough people with taste and understanding to make it popular. It's the cheap imitations of art that are sold by the million."

The cheap imitations of jazz caused the scarcity of records we considered of permanent value. When a popular record sells no more than a thousand copies a year it becomes impractical to continue manufacturing it, though the master, of course, remains in the recording company's files. Thus *Riverboat Shuffle*, a jazz classic, died with *Yes, We Have No Bananas*, a popular tune; so far as the public was concerned both were in the same

237

category; so far as the record companies were concerned it was uneconomical to keep either in circulation. How to get *Riverboat Shuffle* and others like it re-issued was a problem which Gabler bravely tackled. He asked the companies how small an order they would accept for a new pressing of a record. The answer was one thousand.

"It may take me two years to sell them," Gabler said, "but I'll do it."

He placed his orders and the re-issues began—records by the Wolverines, by Pine Top Smith, and by studio bands such as the one I had not assembled and not rehearsed with Fats Waller. On the label appeared the date of the original recording and the names of the men participating. The records were priced at a dollar; they sold quickly. One day a Yale student named Marshall Stearns dropped in to buy some and talked to Gabler about a hot club he had organized at New Haven; he had patterned it after the hot clubs of Europe, whose members were embarrassing American tourists by taking it for granted that all of them were experts on jazz.

"I've got a hot club of my own," Milt said. "It's informal but all the members show up when a re-issue is due."

Stearns wanted to make the re-issues available to the members of his club, and to other hot clubs which were being formed over the country at various colleges. Gabler offered an idea; he would change the label on the re-issues to UHCA— United Hot Clubs of America.

"You get the clubs and organize them," he said to Stearns. "I'll get the records."

At the time fourteen re-issues had appeared. The fifteenth was the first UHCA record; it was *China Boy* and *Bull Frog Blues*, made in Chicago by Charlie Pierce, with Muggsy and

238

Tesch in the band. After that came some of our records, including, *I Found A New Baby*. The next was Bessie Smith's *Young Woman's Blues*. The records were sold only to hot club members; in a short time they were also collector's items, and the problem of keeping the jazz classics available was right back where it started.

"We will have to do some missionary work," Milt said. "We will have to arrange some jam sessions and let people hear the music as it's being created. Then they will want the records and gradually a demand will grow up until there is a market large enough to absorb regular commercial re-issues."

The first session was held in a studio at Decca on a Sunday afternoon. I assembled the musicians; Gabler paid the expenses; his mailing list brought an overflow of guests. Pictures were taken, and some of them appeared in newspapers during the following week. A few of the participating musicians got jobs as a result of the publicity. Gabler's mail increased. The theory seemed to work.

That summer we rehearsed a band for the Onyx, which had suffered a fire and was being redecorated; Jack Kapp of Decca let us use one of his studios. By August the band sounded almost musical; it contained a couple of men I hadn't previously known, Mike Riley, a trombonist, and Ed Farley, a cornet player. One day a girl wandered in and began talking about a gag tune she had heard in Chicago, something called *The Music Goes 'Round And 'Round*. She sang it for the boys:

> You push the middle valve down,
> The music goes 'round and 'round,
> Oh-oh-oh, Oh-oh-oh,
> And it comes out here.

239

We played the chordal structure of *Dinah* for background and Riley tried it out.

"Not a bad novelty," he said.

Paul Smith took charge of the decorating at the Onyx; it was painted in simple bands of color, graduating from light gray near the ceiling to black at the floor. I was without an instrument, so Paul let me take a small four-string guitar, tuned like a banjo. We opened and I found out about Riley and Farley. During rehearsals they had conducted themselves as musicians; an audience transformed them into clowns. They poured water over each other, scuffled, mugged, and did everything but play music. Manny Klein, a cornet player who dropped in for a drink and saw the slapstick, went to a bakery and bought a lemon meringue pie. He gave it to Riley and said, "I dare you." Riley took the pie and hit Farley in the face with it. After that it happened every night, and I nicknamed Riley and Farley Lemon Meringue and Mince.

When the clowning started I left the stand and went to the bar. No matter how low you fall, I thought, there's always room underneath: wearing a jersey and cap and playing a lute, keeping a band in the key of F for fourteen thousand miles, and now a trombone player who throws lemon meringue pies. But a man isn't compelled to step down. I didn't. I was fired.

McKenzie and I moved to an opposition club across the street, the Famous Door. It occupied the old quarters of the Onyx, with a downstairs room added. Billie Holiday, the singer, had preceded us, with Teddy Wilson on piano. We took over the relief piano player, a young New Yorker named Joe Bushkin; Bunny Berigan played trumpet. We used a saxophone and string bass and got along without drums. Lee Wiley, a girl from Oklahoma, dropped in to sing occasionally. The manager,

240

Jim Doane, liked our music and let us play it without interruption. He agreed with us that the decorations on the mirror panels which ran around the room were insulting and in bad taste—they consisted of musical notes. One night after closing he and Johnny DeVries, the illustrator, and I went to work on the mirrors. I had a bottle of paint remover and Jim had a bottle of whiskey; between us we wiped off the notes. DeVries came along behind us, painting caricatures of frowsy blondes, gentlemen drunks, dancers, and a frightening representation of an alcoholic stomach, filled with beer caps, cigarette butts, ash trays, broken glass, burnt matches, and ice. There were fourteen square mirrors and two rectangular ones; Johnny painted something on each one. He was a practiced improviser; once he decorated George Wettling's room with toothpaste.

The club took its name from a small door made of plain wood on which visitors scribbled their names. The signatures I remember as memorable were those of the musicians who came to the jam sessions we held on Sunday afternoons. We didn't charge admission; the audience sat around buying drinks while the best jazz men in the country played for their own amusement. Bessie Smith was in town for a while; she came over and sang: *Baby Won't You Please Come Home, Mama's Got The Blues, I'm Wild About That Thing, The Gin House Blues, Dirty No Gooder's Blues,* and *Nobody Knows You When You're Down And Out.* She was still the great Bessie; hearing her magnificent voice complain about the sadness of living made life a lot easier to bear. On that Sunday afternoon Bessie seemed immortal; she had one more year to live. Mildred Bailey was there that day but she refused to sing. She was right; no one could follow Bessie.

One of the audience that afternoon was a young intern from

Polyclinic Hospital. I had met him a few months before, when I went to the hospital to have some abscesses lanced. At the Onyx I had been forced to wear a uniform; the jacket was too small and the cheap dye ran and irritated the skin under my arms. When the abscesses appeared I had been fired and was too broke to go to a doctor. I walked to Polyclinic and went to the emergency room. An intern worked on me.

"That will cost you a quarter," he said when he was through. I searched my pockets. "I haven't a quarter," I said. The intern was puzzled. I was too well-dressed to be that empty.

"You haven't a quarter?" he said. "What do you do for a living?"

"I could be an intern," I said, "but I'm the next lowest thing —a musician."

He smiled. "We have a combination of that here—an intern who is a musician," he said. "I'll introduce you to him."

He brought in a black-haired, friendly young man whom he introduced as Dr. Joseph Slovak. Slovak said he had earned his way through Union College playing the saxophone and had worked as a professional musician in Albany for a year before coming to New York.

"Any time you need a doctor, call me," he said. "I owe music something—it gave me my education."

One morning early in 1936 Joe Bushkin and I left Dave's Blue Room at five-thirty and took a taxi home. I got out at the Elk Hotel. "See you tonight," I said to Joe. Two hours later I woke with a blazing pain which filled me from my neck to my hips. Whatever it is, I thought, it's bad. McKenzie came by and found me doubled up and moaning. He went to Polyclinic and came back with Slovak, who gave me an injection of morphine.

242

"Let me know when the pain goes away," he said. "If it means an operation you'll be better off at the hospital tomorrow, when Dr. McGrath is operating."

The pain didn't stop. McKenzie and Bushkin took turns sitting with me. Slovak returned every few hours; when it was necessary he gave me more morphine. At four o'clock the next morning he said, "If the pain hasn't eased by eight o'clock come to the hospital."

At eight o'clock it was worse. Bushkin helped me into my clothes; I was bent over like a horseshoe. At the hospital I was placed on a table and six doctors tried to diagnose the trouble. One of them was Dr. John J. McGrath; he was then over seventy; he had been a surgeon for fifty years.

"Please, Doc," I said to him, "operate here"—I drew a finger across my throat.

The blood count on my white corpuscles was high, indicating infection. It was decided to operate immediately. I was put behind a screen. Someone asked me my religion. An orderly came with a dull razor and shaved the hair from my chest and abdomen; he could have peeled the skin from me with less pain. Then a priest came and touched my forehead. "This may be your last confession," he said. "What do you wish to tell me?"

I can't go through all that now, I thought. Bless me, Father; I disobeyed my parents, I disobeyed my sisters, I disobeyed the nuns, I disobeyed you, Father. Say seven Hail Mary's and the stations of the cross and go home and wash your face.

"I can't be put in jail for anything I've ever done," I said. "You'll have to settle for that."

They gave me ether and operated. My pancreas had burst and its juice was dripping into my abdomen, trying to digest

243

whatever it touched. Half of my appendix was gone. Such cases had a 99.9 per cent mortality; in his fifty years of surgery Dr. McGrath had operated on five; all had died. No one held any hope for me.

When the operation was finished I was wheeled into the deathroom, a small cubicle where a man can pass out without bothering his fellow ward patients. My temperature went to 106 and I began to sink. Slovak was in charge of my exit; he called McKenzie and told him I needed a blood transfusion. Red arrived with Joe Bushkin, Bud and Artie Freeman, and Mike Gould. Joe was ruled out as a minor; it was all right for an eighteen-year-old boy to work in a night club but he couldn't give blood to a friend. None of the others was the right type. "We'll have to use a professional donor," Slovak said. Bud, who had a bank account, put up the money. While this was going on I thought I was at Decca making a record and kept shouting for Harry Kruse. I woke once and saw blood on the linen and a transfusion apparatus. It must be bad, I thought. Then I went back to Decca. I still couldn't find Harry.

The fever lasted for three days and three nights. I was rubbed with whiskey and wrapped in hot blankets. When McKenzie found out about the whiskey massages he brought a bottle from the Famous Door.

"What's that for?" Miss Roach, the nurse, asked.

"It's to rub Mr. Condon with," McKenzie said.

Miss Roach sniffed. "We only use bonded whiskey!" she said.

McKenzie stared. "To rub a guy with?" he said.

He opened the bottle and he and Berigan and Bushkin drank it.

There was no chance for me, but Slovak kept trying. I was given extreme unction, the church's sacrament for the dying.

244

Then my temperature came down, my mind cleared, and I began to get well. Dr. McGrath was digging for dandruff; he was glad I was improving but he wondered why. I tried to give the credit to Slovak but he declined. "It's because of the life you lead," he said. "Drinking a quart of milk at five o'clock in the morning is the secret of better health."

I remained in the deathroom until the day before I left the hospital; Miss Roach gave McKenzie, Berigan, and Bushkin special dispensation to visit me after work, at four-thirty in the morning.

"I don't like this little room," McKenzie used to say. "They still must be betting on you to blow the race."

The day I was moved to a ward Mezzrow came to see me; he brought a box of Persian dates. The door to the deathroom was shut. Thinking I was sleeping he opened it slowly and looked in. He saw a figure covered completely by a sheet—the tenant who succeeded me died in a hurry. Mezz backed out, dropped the dates, and turned to run just as Miss Roach came along.

"Are you looking for Mr. Condon?" she said. "He's down the hall in the ward." She helped him pick up the dates and led him to my bed.

"Perhaps you ought to get up and let your friend lie down for a while," she said to me.

Mezz dropped the dates again, this time on my stomach.

"I b-b-b-brought you something," he said. "Thanks for not being dead."

Burris Jenkins, the cartoonist, invited me to spend a few weeks of convalescence at his home in Pelham. He picked me up at the hospital the night I was discharged. We stopped at the Famous Door to say good-by to the boys. Tommy Dorsey, Bud Freeman, and Dave Tough were there; as we came in they were sitting in with the band, tearing the clothes off Dinah. Burris was fascinated. "I've never heard music like that," he said to me. "What is it?" I told him. It's amazing how many North Americans have never heard jazz, I thought.

Berigan came over and put a twenty-dollar bill in my hand. "I owe you this," he said. "I thought if I kept it until you got out you'd have a better chance of making it." I thanked him. I was broke, as usual. "This is the best hypodermic I've had in three weeks," I said. Bunny smiled. "Someday I may be in the same spot myself," he said. He was. A few years later he died in Polyclinic.

Fifty-second Street was booming when I got back to work. A jazz term I first heard in Chicago had caught on with the kind of people who demand something new. The word was swing and it was the "new music." Swing bands took the town over; some played jazz, some played garbage. After the Famous Door closed I worked successively at the 18 Club, the Hickory House, and the Red McKenzie Club. Red's backers were a restaurant family trained in serving good food to quiet people; they were puzzled by the patrons who came to hear our music; business was fair but the service was so bad the place failed anyhow. We had an excellent band: Joe Bushkin, George Wettling, Artie Shapiro on bass, and the Marsala brothers from Chicago, Marty on trumpet and Joe on clarinet. Wettling and I were living together on East Thirty-eighth Street, along with my brother Pat, who had finished another course in bumology.

At the time Artie Shaw had a string sextet. His playing impressed George Gershwin, and Artie found himself booked for a run at the Paramount Theater. He organized a full band for the date, with Wettling on drums. Just before the opening

246

his guitar player went to a hospital with appendicitis and I re-placed him. The band wore uniforms and ugly brown suede shoes. At one point in the performance I had to stand up, put my right foot on a chair, and play a sixteen-bar solo. Otherwise both my feet were hidden by a music stand. Wettling's right foot was hidden by his bass drum; his left was visible to the audience. We wore the same size shoe, and since each musician had to buy his own uniform and accessories, we shared a pair of the brown suede atrocities. George wore the left one, I wore the right one. The band sat in the pit, which was elevated for the stage show. The movie was *Pennies from Heaven* with Bing Crosby and Louis Armstrong. I stayed in the pit and watched it again and again. During one performance I had Colin Campbell, a friend, with me. When it was time for the stage show Colin said, "I'd better get out of here or I'll be lifted up with the rest of you."

"Sit by the organ," I said. "It doesn't go up."

But it did. I turned around just in time to see Colin frantically scrambling off as the spotlight picked us up.

By December the Red McKenzie Club was well on its way to failure. One night Paul Smith dropped in and suggested that I spend the holidays cruising on the *Empress of Britain*.

"All you've got to do is organize an eight-piece band for a nine-day cruise," he said. "The sailing date is December 28th; the ship stops at Havana and Kingston, Jamaica. You'll be back in time for the cold weather."

Over McKenzie's protests I got together the Marsalas, Bush-kin, and Artie Shapiro. I also hired Al Seidel, a drummer. I needed two more men, but every other good musician I knew was engaged for the holidays. I called Max Kaminsky in Pitts-burgh. "Can't you hold the boat until January 2nd?" Maxie said. "I'd love to go." I even tried to get Dr. Slovak, but he had agreed to stay at the hospital so the other interns could be home for Christmas. In desperation I decided on Pat, which gave me two guitar players. The day before sailing I was still short a man. "It looks as if you're going to be the third guitar player," I said to Paul.

I barely escaped from Fats Waller in time to make the sailing; I was on the wagon except for wine, but there was plenty of that around. The next morning I hung over the rail, sick; the sea was smooth. That afternoon we played an introductory cocktail party. First we listened to the fifteen-piece English band with which we were to alternate. Since we had three guitar players I decided to act as conductor. The room was hot; we were dressed in tuxedos. My shoes had hard heels, the small podium was slick, and the roll of the ship worried me. I had no baton. A tall steward named Flack stood near by and stared at me all the time we were playing. He can't throw us off now, I thought; some of these boys can't swim.

At night there was a floor show. We assembled to play and the master of ceremonies said, "Ladies and gentlemen, there is a question we all ask these days. What is swing? Tonight Eddie Condon and his boys will answer that question." He extended his hand toward me. I turned to check the band. Marty Marsala was missing.

"The answer will be slightly delayed," I said. "We were to open with *Bugle Call Rag*, which begins with a trumpet solo. As soon as we find our trumpeter we'll begin."

Marty was on deck with Colin Campbell, who had come along for the ride; the two were gazing at the moon. Probably the delay increased the interest of the audience in what we were going to play; our concert was enthusiastically received.

Afterward we played for dancing, alternating every half hour with the English band. One of the women passengers, an American, invited us to the Knickerbocker Bar for champagne. "It's nice to have a good band on board," she said. "It makes me feel at home." "That makes everyone at home but us," I said. Flack, the steward, was still watching me.

The next day Paul and I were in the Knickerbocker Bar. I was drinking fernet branca, an allegedly medicinal drink which betrayed me. Arthur and Schuyler Kudner, Chicago boys who had migrated to New York and opened an advertising agency, came in, followed by Vincent Bendix and Bob Neely, our sponsor at the Bath Club. The lady who had been our hostess the night before joined the Kudners; she was Bunny McLeod, wife of Norman McLeod, director of *Pennies from Heaven*. Neely ordered drinks for us.

"We'll get a piano in here," he said, "and have some music."

Flack shook his head when we asked that one of the small uprights be brought into the bar. "Absolutely not," he said quietly.

Neely went to the captain. Flack disappeared and returned with two deck hands and a piano. The piano got stuck in the doorway. While the deck hands shoved and pulled we surrounded Flack and gave him advice. His mouth tightened and his face turned red, but he only said, "Possibly you're right, sir. . . . Perhaps that is the correct technique, sir. . . . It may be the best approach to the problem, sir." When the piano was inside Bushkin came up and played for several hours. Later I was called to the office of one of the cruise supervisors, a woman.

"Mr. Condon," she said, "as leader of the orchestra you are entitled to freedom of the ship. I must remind you, however, that this is not true for the musicians under your direction. They must not gather socially in places reserved for passengers."

"Such as the Knickerbocker Bar?"

"Precisely."

I took a firm grip on my temper and then let go of it.

"My dear lady," I said, "the musicians in my band did not come on this cruise to make money or to provide themselves with employment. They are on vacation from work which pays five times the coolie wages you are giving them. They are here to enjoy themselves and to relax, not to be locked in a coal chute during the time they are not performing.

"If you want them to sleep with the cargo and drink off the rudder, and if you can force them to do it, don't exclude me. Wherever they go I'll go with them, and I'll go first."

I didn't wait for her to answer; I walked out and called the boys together.

"From now on I want all of you in the Knickerbocker Bar as often and for as long as possible," I said. "That's all."

I went into the bar and sat down with Paul and Pat. I was so angry I forgot about medicinal drinks and ordered whiskey. In somewhat less than a hundred thousand loosely chosen words I described my encounter with the supervisor. Paul sipped his drink thoughtfully.

"Now that you've started talking for the boys, why don't you keep on doing it?" he asked.

"Just let anybody start pushing them around," I said. "Just let that steward Flack—"

"I don't mean that," Paul said. "I'm thinking of jazz musicians in general. Ever since I've known them they have been playing in night clubs and saloons and dance halls, being hired with no one to bargain for them, being fired with no one

250

to argue for them. Like most artists they are inarticulate outside of their own medium of expression. A lot of articulate people are enthusiastic about their music, but is there a jazz man who can talk for his music, bargain for it, publicize it, and demonstrate to people what jazz really is?"

I had to admit there wasn't.

"There are men who misrepresent jazz," Paul went on. "They commercialize it, organize it, prostitute it, and convince the public that jazz can be played from arranged music by sixty men whose only qualification for musicianship is that they read notes. They play on radio programs and tour the country; they pick off the good jazz men one by one and bury them in their tiers of horns and reeds. You don't like it and the guys don't like it, but what do you do about it?"

"Except when he's sleeping," Pat said, "he talks about it. We all do. Music is like everything else; it suffers from monopolistic control. The public never hears what it wants to hear; it gets a prize package with a tin whistle at the bottom."

"How many capable jazz men are there in the country today?" Paul asked. "Are there a hundred? Probably not. The percentage is the same in any art—thousands try to write or paint or sculpt or compose and a handful really qualify. How many great concert artists are there in classical music? If you match them with top jazz players the lists would probably be about even.

"Jazz is one of the forms of musical art. It has its *virtuosi*. Where are they? They are playing in saloons and cellars, or in a tier of trumpets or clarinets in somebody's symphonic swing band, or on the *Empress of Britain* for board and room and cigarette money."

Pat struck the table with his left fist, the revolutionary one.

251

"They should organize!" he said. "They should have a leader and a spokesman. They should hold meetings and—"

"Why don't you be it?" Paul said to me quietly. "You know the musicians, you know people such as I, who want to do something for jazz, and you have hemophilia of the larynx. You couldn't stop talking if you wanted to. Why don't you put your monologues to a good purpose?"

The whiskey was the first I had drunk in eleven months; it affected me. I talked briefly for half an hour.

"That's precisely what I mean," Paul said. "You said it very well, especially during the first ten minutes."

"What did I say?" I asked.

"You said jazz asks for only two things—the respectability accorded other forms of art, and a chance to be heard."

I sipped a fresh drink. "That's fine," I said. "Now how are we going to get those two things?"

Pat tapped on the table with his left forefinger, the conniving one.

"Organize the parish," he said. "Circulate among the boys and let them know they have a unity and a common strength. Locate a few places of assembly—"

"We can't have meetings and offices," I said. "This is something else—we need jobs for the men and publicity for the music."

"Exactly," Paul said. "You've already begun. Just keep jabbering. Why did you take so long to start?"

I ordered another drink. "It took me a long time to get mad," I said.

Pat banged for attention with his revolutionary fist. "Let me tell you about places of assembly," he demanded. "You don't need offices and you don't need meeting.. Adapt your technique to the natural habitat of the musician."

"The saloon?"

"What else?" he said. "The saloon is where the jazz man eats, drinks, talks, makes his telephone calls, gets hired, gets fired, meets his girl, changes his shirt, spends his money, borrows it back, gets his mail, answers it, and leaves his instrument for safekeeping."

We ordered more whiskey and drank a toast.

"To the revolution of the saloons," Paul said, "to the emancipation of jazz."

What am I getting into? I thought; I must be loaded.

Flack, the steward, stood near whenever we played. After the first day he kept his eyes on the two guitar players. One night between sets he spoke to Paul. "Do you do something else besides play that guitar?" he asked. Paul knew he was discovered; he took out his wallet and showed Flack his pilot's license and membership cards in various clubs. "I thought so," the steward said. Then he smiled and invited Paul and me to his stateroom. We were nervous but we went. He closed the door carefully, took a bottle of whiskey from a cabinet, and offered us a drink. Then he sat down and smiled again.

"I like American music very much," he said. "You chaps do it as well as any I ever heard." He looked at Paul. "Fast company, isn't it?" he said.

Flack became our pal. He saw to it that we were sufficiently supplied with various types of nourishment, and he stood near the bandstand every night while we played, apparently rigid but rocking almost imperceptibly to the music. For New Year's Eve the sports deck was waxed and we played there for dancing. At Kingston we drank daiquiris; Pat went off to take the pulse

253

of the revolution. That night at the Myrtle Bank Hotel I was paged. It was Pat; he was running a temperature* and had a guitar in his hand. "Come on," he said. "I've got eight saloons lined up for the jazz revolution!" I sent him away.

At Havana we were driven into the country to a native night club with a dirt floor. The musicians used tom-toms and a young girl danced with a glass of water on her head. At a certain point in the performance she stopped in front of Colin Campbell and put the glass of water on his head. Colin, a shy Scotsman, sat quietly and blushed. Pat took the manager of the place aside and organized him for the jazz revolution. Paul and I listened carefully to the tom-toms; the beat was familiar—Krupa, Tough, Wettling, Zutty Singleton, Baby Dodds, they all had it.

On board ship the next day we met our captain, whose name was Hilton. "I have enjoyed your music," he said to me. We began talking about it, while Paul stood aside and drew a caricature of the captain. When it was finished Hilton accepted it, looked at it, and said, "Very good." Then he turned the sheet over, took a pencil from his pocket, and drew an excellent caricature of Paul. After that he invited us to his cabin. When the door was closed and a drink was poured he went to a wall safe and took out a beautiful Hawaiian guitar, inlaid with mother-of-pearl.

"I wonder if you could tell me if this is a good instrument," he said to Paul. "I'm only an amateur performer; I wouldn't know. I'd appreciate the judgment of a professional."

Paul avoided my eyes while he tried a few chords and assured the captain that he had not been cheated. I listened and watched enviously; I still did not have an instrument of my own.

* mildly intoxicated

The banjo had gone out of fashion while I was playing a lute with the Blue Blowers. The six-string guitar, tuned like a ukulele, with two bass strings added, did not appeal to me. Ukulele tuning lacked the wide chordal possibilities and the rich voicing of banjo tuning. For setting the beat and giving the structural background in a jazz band the guitar with ukulele tuning was, I thought, inadequate. Experimenting with Paul's four-string guitar tuned like a banjo, I had discovered resources which intrigued me. I decided to get a full-sized guitar, use four strings, and stick to banjo tuning. I had never had a desire to play solos; neither the banjo nor the guitar, in my opinion, is suited to such individual performance. I wanted only to remain where I belonged, in the rhythm section.

"What instrument do you play, Mr. Condon?" the captain asked.

"At this point," I said, "I'm not sure."

NICK'S
AND THE REVOLUTION

BACK in New York I was inclined to forget the jazz revolution, but neither Paul nor circumstance would let me. I went to work again at the Hickory House, with Joe and Marty Marsala. One night Paul dropped in and brought a girl with him. Her name was Phyllis.

"There are five Smith brothers," she said. "I'm one of the two sisters."

She had come to town to work as an advertising copy writer. She began scribbling publicity ideas for the jazz revolution. "You've got to get this music out of the saloons and into the concert halls," she said.

Who the hell are you? I thought, to be telling me what to do.

She had a definite air about her; she was also attractive. She began calling me on the telephone in mid-afternoon. "Time to get up and take a look at the trap line," she would say. I would find myself at Reilly's saloon on Fifty-second Street at five-o'clock, wondering why I was up before dark. I'm a conservative guy and I like sleep, I thought; what am I doing up at sunset starting a revolution?

My father died that spring. Pat didn't come back to New York after the funeral, but he left a memory. He had been eating at the Hickory House and charging it. One night I had to ask for an advance in salary. The boss had a prominent abdomen; I tapped it playfully and forgot to pull my punch. At the same time I said, "How about a few of your ill-earned bucks in advance of my honest wages?" He grabbed his middle and sat down. When his breath returned he blew it at me. "You're fired!" he bellowed.

Joe Marsala and I were living at the Plymouth Hotel on West Forty-ninth Street. During the next few weeks I sat around watching the rain come down and the rent come up. Bobby Hackett, a Rhode Island boy, arrived in town with his orchestra, following a successful run in Boston at the Theatrical Club. A club was to be opened for him in New York, but the idea was abandoned and the band had to break up. Bobby, a fine trumpeter, also played guitar; he took my place at the Hickory House.

"It's disgraceful!" Phyllis Smith said. "It shouldn't be possible for things like that to happen. You shouldn't have been fired and Hackett's band shouldn't have had to break up. But as long as you have no organization, no recognition, and no spokesman, nothing can be done about it."

She looked at me with very blue and serious eyes. What's it to her, I thought?

"It's a matter of recognition," I said. "As long as a jazz man is just a musician in the opinion of those who hire him and those who hear him, he can be replaced by anyone who can hold an instrument."

One day I was meditating in my room with a few lay brothers, including Colin Campbell, when Joe Marsala came in looking illegally happy. He called me into the bathroom and showed me a roll of bills thicker than a wrestler's head.

"Belmont," he whispered. "Take whatever you need."

257

I peeled off enough for the rent and went back into the room. "Colin," I said, "you have just acquired a roommate." Colin lived at the Beaux Arts Apartments on East Forty-fourth Street. He helped me pack, I paid the bill, and we went to the Beaux Arts, where the air was better and I could look at the river while contemplating my sins. Not far away, on the southeast corner of Forty-fourth Street and Third Avenue, was Tim Costello's saloon, a watering place for writers, newspapermen, Irishmen, and residents of the neighborhood. During the dull hours Tim and his brother Joe discussed points in James Joyce's *Ulysses*, citing page numbers and paragraphs from memory. On the walls were decorations by James Thurber, a customer. John McNulty, a reporter who had won a brogue on a punchboard, was usually there; he was fine company for me and he never seemed busy. He drank vichy water.

"What does he do?" I asked Joe Costello.

"He's a chronicler," Joe said. "In ancient Ireland every important family had its chronicler, to keep a record of important events and to make sure that a few legends grew up along the way. McNulty is our chronicler. He is also something of a brehon; a brehon is an expert on law. In ancient Ireland every family had a brehon too. Around here it is more ritual than law, but McNulty is our expert. He writes little magazine articles about how things are done here.

"You see," he went on, "in order for a civilization to remain healthy it must adequately support the ornaments of its culture."

He paused politely while I swallowed my drink. When he had poured me another he said:

"The delight of a good society is that a man can develop the best part of himself and use it to give pleasure to others. It may

258

be as small a thing as painting a pole, but if he does it better than anyone else he is distinguished and happy and the country is full of beautifully painted poles."

He gave me some water in a small glass.

"Over here," he went on, "a man is expected to do his job poorly for as much money as he can get from his employer by either personal or collective bargaining. Usually his employer doesn't know the difference between a good job and a bad job so it makes no difference; the high price and the bad work are passed on to the consumer. There are a lot of poles and they all have flags on them but very few are beautifully painted. It's a wonderful country but it has very little art; everyone is too busy being successful—getting more money for doing less work. McNulty writes well and is poorly paid for it. He is an artist."

"Do you charge for the conversation or just for the whiskey?" I asked.

"Just for the whiskey," Joe said. "The conversation is part of the entertainment. In places where the customers don't want to think the management hires musicians. In here the customers think."

A few blocks away was the Commodore Music Shop. I sat and talked with Gabler and listened while he played records. The re-issues were selling out as fast as they appeared; originals of the jazz classics were harder and harder to find.

"The trouble with re-issues is that when they are sold I am no better off than I was in the beginning," Milt said one day. "I don't own the master records and I can't get the rights to them. I've been thinking of making some records myself, under my own label. Most of the men who played on the discs I've re-issued are still available. Why can't we get them together and make some new ones?"

"They're not only available," I said, "they're better musicians. It's ten years since I made my first record in Chicago. Except for Tesch and Jim Lannigan—he's with the Chicago Symphony Orchestra—all the boys are active. Ten years of additional experience hasn't hurt their playing."

Gabler nodded. "The trouble is they are scattered all over the country, playing with the big bands," he said. "It would take a lot of planning and some delicate timing to get the right ones together for a recording date. Bud Freeman is with Tommy Dorsey, Jess Stacy is with Benny Goodman, Jack Teagarden is with Whiteman. . . ."

"You can try," I said. "Sooner or later they'll all be in town at the same time."

"I think I will," Milt said. "Somebody's got to do it sometime."

That fall McKenzie turned up with a job in Greenwich Village, at a place called Nick's.

"Guy named Nick Rongetti owns it," he said. "He went all the way through Georgetown and Fordham to be a lawyer—wish I had his nose full of information. He's a Dixieland guy; likes to play the piano. The place is a cigar box down on Seventh Avenue at Tenth Street. He's building a new place across the street. Sharkey Bonana is playing for him now; he wants another band."

"Did he ever pass the bar?" I asked.

"What's the difference?" McKenzie said. "He owns one."

Nick had a long chin and a lot of ideas. He liked jazz and wanted a lot of it, created by the best men available. His club was a place on the west side of the street; it was drawing the jazz audience downtown. Sharkey Bonana, an excellent trumpet player from New Orleans, had Dave Bowman on piano and

George Brunies, of the old New Orleans Rhythm Kings, on trombone. I had a curious feeling the night McKenzie took me into the place and I heard the music. Greenwich Village was supposed to be a district where good things were given a chance. McKenzie must have known what I was thinking. "This guy likes music and he leaves the musicians alone," he said. "It's not like the old days in Chicago, but it's not like Fifty-second Street either."

Across the street on a vacant lot Nick was putting up a one-story building with store fronts grouped around a club cut like a piece of pie—the entrance was at the point, the bandstand was in the center of the crust. We began rehearsing a band for its opening; we borrowed George Brunies and Dave Bowman from Sharkey and added Bobby Hackett, Pee Wee Russell, a drummer named Nunu, and Clyde Newcomb, a bass player. A building strike delayed things across the street; we went into the cigar box, alternating with Sharkey. In the middle of December we lugged our instruments across Seventh Avenue and Nick proudly showed us the two pianos he had installed, one for himself.

"I hope you'll be happy here," he said. "Now get up on the stand and play."

For the next eight years I was in and out of Nick's more often than the mailman. He fired me regularly—it may have had something to do with sunspots—and sent for me on schedule. He was always justified in bouncing me, and he was always logical in hiring me again. Actually we had the same enthusiasm and the same point of view—we believed in jazz and wanted others to believe in it—but Nick had one theory of propaganda and I had another. "Play the music," Nick said. "Play the music and talk about it," I said. "Talk about it to the right people. Get

261

pictures and articles in newspapers and magazines. Get it played on the radio." "Get up on the stand and play that guitar," Nick said.

Between sets I talked with the customers, particularly those whose written or spoken word might help the cause. Sometimes I considered that my presence at one of the tables was doing more for jazz than my appearance on the stand. Nick disagreed with me. "I want you on the stand," he said. "I am not paying you to talk." I tried to explain to him that because of talk the club might be mentioned in newspaper columns. "Will that make the music better?" he said.

Usually between sets I went down the street to Julius' saloon, fifty yards east on Tenth Street. It had sawdust on the floor, the best hamburgers in town, and decorations from the days when the place catered to the carriage trade. It admitted to being the oldest saloon in New York; it had remained open during prohibition without locking its door. Usually I took some of our customers with me when I went there, and this irritated Nick all the more. I admitted his point. I spent the money he paid me in Julius', took his customers with me, and was late getting back to the bandstand. But references to Nick's began turning up in newspapers and magazines; business was better and better. One night I met a quiet young fellow with round spectacles who said he worked for a magazine publishing company. His name was Ernest Anderson.

"How can this music be promoted?" I asked him.

He told me. I missed one whole set and part of another. "You're fired!" Nick said. Anderson and I became partners.

In January, 1938, the first records were made for Milt Gabler's Commodore label. The date was changed again and again; the men we wanted were in and out of town half a dozen times

262

before all of them were available on the same day. Jess Stacy was the last to shake himself free. He played a concert with Benny Goodman at Carnegie Hall the night before. In the morning the Goodman band had a recording date. Gabler explained the situation to Benny.

"Everyone else is ready," he said. "Eddie is bringing Hackett and Pee Wee and Brunies from Nick's. Bud Freeman, George Wettling, and Artie Shapiro are here. All we need is Jess."

"He'll be there," Benny said. "I'll postpone our date."

In honor of Benny we named the first two sides *Carnegie Jump* and *Carnegie Drag*. They were improvisations on ideas contributed by Jess and Bud. They were made on a twelve-inch record—Gabler realized that a jam session needs room for development. On a ten-inch record we made *Ja-Da* and *Love Is Just Around The Corner*. Then Jess, Bud, and George Wettling made some sides as a trio. Gabler was happy. He had shuffled the arrangement of men to get better balance and to suit his notion that all the instruments should be audible during all of the record.

"I want to be able to hear any instrument in the band any time I want to listen to it," he said, "and I want it that way on all my records. Well, we're on our way with the first independent label in the recording business. The rest will be history."

It was; the records were an instantaneous success. Gabler set a second date for April.

I shadow-boxed myself into some courage and went to the Chrysler Building to see Hank Brennan, art director of *Fortune* magazine, and Richard Edes Harrison, the cartographer. My mission was simple; I wanted reportorial and photographic coverage on a Commodore recording. I talked in a normal tone of voice for somewhat less than an hour; I mentioned the condition

263

to which jazz had been reduced by public indifference; I gave the personnel of the band being assembled, the system of free enterprise employed in the music, and the popularity of the first record. Brennan and Harrison sent for Alexander King, one of the editors of Life magazine and a jazz fan. King listened to a summary of my argument and said, "Fine. Let's get a photographer and cover the date. We'll do the story in Life."

"I have the photographer," I said. "There is a guitarist named Charlie Peterson who played with Rudy Vallee and who saved his money. He is now a professional photographer and he knows how to handle musicians. He won't bother them when he shouldn't bother them and he'll get what you want."

Gabler had difficulty again in finding a day when all the men were free and in town. We finally assembled with the same line-up except for Brunies, who was replaced by Jack Teagarden. For the twelve-inch sides we did Embraceable You and a blues featuring Pee Wee Russell, which we called Serenade to a Shylock. Jack Teagarden sang an improvised chorus beginning:

Oh, Mama, Mama, Mama, where did you stay last night?
Oh, Mama, Mama, Mama, where did you stay last night?
'Cause the last I saw you, your hair didn't look just right.

For the ten-inch record we played Meet Me Tonight In Dreamland and Diane. Peterson took pictures of everything but the inside of our shoes. The reaction at Life was enthusiastic; Pee Wee and his elastic face were to be on the cover. I told Nick. "Get on the stand and play," he said. I explained to him about the circulation of Life. "I can't hear pictures," he said.

That spring the British Broadcasting Corporation organized a jam session in New York for a broadcast direct to England. It was to be a special treat for English jazz fans, who were confined like the Europeans to hearing the music on records, most of them old and the majority of them collectors' items. The party was held during the afternoon in the Viennese Room of the St. Regis Hotel, with Alastaire Cook in charge. Admission was by invitation; the audience sat at tables and sipped drinks while the best musicians in town, assembled by Joe Marsala, played. Bobby Hackett, Hot Lips Page, Marty Marsala, and Yank Lausen alternated on trumpet; Zutty Singleton and Dave Tough spelled each other at the drums; Joe Bushkin and Jess Stacy played piano; the clarinetists were Mezzrow and Joe Marsala. Lee Wiley sang Sugar, W. C. Handy spoke, and once during the broadcast Mezz edged up to the microphone and said, "Hello, England, this is Mezz!" I left in time to hear Benny Goodman play his first Town Hall concert with the Budapest String Quartet. The obvious success of the BBC party and the presence of Benny at Town Hall playing Mozart started something mixing in my mind. John Chapman of the Daily News took me with him from the broadcast to the concert; the next day his column, "Mainly About Manhattan," concerned itself with the two musical occasions. Why couldn't the jazz concert have been held in Town Hall? I wondered. "It could," Phyllis Smith said.

Ernie Anderson and Paul Smith thought we ought to begin jam sessions patterned after the BBC party. We considered a subscription series and organized the New York Society of Musicians; the title carried neither appeal nor information, and across the first set of tickets we stamped a new name, The Friday Club. When we tried to rent a hotel room we were turned down by the Waldorf Astoria, the St. Regis, and the Ambassador; one mention of jazz and the doors were shut. Finally the Park Lane, a quiet, residential hotel at 299 Park Avenue, allowed us to hire its main ballroom for a Friday afternoon concert from five until eight o'clock. Since there was to be no dancing we filled the entire room with tables and sold five hundred tickets at a dollar each. Ernie used a simple suggestion in his publicity: do your night-clubbing in the afternoon and be home for dinner. For the first session I got twenty-two musicians. Among them were Sidney Bechet, Sidney Catlett, Jimmy Dorsey, Willie the Lion Smith, Arthur Schutt, Joe and Marty Marsala, Zutty Singleton, Bobby Hackett, Hot Lips Page, Bud Freeman, Pee Wee Russell, Brad Gowans, and the Spirits of Rhythm. Joe Marsala was master of ceremonies.

It was an upsetting experience for the Park Lane. The cocktail lounge outside the ballroom, gaited to the sale of a few Pink Ladies and Manhattans in the late afternoon, ran out of Scotch, waiters, ice, and several other natural resources. Every seat was occupied, and the applause was in the ovation bracket. The next week we had another sellout; we settled down to what we hoped would be a long and successful run. During the fifth session two vice-presidents of the New York Central Railroad walked into the cocktail lounge and ordered drinks.

"What is that noise?" one of them asked the bartender.

"There is a jazz concert going on in the ballroom," the bartender said.

"Send for the manager!" the other vice-president said.

The New York Central owns the Park Lane. We were informed that we could no longer use the ballroom for our concerts; the manager of the hotel was fired for renting it to us. Jazz went back to the saloons.

One night I returned to Nick's after a brief visit to Julius'. Nick was waiting for me. "When is that story coming out in Life?" he asked me. "Any week now," I said. "It's been made part of a photographic story of the history of jazz. It has to run when there isn't much news. There's an old picture of Bix and the gang at White City—"

"I don't believe it's going to run at all," Nick said. "You're fired!"

It was summer so I went to visit friends at Lyme, Connecticut. While I was at a party with some youngsters who were jazz fans I received a telephone call from Alexander King. He had news for me. He had invited Nick to his office and shown him the layout of the jazz article, which was scheduled for appearance in the issue of August 8th. It was entitled "Swing: From a Dark Past It Comes Into Its Golden Age." There was a full page picture of Pee Wee in the throes of *Serenade To A Shylock*; there was a page of shots of the recording date. There was a page devoted to Bix. The White City photograph, taken on a prop representing the rear platform of a train, showed Pee Wee, Mezz, Bix, George Rilling, Sonny Lee, and me. There was a double page spread of the great colored jazz men—Louis Armstrong, Duke Ellington, King Oliver, and Count Basie. There was a picture of Benny Goodman's band, which then had Jess Stacy, Bud Freeman, Harry James, and Dave Tough.

"By the way," King said to Nick, "what's happened to Eddie? Is it true that you have fired him? He's in several of these pictures. We probably ought to take them out if—"

"I love him like a brother," Nick said. "He can go to work tonight."

I thanked King and waited a few days. When I returned Nick bought me a drink.

"Why have you stayed away so long?" he said. "I've missed you. Get right on the stand and play. The band isn't the same without you. Would you like a week's salary in advance?"

267

"I would like two weeks' salary in advance," I said.

The night after the article appeared people stood along the walls and customers were six deep at the bar. Some of them carried copies of the magazine; some of them pointed at Pee Wee and stared. Pee Wee, unconcerned, continued to pour his countenance into his clarinet; his facial contortions and the notes he forced from his instrument fascinated the crowd. Nick was impressed. "Pee Wee's quite a sight, isn't he?" he said to me. "You can't hear a face," I said.

That fall Milt Gabler opened a branch store on Fifty-second Street; his mail order business was increasing and he was now serving most of the radio disc jockeys, who were continuously in search of rare records. During the winter he began a series of Sunday afternoon jam sessions at Jimmy Ryan's, a night club opposite his Fifty-second Street shop. I got the musicians, and Milt finally succumbed to the necessity for paid admissions; he charged a dollar. The sessions ran from five to eight; going from Ryan's to Nick's, which was open on Sunday, I found I was tired by the time I got to work. Usually I had some of the boys with me and they were also tired. Nick objected. Eventually he made us play a Sunday matinee at his place in order to keep us from going to Ryan's.

In the spring he fired me again. I got a band together to play at Princeton for the tenth anniversary of Squirrel Ashcraft's class. Sitting around a barrel of beer we remarked on what a fine group of musicians we had, and how much we enjoyed playing together: Pee Wee, Bud Freeman, Dave Tough, Max Kaminsky, Dave Bowman on piano, Brad Gowans on trombone, and Morty Stuhlmaker on bass. We decided to form a co-operative band. We would play music our own way for what we could get and divide the take equally. When we got back to New York there was a message for me from Nick. I was in again. I took the band with me.

"This is a co-operative outfit," I explained to Nick. "It won't make any difference what you pay us as individuals. We'll put it in a pool and divide it equally."

"Do what you like," he said. "What about a name for the band? How about the Wildcats?"

"The basketball season is over," I said.

"Get a name yourself or you'll open as the Wildcats," he said.

I called up Phyllis Smith; she was working in an advertising agency.

"Give me a name for a jazz band composed of hand-picked musicians," I said.

"Summa Cum Laude," she said.

"Don't talk with your mouth full of food," I said. "I'll wait until you finish."

"It means the very best, the tops," she said. "It's a Latin phrase—in college if you win highest honors you are graduated summa cum laude. It's just right for your mob."

I told Nick. He nodded. "I almost was graduated with it," he said, "but who can pronounce it?"

"What difference does it make so long as we don't play it?" I said.

"Move in," Nick said.

SUMMA CUM LAUDE

NICK was happy with the Summa Cum Laude band. He had reason to be. We were a co-operative organization musically as well as financially; we rehearsed; we were not confined to classic jazz tunes and Dixieland numbers— *At The Jazz Band Ball, Muskrat Ramble, Sensation Rag, Fidgety Feet*, etc. Jazz had never been confined in its material; it was always a way of playing music, and its manner—freedom of improvisation on a basic chordal structure—could be applied to any standard song. At Nick's we did a lot of Dixieland numbers because the customers identified them with our music and asked for them; we could have played the most recent popular hits, giving them our interpretation, but many of the listeners would not have believed they were hearing jazz. Decca, for instance, asked us to make an album of tunes which Bix had played on records, numbers popularly identified with jazz. I wondered, as we were cutting the sides, how many of the tunes Bix would have been playing were he alive—*Goosepimples, Royal Garden Blues, Louisiana, Wa-da-da, Sweet Sue, For No Reason At All In C.* Bix was also the hero of a novel, *Young Man With A Horn*, written by Dorothy Baker, a Harvard professor's wife. In the book a girl finally got Bix; her name was Amy North and in real life Bix would have outrun sound getting away from her.

That winter Erik Charell, a European producer, decided to

give New York a jazz version of Shakespeare's *A Midsummer Night's Dream*. It was to be staged at the Center Theater in Radio City, and the title was *Swingin' The Dream*. The Summa Cum Laude band was invited to participate, along with Benny Goodman's septet, Louis Armstrong, Maxine Sullivan, Bill Bailey the dancer, and a cast large enough to found a small city. We were put in a box at one side of the stage; Benny and his septet were in a box on the other side. The Don Voorhees band was in the pit.

Charell had a curious idea about jazz.

"Play soft!" he said to us. "Play soft! Like Count Basie."

Basie was in town at the time, and when his band played *One O'Clock Jump* it could be heard in the foothills of Connecticut. Charell is mixed up in his English, I thought.

"He wants it louder," I said to the boys.

We poured it out. Charell rocked back and forth in pain. As rehearsals went on the show looked worse and worse; more talent than I have ever seen in one place was being completely mismanaged. By opening night our part in the show had been cut to two numbers, played as preludes to the first and second acts. We were scheduled to begin *Muskrat Ramble* at eight-thirty-five. I got into the white uniform I was forced to wear and went across the street to Dillon's bar. By then I knew beyond a doubt that we were swinging a flop; it was the first time I had ever worn white to a funeral. While I was brooding and sipping, the time for our number was put forward ten minutes; I met the band as it came out of the stage door. I managed to make the second turn; we sat up after the show and read the notices. They were definite. *Swingin' The Dream* was embalmed. It gave thirteen performances.

Nick disliked the idea of sharing us with Shakespeare. We

were fired. After the show closed we went into the Brick Club on West Forty-seventh Street, between Sixth and Seventh Avenues. It had a water-front atmosphere, an alternate band, a floor show with which we didn't get stuck, and a place called the Palm Room, in which we played. It was the kind of place I wouldn't be found dead in, but I was afraid I might be. When summer came the William Morris agency saved us; we were booked for four weeks in the Panther Room of the Sherman Hotel in Chicago, formerly the College Inn. After twelve years I was going home.

Before leaving we played for a house party at Princeton. Some students put us up in their dormitory rooms; Bobby Hackett made a bed on the cushions of a window seat. He fell asleep while smoking and his cigarette set fire to a drape. The boys whose beds we were occupying must have spent the night on the lawn because they saw the smoke. They rushed into the room where the drape was burning and tried to wake us up. We finally got on our feet and helped them carry water from the shower room; we used everything from buckets to shot glasses. When the flames were almost smothered Bud Freeman, who like the rest of us had been running in and out of the shower room in bare feet, said, "Don't put it all out yet! My feet are wet. I want to dry them." One of the students brought him a towel.

In Chicago we checked in at the Knickerbocker Hotel; Ernie Anderson came along with us as adviser and manager. Slim Kurtzmann and Josh Billings dropped in before the luggage arrived; Squirrel Ashcraft called up; Murphy Podolsky was announced; somebody told me my Uncle Dennis had retired from the police force. Somebody said, "Who wants a drink?" Things hadn't changed.

272

We alternated with Stuff Smith and his band, but we were stuck with the floor show and two half-hour network broadcasts every night. Lee Wiley was another attraction; we accompanied her when she sang. It was a lot of work and we had little opportunity to play for dancing; the broadcasts in particular demanded the latest of songs, however soupy: *Careless, I'll Never Smile Again, Only Forever, When You Wish Upon A Star,* and *With The Wind And The Rain In Your Hair.* The weather was hot. The saloons in the neighborhood were air-conditioned.

We didn't work Monday, which was fortunate; Monday night is open house at the Ashcraft home in Evanston. Jam sessions are held in the living room and Squirrel transcribes them on a home recording machine. We went out early in the day on our first Monday and spent the afternoon playing bocci, an Italian game, on the lawn. At night we drank and talked about the good old days. One of Squirrel's friends, a bass player named Joe Rushton, wanted to make some records. Again and again he tried to get us together long enough to play a few numbers. Finally in disgust he wheeled his motorcycle into the living room, started the motor, turned on the recording machine, and transcribed the noise. At four o'clock in the morning Squirrel said to me, "Albert"—he is always correct—"you know where things are. I shall leave you in charge. I am going to bed. I must be in court at nine o'clock in the morning and I must be kinda smart."

It was a pleasant month, but between long working hours and long visiting hours I found myself continuously tired. One night we were sitting around a hotel room drinking and talking about the good old days. Suddenly I stood up, took my hat, and said, "Fellows, I can't stand this any longer. I've got to get

273

out of here and get some sleep." I put on my hat and walked out. It was my own room.

The band disintegrated after we returned to New York; we were still co-operative but all we had to share was an absence of work. One day Nick sent for me. "Why don't you come to see me?" he asked. "I love you like a brother." I was in again. I asked for volunteers from the remaining Summa Cum Lauders. Pee Wee, Max Kaminsky, and Brad Gowans put up their hands. The remnants went with Bud Freeman on a tour through New England. It was over in a hurry. Jazz still had few takers in the Coolidge country.

That fall a fight developed between the radio networks and the American Society of Composers, Authors, and Publishers. ASCAP asked for more money for the use of its music; the networks said no. The existing agreement expired at the end of the year. After midnight on December 31, 1940, every station over which an ASCAP tune was played was subject to a fine of five hundred dollars. Since ASCAP owned an overwhelming majority of the music used in radio the networks were in an awkward position; they threw up a rival, Broadcast Music Incorporated, but ASCAP wasn't worried. BMI didn't have Victor Herbert, Irving Berlin, Jerome Kern, George Gershwin, Richard Rodgers, or Vincent Youmans. Tune sleuths from ASCAP sat in the broadcasting studios and checked on the numbers listed for each musical program. About the middle of January, while people all over the country were learning to like prose programs, I was asked to assemble a quartet of Chicago jazz players for The Chamber Music Society of Lower Basin Street, a National Broadcasting Company program allegedly devoted to hot music.

The broadcast happened to fall on Joe Sullivan's night off

and I had to argue with the union about using him. The union does not allow a man to work on his night off lest he deprive some other musician of a job. I remembered how Charlie Straight had gotten around the rules when he wanted Bix to play for him in Chicago; I used the same argument. Chicago style jazz, I pointed out—I didn't believe this but I said it—is a specialized music which can be played only by certain men.

"There is no substitute for Joe Sullivan," I said. "He is unique."

In that statement I believed sincerely, and the union agreed with me. We assembled for rehearsal in an NBC studio in the afternoon of the day we were to broadcast—Pee Wee, Dave Tough, Joe, and myself. Two tune sleuths came to me and asked for the names of the numbers we were to play. The first was a piano solo by Joe, one of his own compositions. The sleuths listened to it and agreed it did not belong to ASCAP. The second number was to be a blues by the quartet; I had instructed Pee Wee, who was playing the only horn in the group, that he was to go along with the story that this was an original composition of mine, untitled and unscored. I told this to the sleuths. They looked dubious. We played it for them, Pee Wee improvising while the rest of us gave him background.

"It sounds all right," one of the sleuths said when we finished, "but how do we know that he"—pointing at Pee Wee—"is going to play it on the broadcast the same way he played it just now? He hasn't a score to go by."

I took him aside and spoke to him confidentially.

"Don't you know about Pee Wee Russell?" I asked. "That's what he's famous for. He has a very retentive mind. Once he has played a thing he never varies it; he repeats the same notes time after time. It's considered one of the most remarkable musical accomplishments in America."

The sleuth nodded. "I remember now," he said. "I knew he was famous but at the moment I couldn't recall why."

That night on the broadcast Pee Wee, who is utterly incapable of playing anything in even approximately the same way twice, gave a fresh improvisation of the blues. When the program was finished the tune sleuth shook hands with me.

"That Pee Wee is surely a remarkable man, isn't he?" he said. "He played it tonight exactly the way he played it this afternoon." He sighed. "If we had as little trouble with other musicians as we had with him," he said, "our jobs would be easy."

That summer Nick fired me again. Jimmy MacPartland came to town and Joe Sullivan returned from a trip to California. There was a job at the Brass Rail in Chicago, a loop club specializing in hot music, and we took it, with Jimmy as leader. Pee Wee and George Brunies went with us. We were supposed to alternate with another band and do three network broadcasts a week; there were no broadcasts and the alternate band was a juke box. Nobody wanted to hear it while we were around so we spent most of our time on the stand; we played until four o'clock in the morning, and for once when work was finished we were ready to go to bed. By the time we were asleep the temperature was above ninety and the heat woke us up.

Pee Wee stayed with Josh Billings and Slim Kurtzmann, who were sharing an apartment. Both Josh and Slim had given up playing the suitcase and Billings was working days as a lithographer. While he slept at night Kurtzmann borrowed his car and drove to the Brass Rail to meet Pee Wee and take him home. They stopped along the way each morning and shopped at a milk wagon. One morning they found the wagon in front of a large apartment house. The driver was in the building; they waited for him to appear, getting sleepier and more thirsty. Finally they decided to take a few quarts and pay the man the next day. Someone saw them as they drove away, took the license number of the car, and telephoned the police. As the two sat in the kitchen of the apartment drinking the milk the doorbell rang: Kurtzmann answered it, a glass of milk in his hand. He opened the door and two detectives walked in. Half an hour later the thieves were in the Chicago Avenue jail. They got word to me and I telephoned Uncle Dennis.

"Why did they want to drink milk?" he asked. "If it was liquor it would be easier to straighten it out; a man can understand the need of another man for a drink of whiskey at half-past four in the morning, but not milk. Well, I'll do what I can."

By the time the case was called at nine o'clock that night everything was arranged. Pee Wee was a pathetic sight as he stood before the magistrate. He was still wearing his band uniform—tuxedo trousers and a tan jacket. He had neither shaved nor slept in twenty-four hours; he was hungry and he needed a drink. The magistrate stared at him. Pee Wee, always shy, dropped his eyes.

"What do you do?" the magistrate asked.

"I p-p-p-play the c-c-c-clarinet," Pee Wee said.

"See that you stick to it," the magistrate said. "Don't let me ever again hear of you drinking milk. Case dismissed."

The only good result of our stay at the Brass Rail was a story about us in *Time* magazine; propaganda for jazz, I felt, was worth anything, even alternating with a juke box. I could still beat Squirrel Ashcraft at *boòci;* otherwise Chicago had lost its charm.

Nick didn't send for me all that fall; I worked on recording dates and parish organization. The network of information centers was now complete. It consisted of three saloons—Costello's, Reilly's, and Julius'. At Costello's on Forty-fourth Street and Third Avenue Tim or Joe would take a message, or maybe McNulty or Oliver St. John Gogarty would answer the phone. At Michael Reilly's on Fifty-second Street between Fifth and Sixth Avenues, Mr. Reilly himself—no one ever dared call him Mike—or Paddy Carlos or Tom Gerraghan, the bartenders, would accept and give information. At Julius' Pete Pesci, the manager, and the bartenders, Joe Gallagher, Bobby Earle, and Harold Fitzsimmons fulfilled secretarial duties. I also had a trap line, consisting of a series of offices inhabited by friends, from which I could telephone and where I received and gave news concerning the movement to put jazz in a rented pew. Some time during each afternoon Phyllis Smith called me and talked to me until I was sufficiently awake to get up. Some time during the evening I met with Ernie Anderson and worked on plots. I seemed always to have a date to meet Phyllis, too.

Ernie wanted to invade Carnegie Hall. Whiteman had been there, and Goodman, but neither had given the customers real jazz. We decided to begin with a Fats Waller concert, using a small band to back him up during parts of the program.

"Fine! Perfect! Wonderful!" Fats said when I asked him. I saw the gin routine coming again so I ducked. Fats now had a manager, Edward Kirkeby, so we completed the arrangements through him. The date chosen was January 14, 1942. Meanwhile an incident occurred at Pearl Harbor. I dropped in at Nick's to see how it was affecting business.

278

"Why don't you ever come to see me?" Nick said. "I love you like a brother. Have a drink."

We had several. Nick was of the opinion that the Japs would not give us too much trouble. A people without jazz, he figured, couldn't be very dangerous.

"I'll let you know after I've taken a crack at them," I said.

Nick blinked. "You?" he said. "How are you going to get into the army? You can't see past my nose and you hear out of one ear."

"I can fight at night," I said. "It only requires a sense of smell."

We had a few more drinks. "What are you doing at the bar?" Nick said suddenly. "Get up on the stand and play."

"I'm not working here," I explained.

"I love you like a brother," he said. "You can start tomorrow night."

TOWN HALL

THE WALLER PROGRAM at Carnegie Hall was a limited success. We arranged it as a tribute to Fats; we listed all the songs he had written, with a note stating that he would play such of them as he chose for an opening group. There were ninety-one of them, from *Squeeze Me*, written when Fats was fifteen, to *All That Meat And No Potatoes*, his latest hit. Included were *Ain't Misbehavin'*, *I've Got A Feelin' I'm Fallin'*, *My Fate Is In Your Hands*, *Honeysuckle Rose*, *Prisoner Of Love*, *Handful Of Keys*, *Blue Turning Gray Over You*. The note said, "Some of the best of Mr. Waller's popular songs (which are *not* included in this list) are not credited to him simply because he sold all rights to them to unscrupulous Tin Pan Alley authors." John Hammond wrote a program note in which he said, "In one sense this concert is an event. America is paying tribute for the first time to one of its great popular artists, Thomas Waller . . . America does strange things to its great artists. In any other place in the world Thomas Waller might have developed into a famous concert performer, for when he was eleven he was a gifted organist, pianist, and composer. But Waller was not white and the American concert field makes a racial exception only for a few singers . . . Waller's great talent for the piano has never received the acknowledgment that it deserves in this country. It was easier to exploit him as a buffoon and clown than as the artist he is . . . Fats is undoubtedly a

280

great entertainer and showman, but tonight there will be a chance to see primarily Fats Waller, the musician and composer." To back Fats up in the closing part of the program I got Krupa, Pee Wee, Bud Freeman, Max Kaminsky, and the bass player, John Kirby.

When I arrived at the hall there were more people backstage than in the orchestra; Fats' friends had dropped in to wish him luck. He had a drink with each of them. When the curtain went up someone turned him around, pointed the way, and he walked on stage and sat down at the piano. He played as he liked from his own compositions for an opening group.

For the second group he was to play spirituals on the organ. He did, but I noticed that every once in a while he slipped into George Gershwin's Summertime. The third group consisted of improvisations, and again I detected Summertime. After an intermission of twenty-three minutes—one minute to get Fats off the stage and twenty-two to get him back on—he played his London Suite and some variations on a Tschaikovsky theme. Afterward Oscar Levant said, "I never realized until I heard Fats tonight how much Tschaikovsky owes to Gershwin."

After Tschaikovsky the program actually listed a group of Gershwin songs; this was the only time during the program when Summertime was not played; apparently Fats identified it with every composer but Gershwin. We finally came to his rescue with a group including China Boy, I Found A New Baby, and Honeysuckle Rose.

"Fats," I said, when we were backstage again, "you're still my nemesis."

"Fine! Perfect! Wonderful!" Fats said.

A jazz band is necessarily small; on the Carnegie stage we were lost. Ernie agreed with me that the place was too large for our purpose; we visited the management of Town Hall, the cultural headquarters on West Forty-third Street. We asked if we might rent the concert hall some Saturday for the twilight hours between five-thirty and seven-thirty. We explained that the music to be presented was jazz. "Are you sure you have the right place?" the man with whom we were negotiating said. We said yes and he gave us a price of $150. The date we chose was February 21, 1942.

We decided to call it "A Chiaroscuro Jazz Concert," meaning that we intended to present both white and Negro musicians. The Negroes were Sidney Bechet, clarinet; J. C. Higginbotham, trombone; Hot Lips Page, trumpet; Zutty Singleton, drums; Willie the Lion Smith, pianist. The others were Joe Sullivan, George Wettling, Max Kaminsky, Bobby Hackett, Pee Wee Russell, Brad Gowans on trombone and Sid Weiss on bass. Milt Gabler wrote the program note and did his best to tell the audience about us and about jazz. John M. Halpern, musicologist for Nelson Rockefeller's inter-American organization, contributed something he called "Good Music, Apologia." It deserves to be remembered:

From a sociological viewpoint, jazz is most certainly democracy set to music. Differences of color, religion, and race seem to fuse themselves into a whole where jazz is concerned. This is interesting, perhaps inspiring, but not important. What is important is the fact that jazz is good music when it is interpreted by good musicians.

Basic principles of art may be applied to all art forms. Design, harmony and color are the signposts of great art. The men you will see and hear today are instinctively acquainted with these principles just as are Toscanini, Stokowski, and Rachmaninoff. Their terminology, when applied to certain technical aspects of music, may be somewhat different than that used by the above-mentioned great interpreters of serious music. Nevertheless, they are driving at the same thing. What is a "cadenza" to Heifetz, is a "ride" to Hot Lips Page. In jazz, the basic harmonic pattern of Boogie Woogie is called a "Boogie Woogie Beat." Such a treatment of basic harmonies was known as a *basso continuo* back in the days of Handel, Bach, and Vivaldi. Both are essentially the same—melodic improvisations over a given harmonic construction.

The gentlemen performing on this program were brought up in a different atmosphere than most interpreters of classical music, but their talents and their love of music are just as great. They took their music where they found it and it wasn't always in an idyllic or inspiring setting. Nevertheless, they found music and they made the most of it. These men make music and they make it good.

We decided to open with a group of Gershwin songs, in order to show how jazz, a way of playing music, can be applied to any standard tune. After a demonstration of jazz piano playing by Willie the Lion Smith the Negroes were to play the blues in various keys and tempi. After that we listed four Beiderbecke favorites, with Bobby Hackett and Max Kaminsky alternating in the role of Bix. Such a program, we thought, would demonstrate at least roughly the origin, the development, the function, and the technique of jazz.

When I stepped on the stage to make the first announcement I took a long look at the audience. Finally I spoke.

"Lady," I said, "and gentleman."

The musicians had a good time and the people who finally arrived made up enough applause between them to give the impression of a full house. The box office statement showed that 346 people sat in the balcony, 147 occupied the orchestra, and no one sat in a loge. The gross receipts were $480. "Shall we try again?" I said to Ernie.

"By all means," he said. "Let's give a series. We'll either get a following or discover once and for all that no audience for jazz exists."

The Town Hall management was helpful; when we asked for a series of dates for the Saturday twilight hours the price was cut to a hundred dollars. We tried again on March 7; a few more people sat in the balcony, a few less occupied the orchestra. The gross receipts were $426. But again the applause was persistent and enthusiastic. We went back on March 21 for a final try before the warm weather. Afterward Ernie was excited. The gross was $516.75. Someone sat in a loge.

"It's the handwriting on the wall!" he said. "Next year we'll give a concert every month. We're on our way!"

I was happy too. "Some day we may have as many followers as the harpsichord," I said.

On the following Monday we received a call from Worthington Minor of the Columbia Broadcasting Company's television studio. He had walked past Town Hall on Saturday afternoon while on his way to Grand Central Station.

"I had half an hour before my train," he said. "I saw the crowd going in and went along. After the first number I decided to miss my train and stay for the whole of the concert. I think you have something ideal for television—relaxed, casual, intimate music. I'd like to talk to you about it."

In a few weeks jazz was the hit of television. We were small enough as a group to be covered by one camera; as each man played his solo improvisation he could be featured in a close-up. The fact that we wore no uniforms, that we lounged, smoked, and whispered instructions even while the music was proceeding, gave action and reality to the scene. After four shows the Federal Communications Commission issued a war ruling on tele-

284

vision. At the time a station had to televise a minimum of eighteen hours a week in order to keep its license; the new regulation forbade any station to televise more than four hours a week. Television was down and we were out.

The draft board finally agreed to see me. I reported one morning to my local station at Eighth Street and Sixth Avenue; a lot of others had received invitations and all of them had accepted. We were given subway passes and someone was appointed foreman to lead us into the sewer. We rode the Sixth Avenue line to Rockefeller Plaza, then marched across Forty-Seventh Street to Lexington Avenue, where we entered Grand Central Palace. Here we prepared for our physical examination; we stripped to our underwear shorts, checked our clothes, and got in line. The poking, tapping, X-raying, and questioning began. It was now half past eight. I had worked at Nick's until four o'clock.

As we approached the various stops in the line signs prepared us for what we would be asked. At one spot there was a question about diabetes. I was supposed to get it after my pancreatitis but it broke the date. I explained this to the examiner and handed him a sealed envelope from Polyclinic Hospital containing the case history of my operation. He opened the envelope, looked over the report, and wrote something on my papers. I moved on to the eye man. I couldn't read the chart with either eye; as I went toward the ear man I peeked at the report on my eyesight; it was, so the examiner had written, almost perfect.

The ear man was a gruff old guy far beyond the danger of active duty. He paid almost no attention to my left ear, with which I do my hearing. The right one intrigued him; he poked, pulled, blew, probed, and tapped; finally he wired it for electric light. Another doctor called to him and suggested lunch, but he kept digging at my ear.

Finally I said, "Doctor, there's a long line behind me. I'm tired and you're ready for lunch. I can tell you how to save time for me, for yourself, for the guys behind me, and for the government—don't mess with that ear. It has no drum; it has nothing; it hasn't heard a sound in thirty-six and a half years."

The doctor roared—I could hear him with my other ear—"I'll decide that! It's what I'm here for."

He finally gave up and passed me on. I looked at what he had written on my papers—my hearing was normal.

After that I went into a booth and an elderly doctor mulled over the reports which had been written on my papers. He himself wrote that in view of my medical history and my age he recommended rejection. He didn't want the entire responsibility for such a decision, though, so he took me into another booth where another elderly doctor also mulled over the various reports and also recommended that in view of pancreatitis and approaching middle age I be rejected. I was then led to a psychiatrist's booth. He asked me whether I liked boys better than girls, whether I wet the bed, and whether I talked in my sleep. He wouldn't take entire responsibility for me either; he asked me to see another psychiatrist in another booth.

For the first time in seven hours—it was now two o'clock in the afternoon—I was slightly cheered. I had spotted the other psychiatrist as he came in from lunch. I could tell he had been to a bar; he looked relaxed, amiable, my kind of a guy. There, I thought to myself as I watched him go into his booth, is a man who speaks my language; I wish I could talk to him.

There was a selectee in his booth; while I waited for him to come out I tried to read what the first psychiatrist had written on my papers; it was the worst scrawl I had ever tried to decipher; I couldn't make out a word. As I entered the second psychiatrist's booth he crushed out the cigarette he had been smoking. The odor of burning tobacco drifting up from the ash tray was almost too much for me. We had not been allowed to smoke since entering the building; we hadn't had anything to eat or to drink either.

"Doctor," I moaned, "I wish that had happened either before I came in or after I left."

He smiled. "I'd light one for you," he said, "but the other day a doctor did it for a selectee and there was trouble."

He smiled again. He was my kind of guy all right, and I was sure now that he had just come from where I wanted to be. At that point I was completely convinced that I could do more for the war effort by staying out of the army—we had been playing for the boys at camps, and I had seen what the music meant to them—but I was certain that despite the recommendations by the elderly medical officers I was headed for a uniform and a barracks.

The psychiatrist had been looking through my papers. He leaned back in his chair, smiled again, and said, "Mr. Condon, I see that you drink. How often?"

"Every day," I said.

"Why?" he asked.

"I work in a saloon," I said. "I'm a musician. My employer is a fellow named Nick. His place is in Greenwich Village and he sells whiskey"—you've been there, I thought to myself; I can tell by the look in your eyes—"and his customers drink. I can't stand the customers when they're drunk if I'm sober, so I drink too. It creates a mutual tolerance."

He nodded. "How many highballs do you drink every day?" he asked.

"I don't count the highballs," I said. "I occasionally check on the cases or barrels, but that's all."

"Hold out your hand," he said.

I stretched my right arm toward him, with the palm of my hand down and my fingers held together. Fairly steady, I thought; this isn't going to be so bad.

"Spread your fingers," the psychiatrist said.

I did, and the dance was on. My hand shook like an electric washing machine.

"You could stand a drink now, couldn't you?" he said.

"Doctor," I said, "I worked until four o'clock this morning. I haven't had a drink, I haven't had a smoke, I haven't had anything to eat since I came in here. There's a saloon called The Boar's Head at Forty-seventh Street and Lexington Avenue. When I get out of here I'm going into it so fast I won't even open the door; I'll tear it off the hinges."

The psychiatrist smiled again. "Don't forget Allan's," he said. "It's at Forty-sixth and Lexington."

He bent over my papers and wrote a single line on the final sheet. Then he got up and put a hand on my shoulder.

"I'll take you to the orthopedic room," he said. "After that you'll be through except for the classification officer."

He folded my papers and handed them to me; then he led me past the double line of selectees and into the orthopedic room.

"You'll be out of here in a few minutes," he said. "Don't worry, and have one for me."

As soon as he had gone I looked to see what he had written on my papers. The single line was in a bold, clear hand:

<blockquote>This man needs a drink right now.</blockquote>

And he had signed it.

He was my guy all right.

I jumped up and down for the orthopedic man, waited while he wrote on my papers, and went to the classification officer, a lieutenant. He sat at a desk and examined the papers of the selectees as they passed. He had two hand stamps, one for approval, one for rejection. He never looked up; without raising his head he reached for the papers of each new man, examined them, and branded them with one stamp or the other. I handed him my papers and waited. He went through them—the reports on my eyes, ears, heart, lungs, etc. He looked at the report from Polyclinic, examined the recommendations of the two elderly doctors, passed over the unreadable scrawl of the first psychiatrist, and came to the single line the second psychiatrist had written.

Suddenly he looked up at me. For a long moment he stared. Then he put his head down, reached for one of his stamps and struck my papers with it. I picked them up. I had been rejected for military service by the United States Army. Twenty minutes later I was at The Boar's Head. Half an hour after that I was at Allan's. I ordered two drinks, one for me and one for my guy. I drank them both.

All that summer we played at camps, participated in service broadcasts, and made V-discs and transcriptions to be sent overseas. The parish organization worked efficiently; by calling Costello's, Reilly's, and Julius' I could round up a band for any purpose in a few hours. I was struck by the tremendous enthusiasm with which the soldiers received our music.

"It shouldn't surprise you," Phyllis Smith said. "Whenever people hear real jazz they like it. These boys are from all over the country; it's the first time most of them have had a chance

289

to hear the music. A lot of them have never even heard recorded jazz. They've had commercialized popular music rammed into their ears."

That fall we resumed our concerts at Town Hall. The crowds increased; there were several people in the loges. We kept the format of the show informal. I introduced the musicians and the numbers; sometimes we stuck to the program, sometimes we didn't. We never rehearsed; everyone participating knew the numbers we played; it was only necessary to indicate the key in which we were to operate and map out a sequence for the soloists. There were no formalities, no tuxedos; we passed instructions and comment while the music proceeded. The parish organization turned up plenty of talent. Lee Wiley sang, Tommy Dorsey dropped in, James P. Johnson played piano, Gilbert Seldes and George Frazier wrote program notes, and Hot Lips Page introduced his blues, Uncle Sam Ain't No Woman, But He Can Certainly Steal Your Man. Our audience was also informal. Those in the front row propped their feet against the stage; everyone beat time, and a good solo passage was applauded immediately.

The first concert was held on November 7, 1942, and the usual mob played: Bobby Hackett, Max Kaminsky, and Hot Lips Page, cornetists; Sidney Catlett, Cozy Cole, and Zutty Singleton, drummers; Ed Hall and Pee Wee Russell, clarinetists; Benny Morton and George Brunies, trombonists; Mel Powell and Harry Gibson, pianists; and Johnny Williams, bass player. We went through a normal program and closed with an ensemble in which the entire cast hemstitched on a basic theme. When it was over the customers stamped, whistled, and beat the seats; Ernie reported a box office high of almost eight hundred dollars. The next morning after finishing work at Nick's I went home, propped myself up in bed, and browsed through the Sunday papers. I expected no reports of the concert; during the spring the music critics had mentioned us politely; they were willing to admit that jazz was an art and that our performers were fine musicians, but it was obvious that they thought we were a little noisy, a little undisciplined, and not quite ready for polite musical society. Halfway through the *Herald Tribune* I came across a piece by Virgil Thomson, the paper's first string music critic. Beside it was a picture of me. I read the piece.

"The jazz concert that Eddie Condon directed yesterday afternoon in the Town Hall," it began, "was to this reviewer one of the most satisfactory musical experiences of the season."

So far so good, I thought. I was still a little confused by finding the concert discussed in a space normally devoted to classical music. I read on; Mr. Thomson was a little irritated by the "affetuòso manner" of the soloists. I'll speak to the boys about that, I thought. Then came the final paragraph:

"All this changed in the final collective improvisation," it began. "The individual melodic elements of this were more lyrical and sincere; there was less of mere nervous animation and less of sentimental phrase-molding. The whole was magnificently sustained and varied, everybody playing something worth listening to and everybody uttering phrases that had to do with those the others were uttering. The nine-part tuttis were of a grandeur, a sumptuousness of sound and a spontaneous integration of individual freedoms that makes one proud of the country that gave birth to such a high manifestation of sensibility and intelligence and happy to be present at such a full and noble expression of the musical faculties."

I read it seven times, once for each member of the "poorest 7-piece orchestra on earth." Then I pushed the papers off the bed, turned out the light, and went to sleep. Just before I dozed off an idea occurred to me. Now I can get married, I thought.

Paul Smith suffered a slight case of extra-sensory perception. The following Wednesday he called me on the telephone and asked me to meet him at a bar. When we were halfway through a drink he began talking about the length of our friendship, its resistance to time and weather, and its firm foundation. I agreed with him.

"Then let me ask you a favor," he said. "Promise me that you will never again telephone Phyllis. She is my sister but she is a woman. She is breaking up our friendship."

I agreed. "I will not only do it for you, but I will do it for your wife and children," I said. "I will not telephone Phyllis but I cannot do anything about it if she decides to telephone me."

"Good!" Paul said. "Now let's have another drink."

So Phyllis and I were married the next week, on my thirty-seventh birthday. Paul was best man. On the day of the ceremony I was at a studio making transcriptions for the BBC. Things got involved and I realized I would barely get away in time to make the church. I broke my promise to Paul and called Phyllis.

"I won't have time to buy a ring," I said. "Pick one up at a dime store on your way downtown. I'll replace it later."

She did, and by dark we were an act. It was a year before I got around to replacing the ring; by then it was green and Maggie had arrived. I got what I wanted and took it to an engraver on West Forty-eighth Street, definitely an out-of-towner. He examined the ring, a plain gold band like the one my mother wore.

"Like the old times," he said to me. "I'm glad to make it for you. It's better than what the women wear now. It's more warm."

I told him what I wanted engraved on the inside: From Eddie to Phyllis to Maggie.

He struck the counter with his hands and looked at me in joy. "Tinkers to Evers to Chance!" he cried. "You love baseball too?"

He didn't wait for an answer; he told me about baseball— about the Yankees and the Dodgers and the Giants, about coming to America as a young man and seeing the great double play combination of Tinkers to Evers to Chance, about the World Series when Babe Ruth was a pitcher, about Walter Johnson and Ty Cobb and Eddie Collins, about John McGraw and Christy Mathewson and Carl Hubbell.

"That is the thing I like most in America, baseball," he said. Then he added, "Baseball and that music, that jazz. I like that too; it makes me move around and feel good."

He looked at me closely. "Do you like that music too, that jazz?"

"Yes," I said, "I like jazz."

He nodded. "I will work on the ring right away. For you I will make a special job of it. I will finish it for next week. It will be the double play ring, Tinkers to Evers to Chance."

That night Virgil Thomson dropped in at Nick's. I took him to Julius', where we could talk quietly about nine-part tuttis. When I got back the band was playing. Nick put a hand on my shoulder.

"I love you like a brother," he said. "You're fired!"

THERE ARE no more than half a hundred first class players of jazz. As musicians these men are unmatched in technical skill and virtuosity; in addition they are composers. They play a music which is spontaneously and continuously created; to meet its demands they employ what appear to be almost limitless resources for improvisation; they are individual performers with a flawless ability to co-operate with other individual performers; what they play comes from themselves. They are pioneer practitioners of the only American art form. They are respected as artists by other musicians, by music critics, and by jazz enthusiasts. They are admired and discussed in Europe, where people talk about jazz as they talk about the music of Bach, Mozart, Handel, etc. By the large number of Americans they are considered to be colorful characters who talk in an amusing private language and who make a lot of noise on instruments. Americans do not believe it when they are informed that jazz players do not understand "jive" talk and that they shrink in terror when it is used in their presence. Jazz came from America, specifically from the Negro; it cannot be important; it cannot be more than a vulgar form of saloon entertainment.

Jazz players have not bothered to protest against any of this; they have worried only about being allowed to play their music the way they want to play it, for a living wage; as Wingy Mannone said, "You can't work all night and fight all day." Jazz players remain a small group; only occasionally does a young-

294

ster appear who is capable of joining them; there is a bare trickle of new names—Ralph Sutton, Johnny Blowers, Peanuts Hucko, Johnny Windhurst. No jazz player expects the majority of Americans ever to think well of him or of his music.

Yet for thirty years critics and composers here and abroad have insisted that jazz is art. In 1918 Olin Downes wrote: " 'Ragtime' in its best estate is for me one of our most precious musical assets." (Musical Quarterly, Jan., 1918) In 1919 Ernest Ansermet, a European conductor, said, "The first thing that strikes one about the Southern Syncopated Orchestra is the astonishing perfection, the superb taste, and the fervor of its playing. . . . They gave the idea of a style, and their form was gripping, abrupt, harsh, with a brusque and pitiless ending like that of Bach's second Brandenburg Concerto." (Revue Romande, Oct. 15, 1919) In 1922 George Antheil, the composer, said, "Jazz is not a craze. . . . Its significance is that it is one of the greatest landmarks of modern art." (Der Quershnitt, Summer, 1922) In 1923 the composer Darius Milhaud said, "One thing I want to emphasize very particularly and that is the beneficial influence upon all music of jazz. It has been enormous and in my opinion, an influence of good. It is a new idea and has brought in new rhythms and almost, one might say, new forms. Stravinsky owes much to it. It is a pity that it is limited at present, practically to dance music, but that will be remedied." (Musical America, Jan. 13, 1923) In 1934 Hugues Panassié, a Frenchman, wrote Le Jazz Hot, a serious, detailed study of the new music. Another Frenchman, Charles Delaunay, has labored for years to present in the various editions of his Hot Discography a complete and accurate history of jazz on records. 'Europeans, unable to hear live jazz, have made an intense study of it on records; they are learned in the

295

styles and techniques of various jazz players; in England alone there are more than a dozen publications devoted exclusively to jazz. Yet Europeans cannot themselves play jazz well. "What no Europeans make as our men do," says Virgil Thomson, "is la musica americana, that spontaneous ensemble of individual freedoms that we call noncommercial swing. The improvising of it in twelve parts by our greatest instrumental virtuosos under Eddie Condon's direction has provided the most absorbing musical experience that I have been through as a consumer in some years, and one of the highest manifestations of the musical faculties it has ever been my pleasure to witness." (Vogue, Feb. 15, 1943)

When in February, 1946, Condon and his virtuosos tried to hire Constitution Hall in Washington, D. C., for a concert they were turned down. The message of refusal said, "This auditorium owned by the Daughters of the American Revolution operates under a policy which is most restrictive as to the type of attractions we may play." The policy, according to the message, "prevents us playing any jazz band, not because of the attraction itself but rather because of the type of audience which attends and which in some cases may be very destructive." Condon and his men offered to post a bond of $100,000 to cover possible damage by the audience; the answer was still no. The concert was held in the main ballroom of the Willard Hotel; on a rainy night six hundred people paid $3.60 each to hear the music; the Willard reported no destruction to its property.

It is all very much like Ireland and James Joyce, the author of Dubliners, A Portrait of the Artist as a Young Man, Ulysses, and Finnegans Wake. Recently an American magazine decided to run a picture story of Dublin, the setting for all of Joyce's fiction. A photographer was sent to Belvedere College, the Jesuit day school which Joyce attended and which figures prominently in A Portrait of the Artist as a Young Man. While the photograph was being taken the Rector of the school said, "Have you heard of the sad case of a certain student, James Joyce, a freak writer?" (Vogue, May 1, 1947)

Q. E. D.

THE CHICAGO BANDS

☆

EDDIE CONDON ON RECORDS

AN INFORMAL DISCOGRAPHY

☆

Material collected and arranged

by J O H N   S W I N G L E

THE CHICAGO BANDS

SOME of the early touring bands from New Orleans, the birthplace of jazz, came to Chicago; The Original Creole Orchestra came in 1911. Later, bands like the Dixie Land Jass Band were especially formed in New Orleans to play Chicago engagements, and these bands, together with individual musicians like King Joe Oliver, who left New Orleans after the closing of Storyville in 1917, made Chicago both historically and geographically the crossroads of jazz. These bands and men brought with them the Negro Creole and the white Dixieland jazz styles often reflected in the names of the bands as well as in their playing.

In Chicago new combinations were worked and new musicians began to play, until there was a feeling of cohesion that suggested old Storyville. The cord from New Orleans had not been cut, and men like Louis Armstrong were still coming from the South to join jazz in Chicago. However, a new vitality, home grown in Chicago itself, activated bands like the Blue Friars. Out of this vitality a new style developed, the Chicago style.

From Chicago, musicians and bands spread out, invading New York, where the McKenzie-Condon Chicagoans fought for an audience and proved that Chicago vitality had given jazz the will to survive neglect, distaste, and perversion.

The stories of ten Chicago bands are told here and their personnels listed. A glance at this record and the Condon discography shows the great combinations and permutations among jazz bands, and gives clear emphasis to the conclusion that jazz is improvisation and jazz musicians are not so much interpreters as creative artists in a really American art form.

ORIGINAL CREOLE BAND*

The Original Creole Band was formed in New Orleans with Freddie Keppard as leader. From 1911 to 1917 it played vaudeville tours throughout the country as The Original Creole Orchestra, appearing at the Grand Theatre in Chicago and the Winter Garden in New York City, the first jazz band to make such extensive tours. In early 1916 Keppard refused the first offer made to a jazz band to put its music on records since he feared that other bands would steal the tunes and copy his band's style of playing. The band played at the Royal Gardens Café in Chicago as the Original Creole Band from 1917 until it broke up in 1918. Songs associated with the band, especially on tour, were *Steamboat Blues, Roustabout Shuffle* and *Pepper Rag.* Personnels:

THE ORIGINAL CREOLE ORCHESTRA	THE ORIGINAL CREOLE BAND
Bill Johnson, Bass	Bill Johnson, Bass
George Baquet, Clarinet	Jimmy Noone, Clarinet
Eddie Venson, Trombone	Eddie Venson, Trombone
Dink Johnson, Drums [Piano]	Paul Barbarin, Drums
Freddie Keppard, Cornet	King Joe Oliver, Cornet
Norwood Williams, Guitar	Lottie Taylor, Piano
Jimmie Palao, Violin	

302

BROWN'S DIXIELAND JASS BAND**

Brown's Dixieland Jass Band was formed in New Orleans around 1914. It accepted an engagement at Lamb's Café in Chicago in June 1915. Originally the band was billed as Tom Brown's Band from Dixieland but an attempt by union officials to smear the band as playing "jass" music backfired, the band became popular, and the new name, Brown's Dixieland Jass Band, was created. The band broke up in 1916 and some of the personnel formed the Tom Brown Band (later the Louisana Five) while Larry Shields went with the Dixie Land Jass Band (later the Original Dixieland Jazz Band). Personnel:

Tom Brown, Trombone
Ray Lopez, Cornet
Gus Mueller, Clarinet (Larry Shields)
William Lambert, Drums
Arnold Loyocano, Bass and Piano

ORIGINAL DIXIELAND JAZZ BAND**

The Dixie Land Jass Band was formed in 1916 in New Orleans for an engagement at Schiller's Café in Chicago. After Brown's Dixieland Jass Band broke up, the band (renamed the Original Dixieland Jass Band) went to New York and became a sudden success at Reisenweber's off Columbus Circle. When the Original Creole Band refused to make the first jazz records, the band accepted, played as the Original Dixieland Jazz Band, and made a fortune. It was the first jazz band to tour Europe. By the early 1920's the band's personnel had radically altered. Personnels:

DIXIE LAND JASS BAND	ORIGINAL DIXIELAND JAZZ BAND
Alcide Yellow Nunez, Clarinet	Larry Shields, Clarinet (Phil Lytell)
Henry Ragas, Piano	Henry Ragas, Piano (J. Russell Robinson) (Frank Signorelli)
Eddie Edwards, Trombone	Eddie Edwards, Trombone (Emil Christian)
Nick La Rocca, Cornet	Nick La Rocca, Cornet
Tony Sbarbaro, Drums	Tony Sbarbaro, Drums

KING JOE OLIVER'S CREOLE JAZZ BAND*

King Joe Oliver's Creole Jazz Band was formed in Chicago in 1920 by King Joe Oliver for the Dreamland Café. It toured California in 1921, and returned to the Lincoln Gardens Café in Chicago where it played until 1924, when Oliver arranged an Eastern tour. The Dodds brothers and Honoré Dutray remained in Chicago and Oliver toured with a large band. When the band returned to Chicago Louis Armstrong left Oliver and the original Creole Jazz Band was broken up, although Oliver continued to form other bands, mostly larger ones. Personnel:

King Joe Oliver, Cornet
Lil Hardin, Piano (Bertha Gonsoulin)
Honoré Dutray, Trombone
Ed Garland, Bass (John Lindsay)
Minor Ram Hall, Drums (Baby Dodds)
Jimmy Noone, Clarinet (Johnny Dodds) (Albert Nicholas)
W. M. Johnson, Banjo (Buddy Christian)
(Louis Armstrong), Second Cornet
(Rudy Jackson), Clarinet and Saxophone

304

NEW ORLEANS RHYTHM KINGS**

The New Orleans Rhythm Kings were formed in New Orleans in 1919. The band made early tours to Mobile, Alabama, and to Texas. It played on the Strekfus Line river boats, and came to Chicago in 1920. The band played at the Cascades Ballroom in Chicago a short time, and then accepted an engagement at Friars' Inn, where it became famous. Personnel:

Paul Mares, Trumpet
Elmer Schoebel, Piano (Mel Stitzel)
Jack Pettis, Saxophone
Arnold Loyocano, Bass (Steve Brown) (Chink Martin)
Frank Snyder, Drums (Ben Pollack)
Lew Black, Banjo [Bob Gillette]
George Brunies, Trombone
Leon Rappolo, Clarinet

BLUE FRIARS**

The Blue Friars band was formed by the Austin High School Gang in Chicago in 1922 and named after the Friars' Inn Society Orchestra, the recording name for the New Orleans Rhythm Kings. The ages of the young musicians ran from fourteen to seventeen when the band was formed. Most of the players later went with the Wolverines and Husk O'Hare's Wolverines, and the band dissolved. Personnel:

Jim Lannigan, Piano [and Bass later]
Jimmy MacPartland, Cornet
Dick MacPartland, Banjo and Guitar
Lawrence Bud Freeman, C-melody Saxophone
Frank Teschmaker, Violin [learning Alto Saxophone]
Dave North, Piano
[Dave Tough], Drums
[Benny Goodman], Clarinet

305

WOLVERINES**

The Wolverines were formed in late 1923 by Dick Voynow. Their first engagement was at the Stockton Club near Hamilton, Ohio. The band played at fraternity dances at Indiana University. In late 1924 Jimmy MacPartland replaced Bix Beiderbecke and slowly the Blue Friars came into band. Personnel:

Bix Beiderbecke, Cornet [and sometimes Piano] (Jimmy Mac-
    Partland)
Dick Voynow, Piano
George Johnson, Tenor Saxophone
Jimmy Hartwell, Clarinet (Jimmy Lord)
Bob Gillette, Banjo
Al Gande, Trombone [Gande did not leave Ohio]
Bob Conzelman, Drums (Vic Moore) (Vic Berton)

HUSK O'HARE'S WOLVERINES**

Husk O'Hare's Wolverines developed in 1925 from the original Wolverines, using most of the musicians from the Blue Friars. The band played White City, a dance hall in Chicago, and other spots in Chicago. It broke up when Teschmaker joined Muggsy Spanier at the Midway Garden Café. Personnel:

Jim Lannigan, Bass
Floyd O'Brien, Trombone
Dave North, Piano
Dave Tough, Drums
Frank Teschmaker, Clarinet
Jimmy MacPartland, Cornet
Dick MacPartland, Banjo and Guitar
Bud Freeman, C-melody Saxophone [Tenor Saxophone]
306

LOUIS ARMSTRONG'S BAND AT SUNSET*

The band at the Sunset Café in Chicago was reorganized by Louis Armstrong, one of its members, in early 1927, and was quickly recognized as the best jazz band then playing; musicians from other bands often came to listen and sometimes sat in. Personnel:

Louis Armstrong, Cornet
Earl Hines, Piano
Peter Briggs, Tuba
Honoré Dutray, Trombone
Bill Wilson, Cornet
Tubby Hall, Drums
Boyd Atkins, Banjo
Rip Bassett, Saxophone
Joe Dixon, Saxophone
Al Washington, Saxophone and Piano

McKENZIE-CONDON CHICAGOANS**

The McKenzie-Condon Chicagoans got together on December 9, 1927, in Chicago for their recording of *China Boy* and *Sugar*. This marked the high point scored by youngsters in Chicago jazz. Later the group, except for Jim Lannigan, went to New York where they played the old Palace Theater, the mecca of vaudeville. But the vicissitudes of jazz in the world of commercial music forced the band to scatter and for the next fifteen years these jazzmen played in small and large bands, and in almost every state. The combination, with the exception of Frank Teschmaker, who had been killed in an automobile accident, reassembled for the first time in the Town Hall concerts and for the opening of Eddie Condon's. Personnel:

Eddie Condon, Banjo (later Guitar)
Jimmy MacPartland, Cornet

307

Frank Teschmaker, Clarinet
Bud Freeman, Tenor Saxophone
Joe Sullivan, Piano
Jim Lannigan, Bass
Gene Krupa, Drums (Dave Tough)

At Eddie Condon's jazz is on a permanent basis in New York. The following musicians have been regular members of his band and almost every other great jazz musician has accepted Eddie Condon's open invitation to join in jam sessions at his club:

Trumpet (or Cornet): Billy Butterfield, Wild Bill Davison, Bobby Hackett, Pee Wee Irwin, Max Kaminsky, Marty Marsala, Joe Thomas.

Clarinet: Joe Barufaldi, Sidney Bechet, Joe Dixon, Peanuts Hucko, Joe Marsala, Albert Nicholas, Tony Parenti, Pee Wee Russell, Bill Wood.

Trombone: George Brunies, Charlie Castaldo, Brad Gowans, Miff Mole, Freddy Ohms, Jack Teagarden, Munn Ware.

Piano: Joe Bushkin, Pat Flowers, Stephan the Beetle Henderson, Art Hodes, James P. Johnson, Gene Schroeder, Joe Sullivan.

Bass: Bob Casey, Bob Haggart, Al Hall, Morey Raymond, Sid Weiss.

Drums: Danny Alvin, Johnny Blowers, Morey Feld, Kansas Fields, Freddy Moore, Specs Powell, Al Seidel, Dave Tough, George Wettling.

Guitar: Eddie Condon.

EDDIE CONDON ON RECORDS

AN INFORMAL DISCOGRAPHY

SYMBOLS:

BB—Blue Bird
Br—Brunswick
BrF—French Brunswick
C—Commodore
Co—Columbia
De—Decca
HRS—Hot Record Society
L—Liberty Music Shop
Me—Melotone

OK—Okeh
PaE—English Parlophone
Para—Paramount
Pe—Perfect
Sa—Savoy
Va—Variety
Vi—Victor
Vo—Vocalion
UHCA—United Hot Clubs of America

[Records listed without record numbers have not been released.]

McKENZIE-CONDON CHICAGOANS

China Boy	OK 41011	UHCA 9	Co 35951
Sugar	—	UHCA 10	—
Nobody's Sweetheart	OK 40971	UHCA 11	Co 35952
Liza	—	UHCA 12	—

Eddie Condon, Banjo; Jimmy MacPartland, Cornet; Frank Teschmaker, Clarinet; Bud Freeman, Tenor Sax; Joe Sullivan, Piano; Jim Lannigan, Bass; Gene Krupa, Drums (1927).

CHICAGO RHYTHM KINGS

I've Found A New Baby	Br 4001	UHCA 7	Br 80063
There'll Be Some Changes Made	—	UHCA 8	—

Baby Won't You Please Come
   Home (Eddie Condon vocal)   Br 80064
      Muggsy Spanier, Cornet; Frank Teschmaker, Clarinet;
      Mezz Mezzrow, Tenor Sax; Joe Sullivan, Piano; Gene
      Krupa, Drums; Jim Lannigan, Bass; Red McKenzie, Vocal;
      Eddie Condon, Banjo (1928).

JUNGLE KINGS
   Friar's Point Shuffle   Para 12654   UHCA 3.
   Darktown Strutters Ball   —   UHCA 4
      Muggsy Spanier, Cornet; Frank Teschmaker, Clarinet;
      Mezz Mezzrow, Tenor Sax; Joe Sullivan, Piano; George
      Wettling, Drums; Jim Lannigan, Tuba; Red McKenzie,
      Vocal; Eddie Condon, Banjo (1928).

RED McKENZIE AND HIS MUSIC BOX
   My Baby Came Home   OK 41071
   From Monday On   —
      Red McKenzie, Blue Blowing; Joe Venuti, Violin; Eddie
      Lang, Guitar; Eddie Condon, Banjo (1928).

MIFF MOLE AND HIS MOLERS
   Shim-Me-Sha-Wabble   OK 41445   Co 35953
   One Step To Heaven   —   —
      Miff Mole, Trombone; Red Nichols, Trumpet; Frank
      Teschmaker, Clarinet; Joe Sullivan, Piano; Gene Krupa,
      Drums; Eddie Condon, Banjo (1928).

FRANK TESCHMAKER'S CHICAGOANS
   Jazz Me Blues   UHCA 61
      Frank Teschmaker, Clarinet and Alto Sax; Mezz Mezzrow,
      Tenor Sax; Rod Cless, Alto Sax; Joe Sullivan, Piano;
      Jim Lannigan, Bass; Gene Krupa, Drums; Eddie Condon,
      Banjo (1928). [This record was dubbed in 1939 off a
      test pressing preserved from the original recording date;
      the master record had been destroyed.]

EDDIE CONDON'S QUARTET
   Oh Baby   PaE 2932   Co 35950
   Indiana   —   —

310

Eddie Condon, Banjo; Frank Teschmaker, Clarinet and
Alto Sax; Joe Sullivan, Piano; Gene Krupa, Drums (1928).

EDDIE CONDON'S HOT SHOTS

I'm Gonna Stomp Mr. Henry Lee   Vi V38046   BB 10163
That's A Serious Thing   —   —

Eddie Condon, Banjo; Leonard Davis, Trumpet; Jack
Teagarden, Trombone and Vocal; Mezz Mezzrow, C-
melody Sax; Happy Cauldwell, Tenor Sax; Joe Sullivan,
Piano; George Stafford, Drums (1929). [Different master
records were used to make the Victor and Blue Bird
records.]

FATS WALLER AND HIS BUDDIES

The Minor Drag   Vi V38050   Vi 20-1583
Harlem Fuss   —

Fats Waller, Piano; Charlie Gains, Trumpet; Charlie
Irvis, Trombone; Arville Harris, Clarinet and Alto Sax;
Eddie Condon, Banjo (1929).

EDDIE CONDON AND HIS FOOTWARMERS

I'm Sorry I Made You Cry
(Eddie Condon vocal)   OK 41142   UHCA 27
Makin' Friends(Jack Teagarden
vocal)   —   UHCA 28

Eddie Condon, Banjo; Jimmy MacPartland, Cornet; Jack
Teagarden, Trombone; Mezz Mezzrow, Clarinet; Joe Sullivan, Piano; Artie Miller, Bass; Jack Powell, Drums
(1929).

LOUIS ARMSTRONG AND HIS ORCHESTRA

I Can't Give You Anything
But Love   OK 8669   UHCA 36
Mahogany Hall Stomp   OK 8680   Co 35879

Louis Armstrong, Trumpet and Vocal; J. C. Higgin-
botham, Trombone; Charlie Holmes, Alto Sax; Albert
Nicholas, Alto Sax; Teddy Hill, Tenor Sax; Luis Russell,
Piano; Lonnie Johnson, Guitar; Pops Foster, Bass; Paul
Barbarin, Drums; Eddie Condon, Banjo (1929).

FATS WALLER AND HIS BUDDIES

Lookin' Good But Feelin' Bad   Vi V38086

I Need Someone Like You   —

  Fats Waller, Piano; Charlie Gains and Henry Allen, Trumpets; Jack Teagarden, Trombone and Vibraphone; Albert Nicholas and Otto Hardwick, Alto Saxes; Larry Binyon, Tenor Sax; Charlie Green, Trombone; Al Morgan, Bass; Gene Krupa, Drums; Eddie Condon, Banjo (1929).

Ridin' But Walkin'   Vi V38119

Won't You Get Off It Please   —

Lookin' For Another Sweetie   Vi V38110

When I'm Alone   —

  Fats Waller, Piano; Leonard Davis and Henry Allen, Trumpets; Otto Hardwick, Clarinet and Alto Sax; Jack Teagarden, Trombone in *Ridin' But Walkin'* only; J. C. Higginbotham, Trombone in *Won't You Get Off It Please*; Happy Cauldwell, Tenor Sax; Al Morgan, Bass; Eddie Condon, Banjo (1929).

RED NICHOLS AND HIS FIVE PENNIES

Who Cares   Br 4778

Rose Of Washington Square   —

  Red Nichols, Trumpet; Jack Teagarden and Glenn Miller, Trombones; Pee Wee Russell, Clarinet; Bud Freeman Tenor Sax; Jack Rusin, Piano; Dave Tough, Drums; Eddie Condon, Guitar (1929).

RED McKENZIE AND HIS MOUND CITY BLUE BLOWERS

Indiana   Co 1946D

Fire House Blues   —

  Red McKenzie, Blue Blowing; Jack Bland, Guitar; Bruce Yantis, Violin in *Indiana* only; Gene Krupa, Drums; Eddie Condon, Banjo (1929).

Tailspin Blues   Vi V38087

Never Had A Reason To Believe In You

 (Red McKenzie vocal)   —

  Red McKenzie, Blue Blowing; Jack Teagarden, Trombone;

Al Morgan, Bass; Frank Billings, Drums; Eddie Condon
Banjo (1929).

One Hour		Vi 38100
Hello Lola		—

Red McKenzie, Blue Blowing; Glenn Miller, Trombone;
Pee Wee Russell, Clarinet; Coleman Hawkins, Tenor
Sax; Jack Bland, Guitar; Al Morgan, Bass; Gene Krupa,
Drums; Eddie Condon, Banjo (1929).

I Can't Believe That You're In Love With Me		OK 41515
Georgia On My Mind		—
Darktown Strutters Ball	OK 41526	Co 36281
You Rascal You		—

Red McKenzie, Blue Blowing and Vocal; Muggsy Spanier,
Cornet; Coleman Hawkins, Tenor Sax; Jimmy Dorsey,
Clarinet; Jack Rusin, Piano; Jack Bland, Guitar; Al Morgan,
Bass; Frank Billings, Drums; Eddie Condon, Banjo
(1931).

BILLY BANKS AND HIS ORCHESTRA

Bugle Call Rag		Pe 15615	UHCA 107
Spider Crawl		—	—
Oh Peter	Pe 15620	UHCA 109	Co 35841
Margie		—	—
Who's Sorry Now		Pe 15642	UHCA 111
Bald-Headed Mamma		—	—
Slow And Easy			HRS 17

Billy Banks, Vocal; Henry Allen, Trumpet; Pee Wee
Russell, Clarinet and Tenor Sax; Joe Sullivan, Piano; Jack
Bland, Guitar; Al Morgan, Bass; Zutty Singleton, Drums;
Eddie Condon, Banjo (1932). [The Columbia *Oh Peter*
was made from a different master with a Henry Allen
vocal.]

THE RHYTHMAKERS

Anything For You	Me M12457	UHCA 105	
Mean Old Bed Bug Blues —		—	Co 35882
Yellow Dog Blues	Me M12481	UHCA 106	—
Yes Suh		—	

Henry Allen, Trumpet; Jimmy Lord, Clarinet; Pee Wee
Russell, Tenor Sax; Jack Bland, Guitar; Pops Foster, Bass;
Zutty Singleton, Drums; Fats Waller, Piano; Billy Banks,
Vocal; Eddie Condon, Banjo (1932). [The Columbia
record was made from different masters.]

JACK BLAND AND HIS RHYTHMAKERS

It's Gonna Be You(Chick Bullock
   vocal)   Pe 15689   UHCA 110
Shine On Your Shoes(Chick Bullock
   vocal)
Who Stole The Lock
   (Henry Allen vocal) Me M12513   UHCA 104   Co 35841
Someone Stole Gabriel's
   Horn (Henry Allen vocal)   —   —
   Jack Bland, Guitar; Henry Allen, Trumpet; Pee Wee
   Russell, Clarinet; Happy Cauldwell, Tenor Sax; Tommy
   Dorsey, Trombone except in *Someone Stole Gabriel's
   Horn*; Frank Froeba, Piano; Pops Foster, Bass; Zutty
   Singleton, Drums; Eddie Condon, Banjo (1932). [The
   Columbia record was made from a different master.]

EDDIE CONDON AND HIS ORCHESTRA

The Eel   Br 6743   Co 35680
Home Cooking   —   —
Tennessee Twilight Br F500406   Co 36009   UHCA 63
Madame Dynamite   —   UHCA 64
   Eddie Condon, Banjo; Max Kaminsky, Cornet; Floyd
   O'Brien, Trombone; Bud Freeman, Tenor Sax; Pee Wee
   Russell, Clarinet; Alex Hill, Piano except in Brunswick
   record Br 6743; Joe Sullivan, Piano in Br 6743; Arthur
   Bernstein, Bass; Sid Catlett, Drums (1933). [Co 36009
   was made from a different master.]

BUD FREEMAN AND HIS WINDY CITY FIVE

The Buzzard   PaE 2210   De 18112
Tillie's Downtown Now   —   —
Keep Smilin' At Trouble   PaE 2285   De 18113
What Is There To Say   —   —

314

Bud Freeman, Tenor Sax and Clarinet; Bunny Berigan, Trumpet; Claude Thornhill, Piano; Grachan Moncur, Bass; Cozy Cole, Drums; Eddie Condon, Guitar (1935). [Decca *Tillie's Downtown Now* was made from a different master.]

PUTNEY DANDRIDGE AND HIS ORCHESTRA

Here Comes Your Pappy	Vo 3291
If We Never Meet Again	—
Sing, Baby, Sing	Vo 3304
You Turned The Tables On Me	—

Putney Dandridge, Vocal; Henry Allen, Trumpet; Joe Marsala, Clarinet; James Sherman, Piano; Wilson Myers, Bass; Cozy Cole, Drums; Eddie Condon, Guitar (1936).

When A Lady Meets A Gentleman Down South	Vo 3315
It's The Gipsy In Me	—
You're The Darnedest Thing	Vo 3351
Easy To Love	—
The Skeleton In The Closet	Vo 3352
A High Hat, A Piccolo And A Cane	—

Putney Dandridge, Vocal; Henry Allen, Trumpet; Joe Marsala, Clarinet and Alto Sax; Clyde Hart, Piano; John Kirby, Bass; Cozy Cole, Drums; Eddie Condon, Guitar (1936).

DICK PORTER AND HIS ORCHESTRA

Sweet Thing	Vo 3355
Swingin' On A Swing Tune	—

Dick Porter, Piano and Vocal; Jonah Jones, Trumpet; Joe Marsala, Clarinet; Ernest Meyers, Bass; George Wettling, Drums; Eddie Condon, Guitar (1936).

SHARKEY AND HIS SHARKS OF RHYTHM

Mister Brown Goes To Town	Vo 3400
When You're Smiling	—
Blowing Off Steam	Vo 3410
Wash It Clean	—

Sharkey Bonana, Trumpet and Vocal; Moe Zudecoff,

Trombone; Joe Marsala, Clarinet; Joe Bushkin, Piano; Artie Shapiro, Bass; George Wettling, Drums; Eddie Condon, Guitar (1936).

Old Fashioned Swing	Vo 3450
Big Boy Blue	—
Swing Like A Rusty Gate	Vo 3470
Swingin' On The Swanee Shore	—

Sharkey Bonana, Trumpet and Vocal; George Brunies, Trombone; Joe Marsala, Clarinet; Joe Bushkin, Piano; Artie Shapiro, Bass; Al Seidel, Drums; Eddie Condon, Guitar (1937).

JOE MARSALA'S CHICAGOANS

Wolverine Blues	Va 565
Jazz Me Blues	—
Chimes Blues	
Clarinet Marmalade	

Joe Marsala, Clarinet; Marty Marsala, Trumpet; Ray Biondi, Violin; Adele Girard, Harp; Joe Bushkin, Piano; Artie Shapiro, Bass; Danny Alvin, Drums; Eddie Condon, Guitar (1937).

EDDIE CONDON AND HIS WINDY CITY SEVEN

Ja-Da	C 500
Love Is Just Around The Corner	—
Beat To The Socks	C 502
Carnegie Drag(Jam Session At Commodore)	C 1500
Carnegie Jump(Jam Session At Commodore)	—

Eddie Condon, Guitar; Bobby Hackett, Cornet; Pee Wee Russell, Clarinet; George Brunies, Trombone; Bud Freeman, Tenor Sax; Jess Stacy, Piano; Artie Shapiro, Bass; George Wettling, Drums (January 1938).

Meet Me Tonight In Dreamland	C 505
Diane	—
Serenade To a Shylock(Jam Session At Commodore)	C 1501
Embraceable You(Jam Session At Commodore)	—

Eddie Condon, Guitar; Bobby Hackett, Cornet; Pee Wee

316

Russell, Clarinet; Jack Teagarden, Trombone; Bud Freeman, Tenor Sax; Jess Stacy, Piano; Artie Shapiro, Bass; George Wettling, Drums (April 1938). [*Diane* was issued under the name of Jack Teagarden and His Trombone.]

EDDIE CONDON AND HIS BAND

California Here I Come   C 515

Sunday   —

Bobby Hackett, Cornet; Pee Wee Russell, Clarinet; Eddie Condon, Guitar; Vernon Brown, Trombone; Bud Freeman, Tenor Sax; Joe Bushkin, Piano; Artie Shapiro, Bass; Lionel Hampton, Drums (December 1938).

EDDIE CONDON AND HIS CHICAGOANS

Friar's Point Shuffle   De 18040

Nobody's Sweetheart   —

Someday Sweetheart   De 18041

There'll Be Some Changes Made   —

Eddie Condon, Guitar; Bud Freeman, Tenor Sax; Pee Wee Russell, Clarinet; Brad Gowans, Trombone; Joe Sullivan, Piano; Clyde Newcomb, Bass; Dave Tough, Drums (August 1939). [These records were released March 1940 in the first jazz album of new records (Decca: Chicago Jazz) ever issued; the project was conceived and produced by George Avakian, and featured three bands— Eddie Condon's, Jimmy MacPartland's, and George Wettling's.]

EDDIE CONDON AND HIS BAND

It's Right Here For You   C 530

Strut Miss Lizzie   —

Ballin' The Jack   C 531

I Ain't Gonna Give Nobody None Of My Jelly Roll   —

Eddie Condon, Guitar; Max Kaminsky, Cornet; Pee Wee Russell, Clarinet; Brad Gowans, Trombone; Joe Bushkin, Piano; Artie Shapiro, Bass; George Wettling, Drums (December 1939).

A Good Man Is Hard To Find—Part One
(Jam Session At Commodore)   C 1504
A Good Man Is Hard To Find—Part Two
(Jam Session At Commodore)   —
A Good Man Is Hard To Find—Part Three
(Jam Session At Commodore)   C 1505
A Good Man Is Hard To Find—Part Four
(Jam Session At Commodore)   —

> Eddie Condon, Guitar; Muggsy Spanier and Max Kamin-
> sky, Trumpets; Pee Wee Russell, Clarinet; Joe Marsala,
> Clarinet and Alto Sax; Miff Mole and Brad Gowans,
> Trombones; Bud Freeman, Tenor Sax; Jess Stacy, Piano;
> Artie Shapiro, Bass; George Wettling, Drums (March
> 1940).

You're Some Pretty Doll   C 535
Oh Sister Ain't That Hot   —
Georgia Grind   C 536
Dancing Fool   —

> Eddie Condon, Guitar; Marty Marsala, Trumpet; Pee
> Wee Russell, Clarinet; George Brunies, Trombone; Fats
> Waller, Piano; Artie Shapiro, Bass; George Wettling,
> Drums (November 1940).

Don't Leave Me Daddy   C 542
Fidgety Feet   —
Tortilla B Flat   C 1509
Mammy O' Mine   —
More Tortilla B Flat(Jam Session At Commodore) C 1510
Lonesome Tag Blues(Jam Session At Commodore)   —

> Eddie Condon, Guitar; Max Kaminsky, Trumpet; Pee
> Wee Russell, Clarinet; Brad Gowans, Trombone; Joe
> Sullivan, Piano; Al Morgan, Bass; George Wettling,
> Drums (January 1942).

Basin Street Blues   C 1513
Oh! Katharina!   —
Nobody Knows You When You're Down and Out

Rose Room

> Eddie Condon, Guitar; Max Kaminsky, Trumpet; Pee Wee Russell, Clarinet; Benny Morton, Trombone; Joe Bushkin, Piano; Bob Casey, Bass; Sid Catlett, Drums (December 1943).

Back In Your Own Back Yard   C 551

All The Wrongs You've Done To Me   —

You Can't Cheat A Cheater

Save Your Sorrow

> Eddie Condon, Guitar; Max Kaminsky, Trumpet; Pee Wee Russell, Clarinet; Lou McGarity, Trombone; Gene Schroeder, Piano; Bob Casey, Bass; George Wettling, Drums (December 1943).

Singin' The Blues   C 568

Pray For The Lights To Go Out   —

Mandy Make Up Your Mind

Tell 'Em About Me

> Eddie Condon, Guitar; Max Kaminsky, Trumpet; Pee Wee Russell, Clarinet; Brad Gowans, Trombone; Joe Bushkin, Piano; Bob Casey, Bass; Tony Sbarbaro, Drums (December 1943).

BUD FREEMAN AND HIS GANG

"Life" Spears A Jitterbug   C 507

What's The Use   —

> Bud Freeman, Tenor Sax; Bobby Hackett, Cornet; Pee Wee Russell, Clarinet; Dave Matthews, Alto Sax; Jess Stacy, Piano; Artie Shapiro, Bass; Marty Marsala, Drums; Eddie Condon, Guitar (July 1938).

Tappin' The Commodore Till   C 508

Memories Of You   —

> Bud Freeman, Tenor Sax; Bobby Hackett, Cornet; Pee Wee Russell, Clarinet; Dave Matthews, Alto Sax; Jess Stacy, Piano; Artie Shapiro, Bass; Dave Tough, Drums; Eddie Condon, Guitar (July 1938).

BUD FREEMAN AND THE SUMMA CUM LAUDE ORCHESTRA

I've Found A New Baby	BB 10370
Easy To Get	—
China Boy	BB 10386
The Eel	—

Bud Freeman, Tenor Sax; Max Kaminsky, Trumpet; Pee Wee Russell, Clarinet; Brad Gowans, Trombone; Dave Bowman, Piano; Clyde Newcomb, Bass; Danny Alvin, Drums; Eddie Condon, Guitar (June 1939).

The Sail Fish	De 2781
Satanic Blues	—
Sunday	De 2849
As Long As I Live	—

Bud Freeman, Tenor Sax; Max Kaminsky, Trumpet; Pee Wee Russell, Clarinet; Brad Gowans, Trombone; Dave Bowman, Piano; Clyde Newcomb, Bass; Al Seidel, Drums; Eddie Condon, Guitar (September 1939).

Copenhagen	De 18064
Big Boy	—
Sensation	De 18065
Oh Baby	—
Tia Juana	De 18066
I Need Some Pettin'	—
Fidgety Feet	De 18067
Susie	—

Bud Freeman, Tenor Sax; Max Kaminsky, Trumpet; Pee Wee Russell, Clarinet; Brad Gowans, Trombone; Dave Bowman, Piano; Pete Peterson, Bass; Morey Feld, Drums; Eddie Condon, Guitar (March and April 1940).

BUD FREEMAN AND HIS FAMOUS CHICAGOANS

Prince Of Wails	Co 35853
At The Jazz Band Ball	—
That Da Da Strain	Co 35854
Jack Hits The Road (Jack Teagarden vocal)	—

Muskrat Ramble	Co 35855
Forty-Seventh And State	—
Shim-Me-Sha-Wabble	Co 35856
After Awhile	—

> Bud Freeman, Tenor Sax; Max Kaminsky, Trumpet except in *Jack Hits The Road* and *Forty-Seventh And State*; Jack Teagarden, Trombone; Pee Wee Russell, Clarinet; Dave Bowman, Piano; Morty Stuhlmaker, Bass; Dave Tough, Drums; Eddie Condon, Guitar (July 1940).

LEE WILEY with MAX KAMINSKY'S ORCHESTRA

I've Got A Crush On You	L 282
But Not For Me	L 284
How Long Has This Been Going On	L 281

> Lee Wiley, Vocal; Max Kaminsky, Trumpet; Pee Wee Russell, Clarinet; Bud Freeman, Tenor Sax; Fats Waller, Piano; Artie Shapiro, Bass; George Wettling, Drums; Eddie Condon, Guitar (November 1939).

MAX KAMINSKY AND HIS JAZZ BAND

Eccentric	C 560
Guess Who's In Town	—
Everybody Loves My Baby	
Love Nest	

> Max Kaminsky, Trumpet; Rod Cless, Clarinet; Frank Orchard, Trombone; James P. Johnson, Piano; Bob Casey, Bass; George Wettling, Drums; Eddie Condon, Guitar (June 1944).

ART HODES AND HIS ORCHESTRA

Georgia Cake Walk	De 18437
Liberty Inn Drag	—
Indiana	De 18438
Get Happy	—

> Art Hodes, Piano; Sidney de Paris, Trumpet; Rod Cless, Clarinet; Brad Gowans, Trombone; Earl Murphy, Bass; Zutty Singleton, Drums; Eddie Condon, Guitar (March 1942).

GEORGE BRUNIES AND HIS JAZZ BAND

Ugly Chile(George Brunies vocal)   C 546
That Da Da Strain   —
Tin Roof Blues   C 556
Royal Garden Blues   —

> George Brunies, Trombone; Wild Bill Davison, Cornet; Pee Wee Russell, Clarinet; Gene Schroeder, Piano; Bob Casey, Bass; George Wettling, Drums; Eddie Condon, Guitar (November 1943).

Sweet Lovin' Man   Commodore
Hindustan
Wang Wang Blues
Doodle-Do-Do

> George Brunies, Trombone; Wild Bill Davison, Cornet; Tony Parenti, Clarinet; Gene Schroeder, Piano; Jack Lesberg, Bass; Danny Alvin, Drums; Eddie Condon, Guitar (January 1946).

I Used To Love You   Commodore
I'm Gonna Sit Right Down And Write Myself A Letter
DDT Blues
In The Shade Of The Old Apple Tree

> George Brunies, Trombone; Max Kaminsky, Trumpet; Johnny Mince, Clarinet; Joe Bushkin, Piano; Jack Lesberg, Bass; Johnny Blowers, Drums; Eddie Condon, Guitar (April 1946).

WILD BILL DAVISON AND HIS COMMODORES

That's A Plenty   C 1511
Panama   —
Riverboat Shuffle
Muskrat Ramble

> Wild Bill Davison, Cornet; Pee Wee Russell, Clarinet; George Brunies, Trombone; Gene Schroeder, Piano; Bob Casey, Bass; George Wettling, Drums; Eddie Condon, Guitar (November 1943).

Clarinet Marmalade   C 549
Original Dixieland One-Step   —

Baby Won't You Please Come Home   C 575
At The Jazz Band Ball   —
> Wild Bill Davison, Cornet; Edmond Hall, Clarinet;
> George Brunies, Trombone; Gene Schroeder, Piano; Bob
> Casey, Bass; George Wettling, Drums; Eddie Condon,
> Guitar (November 1943).

Confessin'   C 563
Big Butter And Egg Man   —
I Wish I Could Shimmy Like My Sister Kate
A Monday Date
> Wild Bill Davison, Cornet; Edmond Hall, Clarinet; Ver-
> non Brown, Trombone; Gene Schroeder, Piano; Bob
> Casey, Bass; Danny Alvin, Drums; Eddie Condon, Guitar
> (January 1945).

I Don't Stand A Ghost Of A Chance   Commodore
Little Girl
Jazz Me Blues
Squeeze Me
> Wild Bill Davison, Cornet; Pee Wee Russell, Clarinet;
> Lou McGarity, Trombone; Dick Cary, Piano; Bob Casey,
> Bass; Danny Alvin, Drums; Eddie Condon, Guitar (Janu-
> ary 1945).

Sensation Rag   Commodore
Who's Sorry Now
On The Alamo
Someday Sweetheart
> Wild Bill Davison, Cornet; Joe Marsala, Clarinet; George
> Lugg, Trombone; Bill Miles, Baritone Sax; Joe Sullivan,
> Piano; Jack Lesberg, Bass; George Wettling, Drums;
> Eddie Condon, Guitar (September 1945).

High Society   Commodore
Wrap Your Troubles In Dreams
I'm Coming Virginia
Wabash Blues
> Wild Bill Davison, Cornet; Albert Nicholas, Clarinet;

323

George Brunies, Trombone; Gene Schroeder, Piano; Jack
Lesberg, Bass; Dave Tough, Drums; Eddie Condon, Guitar (January 1946).

MUGGSY SPANIER AND HIS RAGTIMERS

Sweet Lorraine   C 1517
September In The Rain   —
Sugar
Oh, Lady Be Good
> Muggsy Spanier, Cornet; Pee Wee Russell, Clarinet;
> Ernie Caceres, Baritone Sax; Dick Cary, Piano; Sid Weiss,
> Bass; Joe Grauso, Drums; Eddie Condon, Guitar (April
> 1944).

Snag It   Commodore
Alice Blue Gown
Angry
Weary Blues
> Muggsy Spanier, Cornet; Pee Wee Russell, Clarinet; Miff
> Mole, Trombone; Dick Cary, Piano; Bob Casey, Bass; Joe
> Grauso, Drums; Eddie Condon, Guitar (April 1944).

Memphis Blues   C 1519
Sweet Sue, Just You   —
Riverside Blues   C 586
Rosetta   —
> Muggsy Spanier, Cornet; Bobby Hackett, Trumpet; Pee
> Wee Russell, Clarinet; Ernie Caceres, Baritone Sax; Gene
> Schroeder, Piano; Bob Casey, Bass; Joe Grauso, Drums;
> Eddie Condon, Guitar (September 1944).

Whistlin' The Blues (Bob Haggart whistling)   C 576
The Lady's In Love With You   —
Sobbin' Blues
Darktown Strutters Ball
> Muggsy Spanier, Cornet; Pee Wee Russell, Clarinet; Lou
> McGarity, Trombone; Gene Schroeder, Piano; Bob Hag-
> gart, Bass; Joe Grauso, Drums; Eddie Condon, Guitar
> (December 1944).

324

MIFF MOLE AND HIS NICKSIELAND BAND

Peg O' My Heart   C 1518
St. Louis Blues   —
Beale Street Blues
I Must Have That Man
> Miff Mole, Trombone; Bobby Hackett, Trumpet; Pee Wee Russell, Clarinet; Ernie Caceres, Baritone Sax; Gene Schroeder, Piano; Bob Casey, Bass; Joe Grauso, Drums; Eddie Condon, Guitar (April 1944).

JOE MARSALA AND HIS ORCHESTRA Directed by EDDIE CONDON

Tiger Rag   Sa 1001
Clarinet Marmalade   —
Joe's Blues
Village Blues
> Joe Marsala, Clarinet; Bobby Hackett, Trumpet; Fred Orchard, Trombone; Gene Schroeder, Piano; Bob Casey, Bass; Rollo Laylan, Drums; Eddie Condon, Guitar (May 1944).

BOBBY HACKETT AND HIS ORCHESTRA

When Day Is Done   Commodore
At Sundown
Skeleton Jangle
New Orleans
> Bobby Hackett, Trumpet; Pee Wee Russell, Clarinet; Lou McGarity, Trombone; Ernie Caceres, Baritone Sax; Jess Stacy, Piano; Bob Casey, Bass; George Wettling, Drums; Eddie Condon, Guitar (September 1944).

EDDIE CONDON AND HIS ORCHESTRA

When Your Lover Has Gone   De 23393
Wherever There's Love(Lee Wiley vocal)   —
* Somebody Loves Me   De 23430
* Someone To Watch Over Me(Lee Wiley vocal) De 23432
* The Man I Love(Lee Wiley vocal)   —

* Issued In Decca Album 398   George Gershwin Jazz Concert

Eddie Condon, Guitar; Bobby Hackett, Billy Butterfield, and Max Kaminsky, Trumpets; Pee Wee Russell, Clarinet; Jack Teagarden, Trombone; Eddie Caceres, Baritone Sax; Gene Schroeder, Piano; Bob Haggart, Bass; George Wettling, Drums (December 1944).

* 'S Wonderful	De 23430
† Impromptu Ensemble No. 1	De 23718
† The Sheik of Araby	—

Eddie Condon, Guitar; Billy Butterfield, Trumpet; Pee Wee Russell, Clarinet; Jack Teagarden, Trombone; Ernie Caceres, Baritone Sax; Gene Schroeder, Piano; Bob Haggart, Bass; George Wettling, Drums (December 1944).

* I'll Build A Stairway To The Stars	De 23433

Eddie Condon, Guitar; Yank Lausen, Trumpet; Edmond Hall, Clarinet; Lou McGarity, Trombone; Joe Dixon, Baritone Sax; Joe Bushkin, Piano; Sid Weiss, Bass; George Wettling, Drums (May 1945).

* My One And Only	De 23431

Eddie Condon, Guitar; Bobby Hackett, Billy Butterfield, and Yank Lausen, Trumpets; Edmond Hall, Clarinet; Lou McGarity, Trombone; Joe Dixon, Baritone Sax; Joe Bushkin, Piano; Sid Weiss, Bass; George Wettling, Drums (May 1945).

* Oh, Lady Be Good	De 23431

Eddie Condon, Guitar; Max Kaminsky, Trumpet; Joe Dixon, Clarinet; Lou McGarity, Trombone; Jess Stacy, Piano; Jack Lesberg, Bass; Johnny Blowers, Drums (June 1945).

* Swanee	De 23433

Eddie Condon, Guitar; Billy Butterfield, Trumpet; Joe Dixon, Clarinet; Lou McGarity, Trombone; Jess Stacy, Piano; Jack Lesberg, Bass; Johnny Blowers, Drums (June 1945).

* Issued In Decca Album 398	George Gershwin Jazz Concert
† Issued In Decca Album 490	Jazz Concert At Eddie Condon's

She's Funny That Way   De 23600

    Eddie Condon, Guitar; Billy Butterfield and Max Kaminsky, Trumpets; Wild Bill Davison, Cornet; Joe Dixon, Clarinet; Bud Freeman, Tenor Sax; Lou McGarity and Brad Gowans, Trombones; Joe Bushkin, Piano; Jack Lesberg, Bass; Dave Tough, Drums (March 1946).

† Stars Fell On Alabama   De 23719

    Eddie Condon, Guitar; Billy Butterfield, Trumpet; Joe Dixon, Clarinet; Bud Freeman, Tenor Sax; Joe Bushkin, Piano; Jack Lesberg, Bass; Dave Tough, Drums (March 1946).

Improvisation For The March Of Time   De 23600
† Farewell Blues   De 23719

    Eddie Condon, Guitar; Wild Bill Davison, Cornet; Tony Parenti, Clarinet; Brad Gowans, Trombone; Gene Schroeder, Piano; Jack Lesberg, Bass; Dave Tough, Drums (March 1946).

† Just You, Just Me   De 23720
† Atlanta Blues(Bubbles vocal)   —

    Eddie Condon, Guitar; Max Kaminsky, Trumpet; Joe Dixon, Clarinet; Fred Ohms, Trombone; James P. Johnson, Piano; Jack Lesberg, Bass; Dave Tough, Drums (July 1946).

† The Way You Look Tonight   De 23721
† Some Sunny Day   —

    Eddie Condon, Guitar; Max Kaminsky, Trumpet; Joe Dixon, Clarinet; Fred Ohms, Trombone; Gene Schroeder, Piano; Jack Lesberg, Bass; Dave Tough, Drums (July 1946).

BING CROSBY with EDDIE CONDON ORCHESTRA

Personality   De 18790

    Eddie Condon, Guitar; Wild Bill Davison, Cornet; Joe Dixon, Clarinet; Brad Gowans, Trombone; Bud Freeman, Tenor Sax; Joe Bushkin, Piano; Bob Haggart, Bass; George Wettling, Drums (January 1946).

† Issued In Decca Album 490   Jazz Concert At Eddie Condon's

Blue   Decca
        Eddie Condon, Guitar; Wild Bill Davison, Cornet; Joe
        Dixon, Clarinet; Brad Gowans, Trombone; Bud Freeman,
        Tenor Sax; Gene Schroeder, Piano; Bob Haggart, Bass;
        George Wettling, Drums (January 1946).

                                                          325
After You've Gone   Decca
        Eddie Condon, Guitar; Wild Bill Davison, Cornet; Joe
        Dixon, Clarinet; Brad Gowans, Trombone; Bud Freeman,
        Tenor Sax; Joe Sullivan, Piano; Bob Haggart, Bass;
        George Wettling, Drums (January 1946).

EDDIE EDWARDS ORIGINAL DIXIELAND JAZZ BAND
    Shake It And Break It   Commodore
    Tiger Rag
    Lazy Daddy
    Barnyard Blues
    Mournin' Blues
    Skeleton Jangle
        Eddie Edwards, Trombone; Max Kaminsky, Trumpet;
        Brad Gowans, Clarinet; Teddy Roy, Piano; Jack Lesberg,
        Bass; Tony Sbarbaro, Drums; Eddie Condon, Guitar
        (April 1946).
    Ostrich Walk   Commodore
        Eddie Edwards, Trombone; Wild Bill Davison, Cornet;
        Brad Gowans, Clarinet; Teddy Roy, Piano; Jack Lesberg,
        Bass; Tony Sbarbaro, Drums; Eddie Condon, Guitar
        (April 1946).
    Maggie   Commodore
        Eddie Edwards, Trombone; Max Kaminsky, Trumpet;
        Wild Bill Davison, Cornet; Brad Gowans, Clarinet; Teddy
        Roy, Piano; Jack Lesberg, Bass; Tony Sbarbaro, Drums;
        Eddie Condon, Guitar (April 1946).

In addition to the records listed, Eddie Condon has made a
number of V-discs for the armed forces and commercial transcrip-
tion records not available to the public.
328

MAJOR AND MINOR CHORDS *

As I mentioned in the beginning, that revolving door at Nick's became less and less exciting as a form of exertion; also, I was getting tired of being somebody else's customer. Pete Pesci and I opened our own shebeen; we were Damon and Pythias with black looks. These appeared on Pete's face whenever I tarried too long uptown discussing my music with Virgil Thompson and others at Tim Costello's or Crist Cella's or Absinthe House. The latter is a drop owned mainly by Marc Rubin and his wife, Edith, and a few scribes: Richard (no relation) Condon, Tim Taylor, Jack Keating, and others who feel that the bottom of a glass is a great place to find material. Some afternoons Lindsay Hopkins would wander up from Georgia, or Miami, or some other Jim Crow camp. Lindsay is also an owner, not only of the Absinthe House, but also of a company that makes typewriters, gyroscopes and farm machinery, and of half the hotels in the Caribbean. He never has been in any special sweat over where his next half-dollar is coming from. Every time he hits town he and I go on it. One afternoon I went up to see him in his suite in the Warwick Hotel. In the front room was a fake fireplace with some fake logs and some red paper covering a couple of electric lightbulbs to ape a fire. I had a chill.

"Lindsay, it's cold in here," I said. "Could you please throw another bulb on the fire?"

That word led to another drink, which happened too often for Pete Pesci's total enjoyment. He was so busy talking to the golf pros and football players who made our place their headquarters he would get in a state of severe annoyance when any of the civilian customers asked for me. Toots Shor, the sage of Fifty-second Street, used to boast that he had the only headwaiter in the world who never smiled. I used to tell Toots that I had the only night damager in the world who was always threatening to fire his boss. Pete was especially fussy over my tardiness. I always felt as though I should have taken him a note from

*This final chapter, written for the 1962 British edition, is included as a supplement to the original (1947) volume reprinted here.

Phyllis, and every month I was disappointed because he wouldn't give me a report card. One night Bud Bohm and Dick Gehman and I were looking at some anthropological specimens at Absinthe House; our own faces in the mirror behind the bar. It was getting late and they were getting nervous about eating. I invited them down to my joint.

"Oh, no," said Bohm. "Every time we go down there Pete gives us hell for keeping you uptown."

He was absolutely right. You were bound to get in trouble if you went to Eddie Condon's with me.

Still, the saloon went along pretty well. Consolidated Edison never once threatened to turn off the lights. On nights when business was slow, Wild Bill, Cutty Cutshall, Gene Schroeder and others would adjourn to the basement, where they were building a miniature railroad. They had more rolling stock than the Long Island, and sometimes they got so absorbed they forgot to report for duty on the stand. The boys' hobbies always were interfering with their playing. For a time, Wild Bill had an antique shop, Trash and Treasures. He had bought a flock of old trumpets, alto horns and other pieces of plumbing and was busy telling Cutty how he was going to make them into lamps. We were ready to beat off; his cornet lay unnoticed in his lap. "Bill," I said. He went on telling Cutty about his lamps. "Bill, let's go," I said. He was still in lampland. "All right, you bum," I said to him. "Pick up that lamp and *play it!*" Another hobby for a time was sports cars. For a couple of years the street in front of our place looked like Watkins Glen on race day. The conversation was chiefly centred around carburettors and cylinders. Before long the trains in the basement were forgotten, and Gene Schroeder finally packed them up and took them home for his children.

One night when I was sitting in the saloon, minding my own whisky, a lady came in and introduced herself as Elaine Lorillard. She was married to a fellow who stemmed from the tobacco business, Louis Lorillard, a clean guy with no shortage whatever of trump. It was obvious from the way she jiggled that our music was one of her main interests. She told me about a plan she and her husband had. They lived in Newport, Rhode Island, and they were planning to hold a Jazz Festival up there the following summer. We were invited. The idea of jazz in Newport struck me as about as sensible as putting Count Basie's band in St Patrick's for vespers, but I consulted the boys and found they all were game. We bussed to Newport and located it after several false leads. The festival was being held at the local tennis club, possibly the oldest in America. Everybody was knee-deep in diamonds and other precious glass. One of the bluebloods asked me what I thought of the proceedings. I looked at that mob of thousands draped over the courts. "It's the end of tennis," I told him.

330

It was only the beginning of the Newport Festivals. We were back again the next year, and the year after that I went up as a correspondent for the New York *Journal-American*. A couple of disturbed editors had asked me to write some magazine articles, and after trying to convince them otherwise I gave in. One was seen by William Randolph Hearst, Jr, who asked me to do a column. *Pro and Condon* ran for about four years, harming nobody except the late Seymour Berkson, the publisher of the newspaper, who hated it. Or maybe he just hated jazz. Anyhow, he cancelled me and I moved over to *The Saturday Review*, where Irving Kolodin was more hospitable.

Early in 1954, a man named Ralph Black startled me by writing me a letter inviting me to take the band to Buffalo, New York, to play a shoulder-to-shoulder engagement with the Philharmonic. One sniff at that letter convinced me that someone in the Philharmonic offices had left a door ajar and some harmless inmate from a nearby loon-lounge had wandered in and used both typewriter and stationery.

Shortly afterwards, this same Black was on the telephone. "Why didn't you answer that letter?"

"Why did you write that letter?" I asked. "Tell me, are you calling with the warden's permission?"

"I'll be in New York tomorrow to discuss this engagement," Black said.

"Bring your warden along," I said.

Black arrived—without roomies—and demanded a hearing. I took Bobby Hackett with me for insurance against making any rash promises that later might have proved embarrassing. Bobby had been bone dry for years. The whole proposition still seemed preposterous.

Black spoke quickly and persuasively. He seemed to think that our appearing with the Philharmonic would be just what the doctor ordered. "You must have some strange doctors up there in Buffalo," I said. "I'll sày this for you. You may be eccentric, but you're dead game."

Hackett and I talked the whole thing over. We'd been in some concert halls before and we'd been locked out of others. The idea of halling it up was not new—but to appear on the stand with a bunch of stiff-fronts playing oboes and other uncomfortable opium pipes made me edgy.

"When we played Carnegie and Town Hole," I said to Bobby, "we had the edifices to ourselves. We didn't have to budge an inch for Toscanini or any of those big-band tycoons. The audiences who came were our audiences. What will they think in Buffalo if they go into Kleinhans Hall expecting Beethoven's fifth and find Condon's full quart? Fruit will fly."

"I've appeared with some large string groups on Jackie Gleason records," Bobby said.

"Any group Gleason is in is a large one," I said. "But maybe we'll give Black a twist, for giggles."

Off to Buffalo we went, with several complications. Bobby and Peanuts Hucko, our clarinetist, had a strolling date in Ohio and had to fly in from there. Cliff Leeman, the drummer, was in the grip of a sinus condition so severe he scarcely could speak to himself, or at least not politely. Sometime previously, some stairs in my house had decided that it would be great sport if I fell down them, and I was a walking roll of Bauer and Black's.

Then too, on the train, Lou McGarity, our trombonist, became slightly invvolved. That second "v" is deliberate. It stands for "vodka". Some idea of his condition may be gathered by what happened in the Kleinhans Hall dressing-room as we were standing around killing time—and a bottle—waiting to go onstage. Ralph Black came in with a young man and said, "Gentlemen, this is Willis Page, our conductor."

"Conductor," McGarity said, "what times does this goddamn train get to Buffalo?"

There were other momentary work stoppages. I was as nervous as Eartha Kitt's vibrato. I had my chop, but in the course of shoving myself into my clothes that morning I'd completely overlooked my picks. A guitarist *sans* pick is like a trumpet player *sans* lip, but Peanuts Hucko was astride the emergency. He improvised a pick for me out of an old clarinet reed, and before we knew it we were in action.

On the stage, the Philharmonic wound up Tchaikowsky's Third Bunny Hug or some other esoteric menace. The entire hall was a sellout. There were around 3,000 in residence, and half again that number had been turned away. As soon as we finished our first effort, everybody showed that he had brought his hands and they were extremely healthy. I don't recall ever getting such an enthusiastic response. If I had been the weepy type I would have shed. And when Willis Page borrowed a string bass and romped with our boys in the final number, the roof was in serious danger.

"History has been made here tonight," Ralph Black said. He meant that this was the first time that jazz and classical music had gone to the post together, and no damage had been done to either one.

That perhaps was putting it too beefily, but it brought home to me the necessity of taking another new squint at our music. During the preceding twenty years even the best of the jazz musicians would have been ordered off the sidewalk outside a concert hall while the services were going on inside. Benny Goodman sometimes was allowed to play nosey-nosey with Mozart, in company with some members of the elongated-locks school, but he was an exception. Artie Shaw played some chamber music with small groups, but they were unusually

332

tolerant. The idea of "jammin' with those symphonic cats", as Mezz Mezzrow unquestionably would have jolsoned it, was as possible as perpetual motion. It was a dream, like the idea of eating was in the old days. Now, it seemed, we were becoming respectable. It gave me the creeps.

When I got back home I had some second and third thoughts, and dubiety prevailed. Buffalo had to be an exception, I reasoned. The proximity of Niagara Falls has made those people up there accustomed to noise. They are like foundry workers who get the shakes in a silent room.

Word got around in some of the loftier circles of the Buffalo Experiment. Bites began snapping in—from Rock Island, Moline, and Davenport, which was not a railroad but a symphony, and even from Texas and other free countries. "Bring your boys and we'll jam it up," they all said. I began to be convinced that Ralph Black had a tittering of blood relatives, all as adventurous—or crazy—as he was.

Some of the offers were impossible for wallet reasons. Most classical ensembles are used to fiddling along on well-frayed shoestrings. By the time those symphonies would have paid us the cost of transporting us by train, plane, submarine, walk, or stagger, the financial jolt would have forced them to suspend for several seasons. It would have been too stiff for them to pay even if we had agreed to go by goat.

For a time, then, I was persuaded that my days as the Barefoot Sir Thomas Beechnut had opened and closed with that one-nighter in Buffalo. Then, around 1955's waist, a call came from Washington.

I'll say one thing for Black: he must be a great pal of the long-distance telephone operators.

"Have you been promoted to trusty?" I asked Black.

"The National Symphony wants you for two concerts," he said.

"If they can stand me, I suppose I can endure them," I told him.

It was settled. I told Phyllis the news: "I'm wanted in Washington," I said, with pride.

"By whom? J. Edgar Hoover?"

The reaction of Maggie and Liza was more demonstrative. Ten and twelve, respectively, they left off wrecking the house to ask if they could go along. It pleased me to think that my little girls wanted to hear Uncle Da-Da play with the National Symphony.

"Oh, we don't care about the concert," Maggie said. "We want to see the sights—the Washington Monument, the Lincoln Memorial, and——"

"And the Tomb of the Little-Known Saxophone Player," Liza finished.

A few rounds with the telephone corralled Hackett, Hucko, and

McGarity (who promised not to get involved again). Gene Schroeder said he would sit at the piano, Bob Carter agreed to bring his bass, and Morey Feld said he would threaten his drums and if necessary beat them.

The contracts arrived from Black. When I saw them I was absolutely positive he couldn't be serious for the second time. The first concert was to be uncorked at the University of Maryland, a few miles outside D.C. That was nothing unusual. But the second had us booked into the place that the National Symphony hangs out habitually—Constitution Hall.

"I'm surprised those dowager DAR dodos would let you in there," I said to Black on the telephone, "considering your last name. I thought they were prejudiced against everything, especially negroes and jazz men." And I told him about what had happened when we'd tried to sit in at the Hall before. Ernie Anderson and I had tried to stage a concert in there and had been turned down.

"This time it will be different," Black said.

We took the plane to Washington on the thirteenth—a Friday, and an ominous omen even to a nonsuperstitious donkey like Uncle Da-Da. When we arrived, there was Squirrel Ashcraft, the old friend from my transparent-hamburger days in Chicago. Squirrel was cloaking and daggering for the Office of Secret Stratagems, or some such spy syndicate. Squirrel offered to serve as guide for Phyllis, Maggie, and Liza while they took Washington apart.

The newspapers indicated that there was some interest in our appearances, but I still didn't feel overconfident, even when I met Howard Mitchell, conductor of the National Symphony, and heard him say, "Having you here is a privilege."

"It's also a risk," I said, "but they can't do more than tar and feather us."

At the University of Maryland in College Park that night it was clear that Squirrel hadn't asked them to keep us a secret. Some folks had heard that we were coming. The crowd crammed in until they were right up against the stage. With associate conductor Lloyd Geisler sticking them, the National boys traipsed on first. They played Mozart's *Overture to the Marriage of Fignewton* and followed it with Strauss' *Blue Danube*. We were to go on with our own version of Straussie-waussie's spasm. I looked at the size of that symphony and then at my own strivers.

"We're giving away some poundage tonight," I mentioned. "There are eighty-seven of them and seven of us."

We went onstage, sidestepping a glockenspiel here, a French horn there, threading our way through the violas. And we tore into *Blue Danube* that would have made Strauss himself happy about having written it. The boys were all in shape; no visits to Vic Tanny's were necessary.

Howard Mitchell later summed up everybody's reaction in one word. "Sensational," he said.

I had to agree. Not only did the audience make the most gratifying noise imaginable, but it was mannerly noise. It wasn't one of those yea-man-go-man-yea-man-go clusters that used to make Norman Granz's concerts a treat for anyone with an emergency call from home. It was a group of people who had learned to wear shoes and eat with tools. When I held up my hand to reintroduce Lloyd Geisler and His Band of 1,000 Melodies, everybody quieted immediately.

The whole thing went off with impressive precision. The Symphony coped with Borodin, Beethoven, Bizet and Tchaikowsky, and we punished everything from *I Ain't Gonna Give Nobody None of My Jelly Roll* to *Saints*. The climax erupted when Lloyd Geisler borrowed a trumpet and stood in with us for one number. He reduced the entire gym to a state of painless panic.

Squirrel and I relaxed later with a cup of soothing beef tea. "You must feel pretty good," he insinuated.

"Tomorrow night is the hospital test," I caromed. "If they take us in Constitution Hall, there'll be no place in the world jazz won't be able to intrude in."

The next day, while Phyllis, Maggie, and Liza were out trying to memorize the Smithsonian, I floated around town trying the patience of several disc jockeys. By seven that night we all had collected ourselves at the imitation funeral monument known as Constitution Hall. There were no members of the flowered hat set in sight. Instead, there were people who looked as though they had opened their minds before they came.

Roy Meachum, a National Symphony straw boss, came backstage and said he had heard from the man in the cage out front that he was selling tickets he never had sold before. I peeked out between the drapes. There were more face colours in that mob than you might find in the average kaleidoscope: pink, tan, black, brown, white, yellow, and John Dewar. All side by side. The hallowed Hall was hardly the kind of place on which a NO BREAD TODAY sign ever could have been hung with grace. It was plain that nobody had put up a neon that said NO COLOURS ALLOWED EXCEPT WHITE.

The place was all but sold out by the time we were ready to go on, and there were no paper-tearers. We had decided to do the same programme we'd done at the University the night before. Again Lloyd Geisler and his soldiers made certain there would be no customers asking for refunds, and then we went on. I know Lloyd and the rest of his Royal Washingtonians won't feel I'm slighting them or being chesty if I say that the reception they gave us was like nothing ever heard before in that mausoleum.

Musically speaking, it was the happiest experience of my life.

335

No, not musically speaking. Personally. As anybody who has ploughed this far will guess, I am no sociologist, and the most profound thoughts that commonly gush out from between my ears are concerned with the Scottish export business, but I thought, as I watched that crowd, that maybe this concert was at last demonstrating that our music was for all kinds of people, and that there was no longer any necessity for confining it to back rooms, gutters, saloons, and wastebaskets.

The bluenosed octogenarian bracket was heavily represented, and none of them tottered out in disgust. Similarly, the black-sweater-and-blue-jeans set sat attentively while the Symphony wailed. Nobody who showed up differentiated or discriminated. The communicants regarded both kinds of music as music, to be enjoyed.

"Your appearance," Howard Mitchell said, "caused a lot of people to come in who never would have thought of coming into Constitution Hall before."

"Including me," I said.

"It would be wonderful," Mitchell went on, "if other symphonic organizations profited by our experience. Jazz bands can help symphonies by bringing in new listeners, and we can help you by introducing our music to people who previously have looked down their noses at it if they have looked at all."

Again I had to agree. I began to see that Ralph Black, who started it all, was not the dreamer (or loony) I'd thought him, but a very broad, tolerant, savvy guy as far as musical appreciation was concerned. It was a fine experience, and if another call comes from a symphony, I won't cringe. I may even buy a baton.

If I do, I don't know if they will ask me to wave it in England.

The next most memorable event occurred in 1957, when the boys and I took a trip.

England, which, the history books say has endured and survived so much over the centuries, finally was called on to withstand another test: me.

Joe Glaser was on the telephone one morning in 1956. Joe was my old friend. I'd known him since the Chicago days, when he was managing the Sunset. He and Louis Armstrong never had widened, and he'd always continued to book jobs for many of the rest of us. If there was any kind of job that needed filling, Joe would book it.

"Do you want to go to Australia?" Joe was asking.

"No," I said, remembering Ruark's jaunt.

"How about England?"

"Maybe."

What is "maybe" to anybody else is "yes" to Joe, and the next thing we knew, Wild Bill, Cutty Cutshall, Bob Wilber, Gene Schroeder, Leonard Gaskin, George Wettling, and I were on a Pan-American DC-7C, with Gehman along as manager.

It was an eventful flight, if you could count bottles. Everybody had a jug, and if I am not mistaken Wild Bill even had poured some vodka into his cornet and corked it.

When we fell off the aircraft at London airport, the Condon Mob, as the British newspapers called us, found a welcoming party. The combined bands of Humphrey Lyttelton, Mick Mulligan, and Chris Barber, plus the skiffle group of Beryl Bryden, all were jamming *At The Jazz Band Ball*. It was organized as well as deafening.

Although there are a good many "progressive players", British jazz is in a state of arrested development. At least, it seemed so to me. What those boys were playing sounded like the music of King Oliver and Louis Armstrong as they were playing it in New Orleans before they got seriously involved in that up-paddling struggle with the Father of Waters. Our music isn't exactly modern, as my friends and I play it, but what Lyttelton, Mulligan, and their gangs were doing sounded prehistoric to me. I asked where the dinosaurs were.

Someone introduced me to Humphrey Lyttelton, a reconstructed Etonian who then was proclaiming his break with his well-brought-up past by wearing a pair of Elvis Presley sideburns. I told him I had to meet his barber at once. Then I saw Beryl Bryden, who was wearing thimbles on all her fingers and slashing away at a washboard.

"Mr Condon, what do you think of the washboard as a rhythm instrument?" she asked.

"I can't say," I said. "I'm not in the soap business."

Somehow, we got to our hotel. There, Harold Davidson, the English booking agent who had arranged the seventeen-engagement invasion with the help of Hurricane Glaser, changed our money into pounds. Everybody scattered immediately. Each musician was followed by a large entourage of musicians and fans. I never heard so many questions in my life, and I never knew any collectors in the United States who were so *keen* on our music.

Somebody asked, "Mr Condon, when you made *Home Cooking*, was Floyd O'Brien on trombone, or was that Jack Teagarden?"

"I have trouble remembering who was in the studio last week," I told him, "let alone on a job in 1932."

"Wasn't that record made in 1931?"

"If you know what year it was," I said, "you tell *me* who played trombone."

The lobby was stuffed with those fans, but the room they assigned me was overflowing. I was glad: the dampness already was setting into my bones. On top of that, I had a complaining arm from a shot I'd had the day before, and my right ankle was beginning to swell, as though I had gout. We had finished all the jugs on the airplane.

337

"Is it possible to get a drink here at this hour?" I asked anybody in general.

The hotel manager was at hand. "Mr Condon, you can get a drink in a British hotel at any hour of the day or night."

"Send out for some naturalization papers," I said. "I want to file for citizenship immediately."

Some Scotch came.

While I was sampling it, the boys began to dismantle London. Wilber and Gaskin, both in their late twenties, had guidebooks. They had their itineraries all mapped. "Remember, boys, this recess is not for the extent of the tour," I admonished them. Wilber wasn't listening. At the opening show, the older members of the band, all of whom had been drinking and might have been expected to pull up lame, were present and accounted for—but Peck's Good Boy was missing. Wilber had taken an overdose of museums. Culture can be much more dangerous than booze.

George Wettling, the band dandy, headed for Burberrys Ltd. He purposely had worn his oldest clothes so he could buy new British ones to wear home. At Burberrys he first bought a tweed topcoat, then a tweed jacket, then another. "Man, oh man, won't these threads gas the cats back home!" he kept saying. George took elocution lessons from Mezz Mezzrow.* On the street he gave his old jacket and topcoat to two British devotees who were following him around. They are now bronzed and being guarded by lions. Cutty Cutshall said, "George had one tremendous disappointment in Burberrys—he found out they don't carry tweed underwear."

There are few decipherable recollections of that first day. We were all over London, in and out of pubs, clubs, restaurants, and after-hours joints. We made Hogarth's characters look like fags. I recall signing some LP's in Dobell's Shop in Charing Cross Road.

Wild Bill got separated from the rest of us somehow. "Where is he?" one of our new friends asked. "He's out trying to unscrew Big Ben," I said. "He's going to take it home and make a lamp out of it." Later Bill told us that he woke up and found himself playing his cornet in a huge room. It developed that he had fallen along with the boys in Chris Barber's band, who were booked for a job in the Recital Room of Royal Festival Hall.

Gene Schroeder was with us, but with difficulty. Some time before our jaunt he had torn a ligament in his left ankle. He was on crutches. Ernie Anderson introduced us to Eddie Chapman, the former bank robber and double agent, and he in turn took us to The Star, a pub in Belgrave Mews. Pat Kennedy, the publican, later said, "The only one in the whole lot who could walk straight was the one on crutches." From The Star we went to The Cottage,

* Readers who wish to do the same should buy *Really the Blues*, by Mezz Mezzrow (Corgi Books, 5s.).

338

a club in Litchfield Street off Charing Cross Road where musicians like to congregate and stagger. It was so packed that Cutshall had to point his trombone towards the ceiling to manipulate his slide. I never touch any instrument but my guitar or my glass, but the festivities got to me. I sat down and began playing piano. Fortunately, no one could hear.

"How do you like British jazz?" somebody screamed in my ear.

"This is no place for a decision," I said.

Bob Dawbarn, of *The Melody Maker*, later said, "Nothing like that night ever happened before." The statement left no room for dispute. One British band showed up for a midnight job two hours later. Mick Mulligan did something totally out of character. Mick is known as The Eddie Condon of England; some day, I hope, he'll beat that rap. He and his band drink as much as I and mine. This night, he had to send one of his men home because he was too drunk to play. "The bloke came on the stand and just stood there giggling," Mick told me. One sideman called his wife at seven and said he would be home at eight. He was: at eight the next evening. Three musicians were tucked into their cradles by constables. Another one stepped into the automobile of a total stranger, believing it a taxi, and was thrown into the gutter, where he slept until some friends found him. The worst casualty was the one who was arrested and spent four days in the Nick.

The next morning, Len Gaskin symbolized the state of our invading forces. He stood in front of a mirror in his hotel room knotting his necktie for ten minutes—until he realized he had not yet put on his shirt. The holdovers were thunderous, but we got cracking early and started all over again. I have no recollection whatever of that day. All I know is that Anderson Bo-peeped everybody together and got them on a train for Glasgow at eleven pm. They had berths, but nobody slept. They took out their horns and played with their new British friends all night long.

Anderson, Gehman, and I flew to Glasgow the next morning. The way I felt, I could have made it under my own power, but we settled for a Viscount. On the way up we read the newspapers. The British press had taken out its razors and slashed us up. I'm sure it was pure jealousy. They'd been the drinking champions before, and now they were smarting.

At the hotel in Glasgow my arm began to ache from the cold and dampness. Anderson, busy welcoming the Glasgow reporters, asked if my room didn't have a heater. "It does, and I'm drinking it," I told him.

One reporter said, "My coming here is a mere formality—my paper is going out of business this evening."

"If I'd known we would cause a disaster like that we'd have

opened in London," I told him. Actually, the Glaswegians were much more civilized than the Londoners.

That day, Glasgow was covered with a thick blanket of grey-yellow fog and smoke. I was afraid the audience would never be able to hear us in that stuff. Everybody was coughing like lungers. When we finally went on stage that night, I opened by saying, "Friends, we're all very glad to be here—but frankly, I've had about as much coal as I can eat."

Humphrey Lyttelton's band had been booked to tour with us. After hearing that antediluvian jazz at the airport, I had been apprehensive. I was not expecting to be impressed. Then I heard them playing the last chorus of *Apex Blues*. Lyttelton's trumpet was coming through sharp and clean. It was not only palatable, it was powerful. I told Anderson that it never would have occurred to me that a guy with a haircut like that could get his instrument out of its case, let alone play it that way. "You ought to get to know him," Ernie said.

As the trip went on, I did. Humph, as everybody calls him, comes from a Family. Raised at Eton, where he first began to blink in 1921, he shocked his family when he was three by picking out *The Whistler and his Dog* on a child's xylophone. He and I may have been drawn together closer when he told me that his first instrument was a banjolele. Humph said, "My mother bought it for me in exchange for my tonsils." Later, he said, he got a used snare drum. Remembering my own two stretches in the hospital, I asked him if he had to surrender anything for that. "Only my interest in studies," Humph said.

In America, we used to woodshed. Humph washroomed, upstairs in his grandfather's house, trying to play *Basin Street Blues* on an old trumpet he'd saved up his farthings to buy. By then our jazz was beginning to roll into England on records, and he attempted to style his playing on Louis lines. Today he has a manner that's all his, but there are still Armstrong traces. He carried his trumpet along with him when he went into the Grenadier Guards; it was with him, in a bag, when he went ashore at Salerno. He used to practise in foxholes and under patient trees. Finally malaria tapped him and he was shipped back home and mustered out.

Lyttelton, Sr wanted him to return to Eton and be a master, but Humph had no taste for standing on a platform and droning Geography at a gang of saplings. He could draw a little. He signed the forms at Camberwell School, an artsy-craftsy centre, and soon wound up with a job on the *Daily Mail* as a cartoonist. There he met another cartoonist who also liked to experiment with jazz, Wally Fawkes, who was playing in a New Orleans-style band led by George Webb. Humph joined the band. They called themselves Troglodytes because of the prehistoric nature of their music. Later Humph went out on his own. By the time our mob arrived in England, he was the country's foremost leader.

All this I found out later. To get back to that first night in Glasgow: we all were pretty jittery as we went out on the stage for our first number. Even the ordinarily infallible Davison blew a clinker or two. Gaskin could not get his bass, a borrowed one, to stay in tune. After I beat the boys off I wandered off stage to complain about Gaskin's bass and to see if the supervisor of the hall couldn't find a functioning one. I understand this caused a minor international incident.

They finished the first number and I went back to announce the second. Anderson had not bothered to explain in front that I've never soloed in my life. "Come on, Condon, play a solo!" they were yelling.

The Prime Minister had just gone out of office. "If that's an example of British manners, I can see why Eden took a powder," I called back.

This made everybody less vibratious. The boys relaxed. They began to sound the way they ordinarily do in our joint, and pretty soon there were no more enemies in the stands. Or, if there were, they were quiet. At the end of the show Humph and his boys joined us for a ham section, and the audience proceeded to demolish the roof.

The Glasgow Jazz Club had a party later. Very little is recalled of what happened there. On the way home, one of the Lyttelton boys was examining a scrap of paper. He looked disconsolate. "There was this absolutely gorgeous chick at the party," he said, "and I asked her to fly to Paris with me next week, and she said she would, and I wrote down her name, and now I can't make it out." Others fared better. Two members of the female race became so enamoured of the bands that they decided to go along to the next town. They carried little baskets— their lunches, no doubt.

Anthony Bracegirdle was waiting for us in Leicester. He had spent some time in Nick's during the war, while on leave from a British ship. He volunteered to chauffeur us in his 2½-litre Jaguar saloon. I was attracted to the car at once because of its type, but I hadn't realized that there are no speed laws in Britain. I realized it as soon as he beat off that accelerator, though. I had to tell him that if I was going to get killed in England, I wanted to be killed by smoke.

At the hall there were some men from *The Melody Maker* who had come up to see how the tour was progressing. One was Max Jones, an unusual-looking chap with a completely clean scalp and a black beret perched behind it. His approach was scholarly. "What do you conceive to be the difference between your music and modern jazz?" he asked. I gave him a variation on my symphony-concert line. "They flat their fifths—we consume ours."

The band jumped the next day to Bristol. There, as Gene Schroeder said later, we really jumped. Bristol was jazz-crazy. The city had four jazz clubs. After our concert, our twin mobs went out with the Cassey Bottom Jazz Band to their club. George Webb proved that he still could play piano, and some of us sat in with some of them, either on the stand or at the bar. Again, two or three of the British cats were so carried away that ultimately they were carried off by the constabulary to the local Nick. Some of us lurched down the street to the station to see if we could vouch for them. In the headquarters a sergeant politely asked us to leave, possibly because Wild Bill took out his horn and rehearsed a few unrestrained arpeggios. "Your friends are sleeping peacefully in their cells," he said. He acted as though he was afraid we would disturb them. I'd never seen such considerate fuzz in my life. It was the first time I'd ever been thrown *out* of a police station, and I'm grateful to Bristol.

The next day was Sunday. There must have been a dozen churches around our hotel. The bells began at six am and became more and more insistent. When I opened my eyes I found that Anderson, Gehman, and I were each in a double bed in a room the size of Stillman's Gym. The bell action persisted until I couldn't stand it any longer. I looked over at Ernie to ask him to do something; Ernie can handle anything. He was asleep, no doubt dreaming of Joe Glaser. Gehman was awake and trying to burn up the bed with a lighted cigarette. "Dick," I implored, "could you please get Norvo to take a nap?"

The bus left at noon. At 12.03 we stopped at a country pub. Some members of the Gabby Hayes set were there, all in thatched suits. Wild Bill saw a golden hunting horn over the bar and could not rest until he tried it. He blew it out the door, and every fox in the county headed for Scotland. Then we went on to Plymouth, which was another success. That night we took the bus back to London, which was another failure. It was a good thing that God didn't equip kidneys with voices. The protests from the two bands would have been deafening.

We had a day off before our engagement at Stoll Theatre, and again everybody scattered. Bob Wilber found himself playing clarinet with a washboard group. He came in late and told me that the washboard was the coming instrument of the future. By then I was convinced that that uncut mutton had gone to his head. Wild Bill and Cutty went jamming in The Cottage, and I'll never forget the sight of the band they sat in with. A dwarf negro was playing piano. Two proper Etonians had guitars. A Romany gypsy with a ring in his ear was playing a "bass" made from a garbage can, two push-brooms, and a clothesline. The strangeness of the combination did nothing to discourage Bill from blowing with his customary force.

Against my will, someone took us to hear a wreck-and-rule

342

band. Two choruses were enough for me. I told my host that I thought rat-baiting had gone out of style, and he seemed to think it was a joke. The dancers made me ponder over the fact that some people have been known to be arrested just for drinking. I had to admit that the band kept time, but I wish they'd given it away.

The concert at Stoll Theatre went off without incident. The thoughtful Harold Davison—Wild Harold—had set up a bar, which put everybody in shape at once. Sinclair Traill arrived. He was the editor of a British magazine—and had some connection with a cousin of the Queen's. The latter bloke was around the corner in a pub, Sinclair said, and wanted to meet me. After protesting that I hadn't brought my robes, I followed Sinclair. The Cousin of the Queen was earnestly trying to get outside several pints, and this proved too distracting to make dialogue necessary.

After a few treaties, we went back to Stoll's and took up where we'd left off. During the last number of the concert Humph and Wild Bill fell into a cutting contest. Next to collecting somebody else's antiques, Bill loves nothing better than a battle. In this one he was determined to come out on top, and Humph later conceded the crown by saying, "Never have I been carved so beautifully, and never have I enjoyed it more." Davison tucked his horn under his arm and came off chewing gum. As he walked by Lyttelton he said, "Good show, Humph."

We went out on the road again early the next morning: to Dundee, Edinburgh, Newcastle, Birmingham, Sheffield, Manchester, Bradford, and Liverpool. Edinburgh, needless to say, was the stop I liked best. It was a pleasure to see one of the sources of supply, and to sample some on the spot. We got back to London and finished the tour with a midnight concert in Royal Festival Hall on February 4th. All the stops were marked by ever-increasing excitement on the part of the fans, and some of them even went along with us from one town to another. By the time the tour was over we were exhausted. "Great Britain is nothing but one big jazz club," Gaskin said. I told him I wished I had the mutton concession. A couple of bands went along to the airport to blow us back to the States, and everybody had his own bottle. "What, finally, did you think of your tour?" Humph asked as we were shaking hands. I knocked back a sip and looked at the fluid remaining in the glass. "At the rate you bums go with this stuff," I told him, "there won't always be an England."

Back home, we settled into our usual routine. We made a few records for Columbia, MGM and Dot, we played some concerts, sometimes with symphonies, sometimes single-o. Then some real estate operators got the bright idea of tearing down the block our club was in, and we had to look around. Pete Pesci and I combed

Manhattan and finally settled on a room in the Sutton Hotel, on East Fifty-sixth, between First and Second Avenue.

The new room has been open nearly four years as I write this. It's smaller, but more accessible. The rope's been up nearly every night since we settled in. I don't kid myself that the reason is our music—it's just that since I wrote the body of this book jazz has been busting out everywhere. There's more interest right now than any of us ever imagined back in the Chicago days. Today we no longer feel like strangers. We're at home everywhere. Why, I've even started going out on the road again—to Chicago, Detroit, Columbus, Toronto, and other stops. Louis Armstrong, Count Basie and other bands have been roving Europe like newspaper correspondents, and Dizzy Gillespie and others have toured the Far East. We called it music—and today people are calling for it everywhere on earth.

INDEX

INDEX *

*The index does not cover the last chapter which was not included in the original edition of this book.

Bland, Jack, 9, 104, 116, 198-199, 203-204, 208-209, 210, 227
Blowers, Johnny, 295
Blue Friars Band, 133, 134
Bohn, Bud, 230
Bolden, Buddy, 25-26, 29, 163
Bonana, Sharkey, 260, 261
Bowman, Dave, 260, 261, 268
Brass Rail (Chicago), 276-277
Brennan, Hank, 263-264
Brick Club (New York), 272
Bright, John, 200-201, 202-203
Broadway Jimmy, 133, 181
Brown's Dixieland Jass Band, 29-30
Brown, Tom, 29
Brunies, Abbie, 101
Brunies, George, 84, 100-101, 108, 165, 261, 263, 264, 276, 290
Budapest String Quartet, 265
Buhl, Squeak, 106-107
Burnett, Don, 76
Bushkin, Joe, 240, 242-243, 244, 245, 246, 247, 249, 265
Busse, Henry, 149

Caffarelli, Gene, 121
Campbell, Colin, 247, 248, 254, 257, 258
Capitol (Strekfus river boat), 79
Capone, Al, 104, 124, 135, 151
Capone, Bottles, 124, 151
Carhart, George, 232-234

Carlos, Paddy, 278
Carmichael, Hoagy, 103, 122
Carnegie Hall, 278, 280
Carroll Dickerson's band, 127, 132
Carroll, Earl, 213, 220
Carson, Kit, 158
Carter, Don, 119
Cascades Ballroom (Chicago), 101, 106
Casey, Bob, 9
Castillian Gardens (Valley Stream, Long Island), 180, 183
Catlett, Sidney, 266, 290
Cattalina, Tony, 79
Cauldwell, Happy, 186, 200
Ceppos, Max, 180
Chandler, Deedee, 99
Chapman, John, 265
Charell, Erik, 270-271
Charlie Straight's Orchestra, 112, 120-121
Chicago Jazz, 100-105, 107-109, 162-163
Clegg, Jack, 44
Clove, Carl, 122
Coburn, Jolly, 172-173
Cole, Cozy, 290
Coleman, Emil, 172
Colonna, Jerry, 229
College Inn (Chicago), 83, 146, 147
Columbia Ballroom (Chicago), 112, 134

Downes, Olin, 295
Doyle, Larry, 204
Dreamland Café (Chicago), 98, 100, 131
Duchin, Eddy, 197
Dunn, Jack, 118
Dutray, Honoré, 107

Earle, Bobby, 278
Eberhardt, Johnny, 83, 85, 88
Eddie Condon's, 8-9
Edison Trio, 59
18 Club, 246
Ellington, Duke, 163-164, 182, 267
Empress of Britain, 247, 251
Engleman, Bill, 67-68, 69
Eppel, John Valentine, 70
Erskine Tate's Orchestra, 132
Etting, Ruth, 130

Famous Door (New York), 165, 240, 245
Farley, Ed, 239-240
Fitzsimmons, Harold, 278
Five Pennies, 152, 164
Flack (*Empress of Britain* steward), 248, 249, 250, 253
Fortin, Johnny, 119
Foster, Pops, 200
Frazee, Harry, Jr., 220-221
Frazier, George, 2, 290
Freedley, Vinton, 7
Freeman, Art, 232-233, 244
Freeman, Bud, 8, 100, 104, 106-108, 126, 131, 132, 133, 137, 145, 146, 150, 152, 153, 158, 168, 175, 193, 244, 245, 260, 263, 266, 267, 268, 274, 281
Friars' Inn (Chicago), 84, 100, 101, 108, 125

Gabe, Dan, 136-137
Gable, Al, 79
Gabler, Milt, 236-239, 259-260, 262, 263, 264, 268, 282
Gains, Charlie, 188, 189
Gale, Harry, 150
Gallagher, Joe, 278
Gamandhi, 234
Gardner, Jack, 140, 142, 145
Garibaldi, Francis, 115
Glassman, Jack (Kubec Glasmon), 201-202
Gedney Farms Country Club, 193, 196
Gerraghan, Tom, 278
Gershwin, George, 163, 246
Gibson, Harry, 290
Gillis, Gerald, 180
Goetz, Ray, 209
Gogarty, Oliver St. John, 278
Goldkette, Jean, 139
Goldman, Chick, 180
Goodman, Benny, 100, 119, 126, 132, 158, 164, 260, 263, 265, 267, 271, 278
Goslin, Ward, 115
Gould, Mike, 244
Gowans, Brad, 9, 266, 268, 274, 282
Greb, Harry, 112

350

Grenwald, Art, 131
Grofé, Ferde, 149
Groody, Louise, 217
Guyon's Paradise (Chicago), 148

Hackett, Bobby, 257, 261, 263, 265, 266, 282, 290
Halfway House (Storyville), 101
Hall, Ed, 290
Hall, Tubby, 123
Halpern, John M., 282-283
Hammond, John Henry, Jr., 222-223, 236, 280
Handy, W. C., 265
Hardin, Lillian, 107, 131
Harris, Arville, 189
Harrison, Richard Edes, 236, 263-264
Helbock, Joe, 229
Henderson, Fletcher, 131, 164
Hickman, Art, 59
Hickory House (New York), 246, 256, 257
Higginbotham, J. C., 200, 282
Hill, Teddy, 200
Hines, Earl, 127, 132, 155, 159, 160
Hixon, Hal, 208
Hobson, Wilder, 236
Holiday, Billie, 240
Hollywood Restaurant (New York), 201
Holmes, Charlie, 200
Horvath, Charlie, 139, 143
Hostetter, Wayne, 83-88

Hucko, Peanuts, 295
Husk O'Hare's Wolverines, 137

Irvis, Charlie, 189, 190

J. S. (Strekfus river boat), 80
Jackson, Tony, 27
Jacobs, Sidney, 181, 183-184
Jacobson, Bud, 126, 127
Jake (Chicago cabaret owner), 124
James, Harry, 267
Jazzbo Jimmy, 181
Jean Goldkette's band, 143, 146, 149, 153, 164
Jenkins, Burris, 245-246
Jimmy Ryan's (New York), 268
Johnson, Bill, 28, 98
Johnson, Charlie, 186
Johnson, James P., 164, 182, 290
Johnson, Lonnie, 200
Jones, Isham, 83, 105
Jones, Richard, 99
Joyce, Peggy Hopkins, 214
Julius' (New York), 262, 278, 289

Kahn, Gilbert, 208
Kaminsky, Max, 9, 193, 230, 231-232, 247, 274, 278, 282, 290
Kapp, Jack, 158-160, 239
Kassel, Art, 128
Katy, Palmer, 106
Kay, Herbie, 118
Kelly's Stables (Chicago), 133

351

MacPartland, Jimmy, 100, 104,
106-108, 120, 132, 137, 149,
150, 152, 153, 155, 158, 168,
169, 170, 175, 192, 193, 236,
276
McVickers Theater (Chicago),
130-131
Mamie Smith and Her Jass
Hounds, 58
Mannone, Wingy, 61, 132, 158,
165, 294
Marable, Fate, 99
Mares, Paul, 101, 108
Markel, Mike, 172
Marsala, Joe, 8, 246, 247, 256,
257, 265, 266
Marsala, Marty, 246, 247, 248,
256, 265, 266
Marshall, George Preston, 204
Marshall, Kaiser, 200
Maurice, 174
Mayo Brothers Clinic, 73-74
Means, Gordon, 206, 208
Mendl, Lady, 213
Meredith, Burgess, 8
Merry Gardens (Chicago), 131,
133
Mezzrow, Milton, 5-6, 119-120,
132, 137, 143-144, 145, 146,
154, 157, 159, 178, 181, 185,
186, 192, 245, 265, 267
Midway Gardens Ballroom (Chi-
cago), 126
Milhaud, Darius, 295
Miller, Charlie, 175
Miller, Glenn, 158, 197

Minor, Worthington, 284
Mitch (Paradise cornet player),
123
Moorehouse, Chauncey, 143,
153
Morgan, Russ, 197
Morton, Benny, 290
Morton, Jelly Roll, 27
Mound City Blue Blowers, 6,
105, 115, 151, 157, 204, 207
Murray, Don, 84, 143, 153

Neely, Bob, 210, 249
Neibauer, Eddie, 170
Nelson, William Warvell, 93
Nest (Chicago), 132, 162
New Orleans Jazz, 19-29, 98-105
New Orleans Rhythm Kings, 30,
84, 85, 97, 100-101, 261
New York Jazz, 162-166
Newcomb, Clyde, 261
Nicholas, Albert, 200
Nichols, Red, 152, 153, 164,
172, 192-193
Nick's (New York), 260-261,
262, 266
Noone, Jimmy, 28, 98, 100, 132,
155, 159-160, 178
North, Dave, 137
Nunu, 261

O'Brien, Floyd, 131, 137
O'Connor, Johnny, 2
O'Connor, Tommy, 198
Oelrichs, Marjorie, 204
O'Hara, John, 2

353

O'Hare, Husk, 106, 137
Oliver, Joe, 26, 28, 30, 98-100, 107-108, 111, 113, 132-133, 155, 163, 227
Olsen, George, 169
Onyx (New York), 165, 240
Original Creole Band, 26, 28
Original Dixieland Jazz Band, 29, 71, 88
Orr, Dee, 137-138
Ory, Kid, 28

Pacelli, Bob, 134
Page, Hot Lips, 265, 266, 282, 290
Palace Gardens (Chicago), 112, 113
Palace Theater (New York), 175
Palmer, Bee, 101, 168-169, 170, 171, 172
Panassié, Hugues, 295
Pancho (band leader), 172-173
Panico, Louis, 83-84, 148, 152, 161, 169
Panther Room (Chicago), 272
Paradise (Chicago), 122
Park Lane Hotel (New York), 265-266
Parkway Hotel (Chicago), 147
Pastor, Tony, 197
Patrick, Mildred, 215
Paul Biese Trio, 59
Peach, Roy, 145, 146, 147
Peavey, Doris Enney, 70-71, 91-92, 96

Peavey, Hollis, 69-71, 73, 74, 75, 78, 79-81, 89, 90-91, 92, 93-94, 96
Peavey's Jazz Bandits, 67-97
Peer, Ralph, 186-187
Pennington, Ann, 209-210
Perez, Manuel, 98-99
Perona, John, 209-213, 214
Pesci, Pete, 8, 278
Peterson, Andy, 41-42
Peterson, Charlie, 264
Pettis, Jack, 84, 108
Pierce, Charlie, 238
Plantation (Chicago), 132
Plunkett, Jimmy, 196-198
Plunkett's (New York), 196-198
Pod's and Jerry's (New York), 181
Podolsky, Murphy, 108, 126-127, 128, 134-135, 272
Pollack, Ben, 150, 158, 167, 169, 193
Powell, Johnny, 180, 185
Powell, Mel, 290
Power, Tyrone, 8
Prima, Louis, 165

Qualey, Dan, 9
Qualey, Jake, 9
Queely, Chelsea, 9, 198-199
Quicksell, Howdy, 153

Rafferty, Mickey, 169
Rainey, Ma, 28, 103
Rank, Bill, 153
Rank, Fat, 69

355

Other DACAPO titles of interest